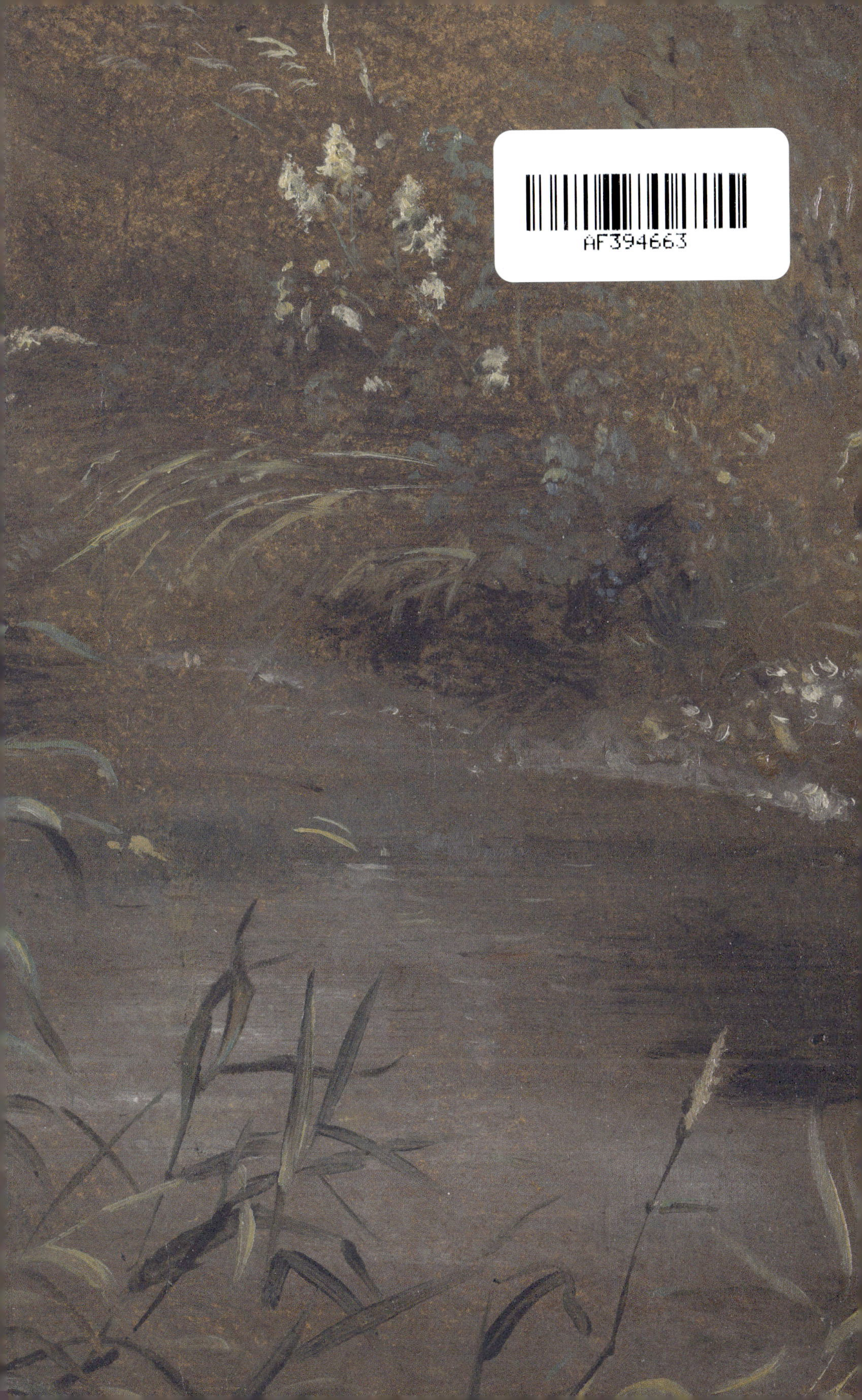

Constable's
Year

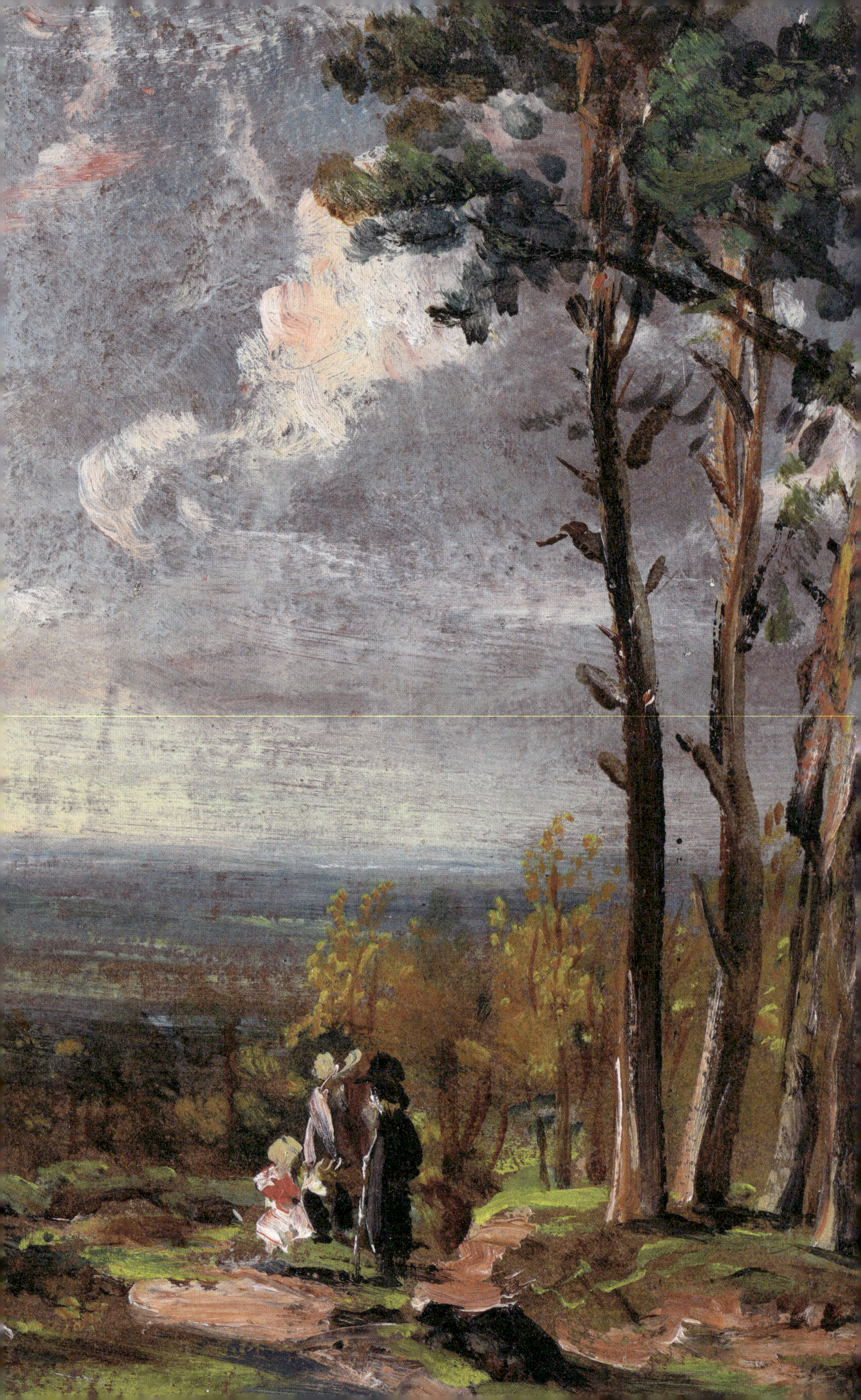

SUSAN OWENS

Constable's Year

AN ARTIST IN CHANGING SEASONS

Over 60 illustrations

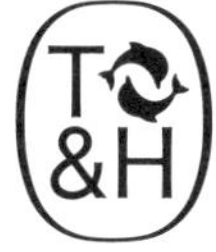

All artworks by John Constable, 1776–1837, unless otherwise indicated.

On the cover, front: *Landscape: Ploughing scene in Suffolk (A summerland)* (detail), 1814. Oil on canvas, 50.5 × 76.5 cm (20 × 30⅛ in.). Private collection
Spine: *The rectory from East Bergholt House* (detail), 1810. Oil on canvas laid on panel, 15.6 × 24.8 cm (6¼ × 9⅞ in.). Philadelphia Museum of Art, John G. Johnson Collection (cat. 856)
Back: *A rainstorm over the sea* (detail), c. 1824–8. Oil on paper, 23.5 x 32.6 cm (9⅜ × 12⅞ in). Royal Academy of Art (03/1390)

Endpapers: *Rushes by a pool*, c. 1821. Oil on paper on board. Oil on paper on board, 22.9 × 29.8 cm (9 × 11¾ in.). Yale Center for British Art, Paul Mellon Collection, New Haven, CT (B1981.25.151FR)

p. 2 *Hampstead Heath looking towards Harrow* (detail), 1821. Oil on paper laid on canvas.

First published in the United Kingdom in 2026 by
Thames & Hudson Ltd, 6–24 Britannia Street,
London WC1X 9JD

First published in the United States of America in 2026 by
Thames & Hudson Inc., 500 Fifth Avenue, New York,
New York 10110

Constable's Year © 2026 Thames & Hudson Ltd, London

Text © 2026 Susan Owens

Cover designed by Steve O Connell

Interior layout designed by Anna Perotti

EU Authorized Representative: Interart S.A.R.L.
19 rue Charles Auray, 93500 Pantin, Paris, France
productsafety@thameshudson.co.uk
interart.fr

A CIP catalogue record for this book is available
from the British Library

Library of Congress Control Number 2025939038

ISBN 978-0-500-02889-6
02

Printed and bound in Italy by L.E.G.O. Spa

Be the first to know about our new releases,
exclusive content and author events by visiting
thamesandhudson.com
thamesandhudsonusa.com
thamesandhudson.com.au

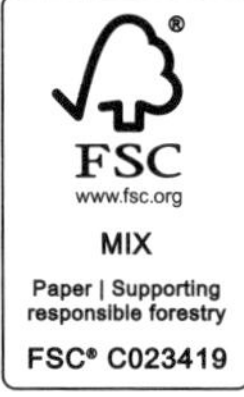

Contents

Introduction   6

I *Spring*   12

II *Summer*   48

III *Autumn*   98

IV *Winter*   146

Epilogue   186

Year By Year   188
Notes   198
A Constable Bookcase   210
Works of Art and Picture List   213
Acknowledgments   217
Index   219

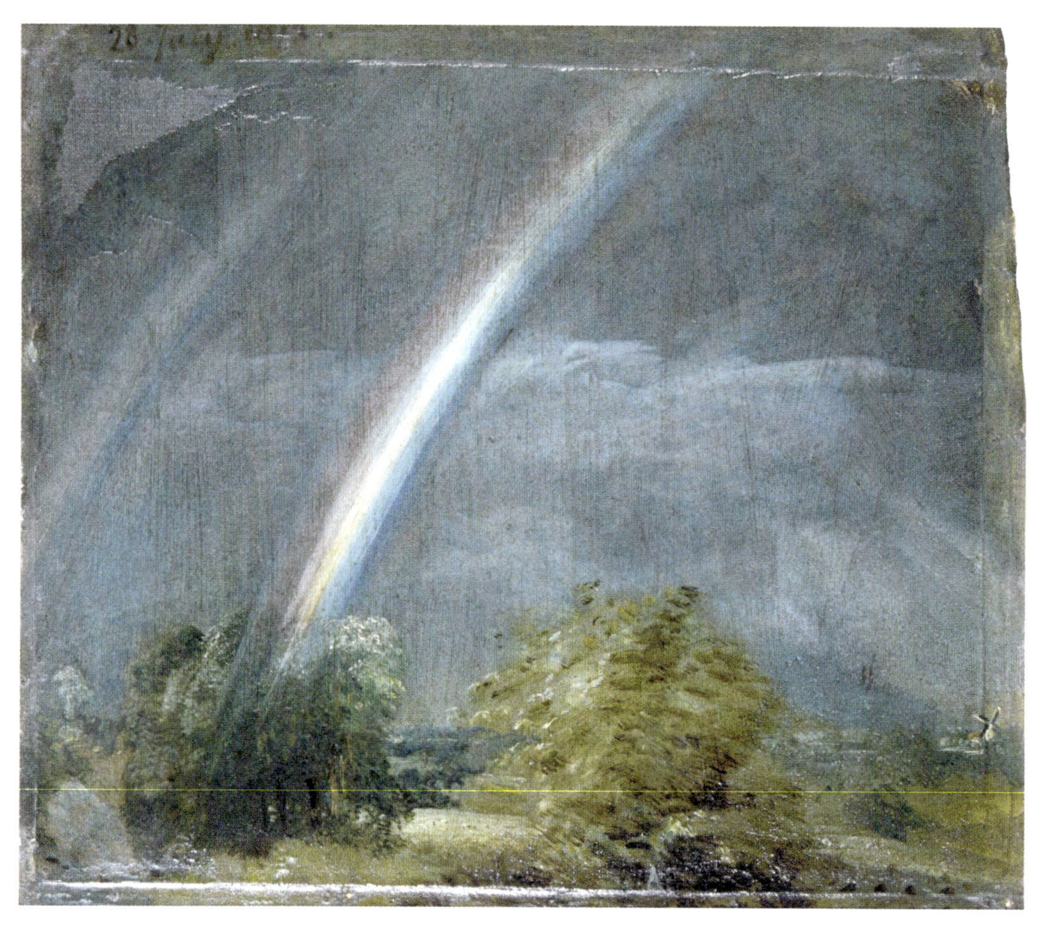

Landscape with a double rainbow, 28 July 1812. Oil on paper.

Introduction

A fellow artist said that John Constable's pictures made him reach for his greatcoat, his umbrella. Constable himself described one of his paintings as 'exhilarating, fresh & and blowing', as though a breeze came from its surface. Stand in front of *The Hay Wain* today, shut out the hum of London's National Gallery and let your eyes wander over the scene: after a few seconds the still warmth of a summer's noon will come to meet you, an atmosphere so rich it could make you drowsy. Or look at Constable's hasty oil sketches, his dispatches from lanes and towpaths. They tell you far more than what the landscape looks like; they tell you about the blustery wind and the flickering of sunlight through leaves, the thickening of the air before a storm.

Constable achieved this by lying down under trees and watching the way the branches moved above him. By lavishing more attention on hedges than anyone but farmworkers. By gazing into ditches, rapt, claiming that he could see great subjects down there. In his day, most artists followed convention when they painted the English landscape; they idealized and generalized and inadvertently lost sight of reality. Landscape painting had become a hall of mirrors, led more by other paintings than by the appearance of nature itself. Constable rejected these ambitions as 'seeking the truth at second hand'. Instead, he set out to paint the country as it actually looked – and felt – under showery, brightening English skies. His passionate, dogged determination to represent the vivid colours of nature and his startlingly fresh evocations of being outdoors on heaths, canal sides and country lanes set him apart from artists of his own time, but resulted in paintings that ring as true as ever today.

For a sense of how far removed Constable's vision of the landscape was from that of his contemporaries, try this: one October day, his close friend John Fisher wrote to him about a fishing trip he proposed to make, to which Constable responded enthusiastically with a list of his own favourite riverside sights, sounds and sensations. They were, to put it mildly, unconventional. 'The sound of water escaping from Mill dams,' he wrote with relish, 'Willows, Old rotten Banks, slimy posts, & brickwork. I love such things'. It is hard to imagine another artist of the era having anything but distaste for the slimy and the rotten. But Constable had grown up in the country, the son of a Suffolk man who owned land, mills and barges that carried goods up and down the River Stour. He had spent his childhood on the riverbank and in the fields. For him, the landscape was not just a visual spectacle; it had an extra dimension that he knew gave him an advantage over other painters. He once compared himself to London artists, remarking that they knew 'nothing of the feeling of a country life' as he did. Feeling is an important word in Constable's lexicon: for him, the landscape had to be felt, both on the skin and in the heart. And that meant experiencing it through the seasons – whether sleet slapped you in the face when you went outdoors or you were thrilled by the song of skylarks in April – not just admiring it on a fine summer's day on an annual sketching tour. 'At all times of the day, at night, and in all seasons of the year', recalled a friend, he 'had inexpressible delight in viewing the works of nature.' It also meant paying attention to fleeting natural phenomena, from rainbows to sun shining through foliage, and recording them in the precious seconds before they vanished. When he was up on Hampstead Heath studying the fast-changing skies, he noted not only the dates but the exact times of day on the backs of his sketches, as though he were collecting data for a scientific experiment. Perhaps, in a way, he was: when giving a lecture one evening, he declared to his audience with particular emphasis: *'we see nothing till we truly understand it'*.

Today, he is often considered a traditional artist. But in truth Constable was radical: radical in rejecting second-hand, slip-shod versions of nature; radical in subjecting natural phenomena to intense scrutiny; radical in doggedly forging a new kind of painting to fit the landscape he saw with his farmer's eye and felt beneath the soles of his boots. He spent his career taking a stand against convention, against habit, against all the tricks and mannerisms that had made art stale.

Constable was radical, too, in viewing the country as an industrial place. His was a working landscape of windmills, locks and watermills. He painted a picture of men building a barge in a dry dock that is so detailed you could use it as an instruction manual, and the technology of ploughs fascinated him to the extent that he recorded regional variations in his sketchbooks. During his lifetime, society, working lives and the countryside itself were transformed as the industrial world we know today began to take shape. In his art Constable had to find ways of balancing the often-opposing demands of landscape painting and the modern farming practices he saw around him. As much as he loved poetry – nature poets James Thomson and William Cowper were particular favourites – it was the prose of the agricultural year that spoke loudest to him.

Constable's life and work were profoundly shaped by the year's cycle. As they were for many other professional artists of his time, summer and early autumn were periods for sketching and gathering material for compositions, while late autumn and winter were for painting in the studio. Early spring was the high-pressure time for completing a picture and meeting the deadline to send it off for exhibition. Other artists tended to tour during the summer, visiting places generally acknowledged to be picturesque or spectacular, but Constable did so rarely. Until he was forty, he usually went back to the village of East Bergholt in Suffolk to stay for several months at his family home, before returning to London for a 'winter's campaign' at the easel; after he married, his wife's health set the agenda. Summers were spent between London and Brighton or Hampstead, where his family stayed because the air was cleaner than in central London, with occasional visits to see Fisher in Dorset or Salisbury. Few English artists of his generation travelled so little.

Things could have been different. Imagine a world in which Constable's mature paintings were not of Suffolk and Hampstead but of Cumbrian lakes and Swiss mountain passes. Would they have been popular in his own time? Probably. Would they strike a chord today? I am not so sure. Constable's oil sketches and paintings resonate now precisely because he was a painter not so much of landscape as of place. He drew and painted where he happened to be, places with which he had – or was developing – a deep connection. A 'landscape' is seen through an imaginary frame placed in front of a view that fits an agreed idea of the picturesque. Place goes deeper. His places were infused with love for his wife, Maria, and with the few, deep friendships that sustained him. Throughout this book I have imagined walking with Constable and seeing what he saw. As the seasons unfolded, I visited the places he knew – most of them surprisingly unchanged by the years – looked at his paintings and drawings and read his letters until I felt I had begun to understand the layers of memories and associations that enriched Constable's own vision.

In the earlier years of his career Constable constructed his sense of place with a wealth of detail. He noted the date he heard the first thrush sing; in April he wrote home about the swallows and the arrival of buttercups in the meadows; and he rejoiced over the cow parsley in the hedgerows in the first weeks of summer. The sketchbooks he filled during the warmer months, when on fine days he would spend long days walking and drawing out of doors, 'never at home 'till night', bristle with daily observations. These and his oil sketches, so often precisely dated, are a visual diary, tracing the passing weeks and the turning seasons, the ploughing, haymaking and harvesting. Together they form an anthology of place. Later, detail became less visible in his work. It had been absorbed, mulched down in his mind to form the rich humus from which his later, expressionistic paintings and drawings grew.

Constable stood at a slight angle to the professional art world he inhabited. He thought differently from so many of his contemporaries because his mindset had been established by the work with which he had been familiar as a youth, which was intimately connected to land ownership and management: the maintenance of towpaths, windmills and barges, for instance, and the timing of sowing and reaping. Occupation shapes the ways we think. If, like Constable, you spend your late teens and early twenties training to run a family business, the habits of mind you acquire during those years are not so easily abandoned, even if circumstances suddenly change and you are, at last, free to follow your inclination. Farming, milling and land stewardship – profoundly seasonal work – were not only in Constable's blood; they shaped his neural pathways. It was a difference that caused him to struggle for acceptance in the art world; but it gave him the power to see what others missed. He once complained that his art was 'to be found under every hedge, and in every lane, and therefore nobody thinks it worth picking up'. Today, 250 years since Constable's birth, that is precisely why it matters. He rethought landscape painting in vital, eccentric, astonishing, necessary ways. By insisting on the importance of weather and season, of particularity and care, he forged a precious connection between us and the natural world that is more important now than ever.

A Note on Spelling

When quoting from letters I have preserved all idiosyncratic punctuation and orthography, such as Constable's habitual spellings 'beautifull', 'beleive' and 'feild', because they are expressive of character and unlikely to be misunderstood. In most cases I have chosen not to disrupt the text with '[sic]' (short for *sic erat scriptum* or 'thus it had been written'); this appears only in the case of misspelled proper nouns.

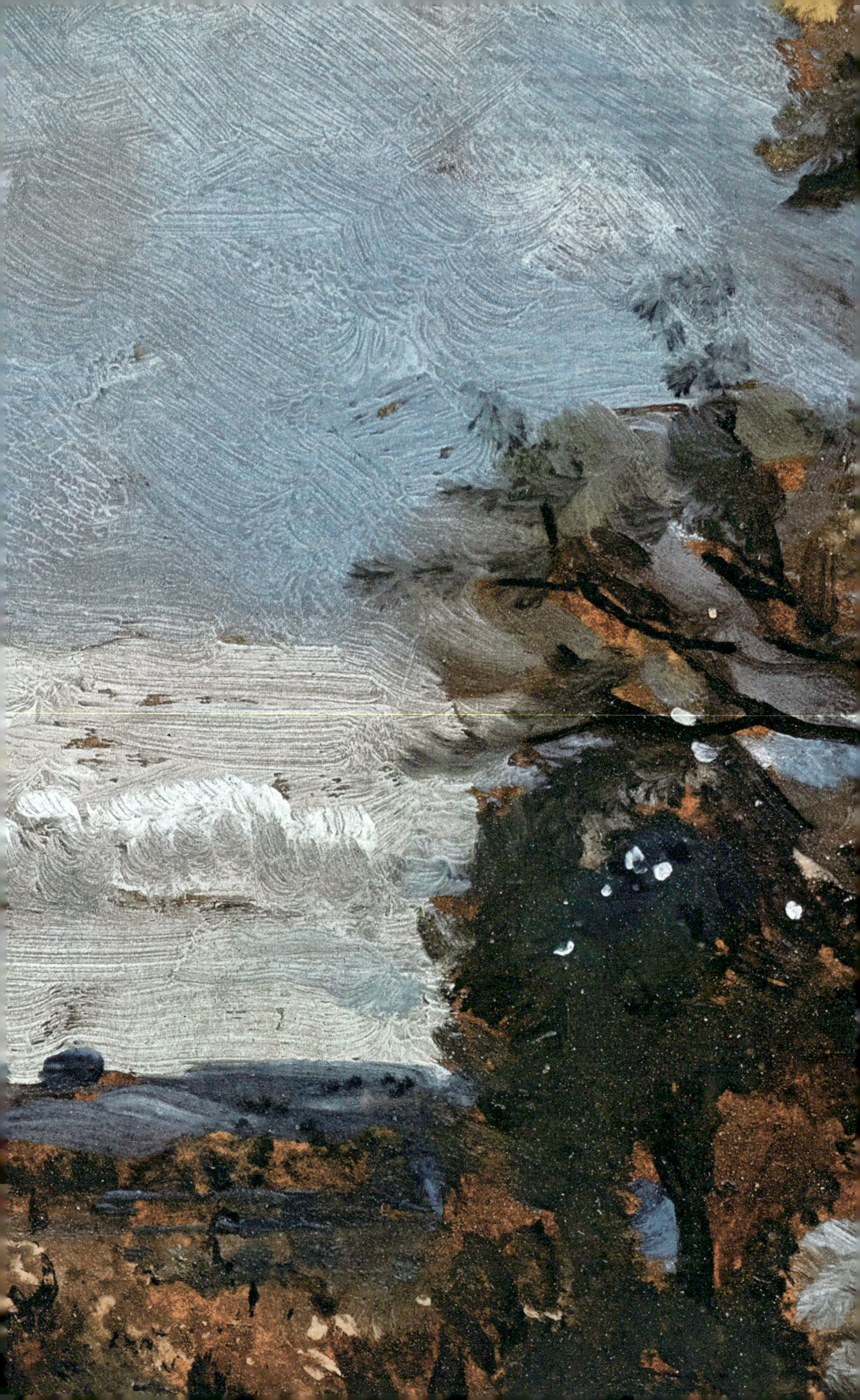

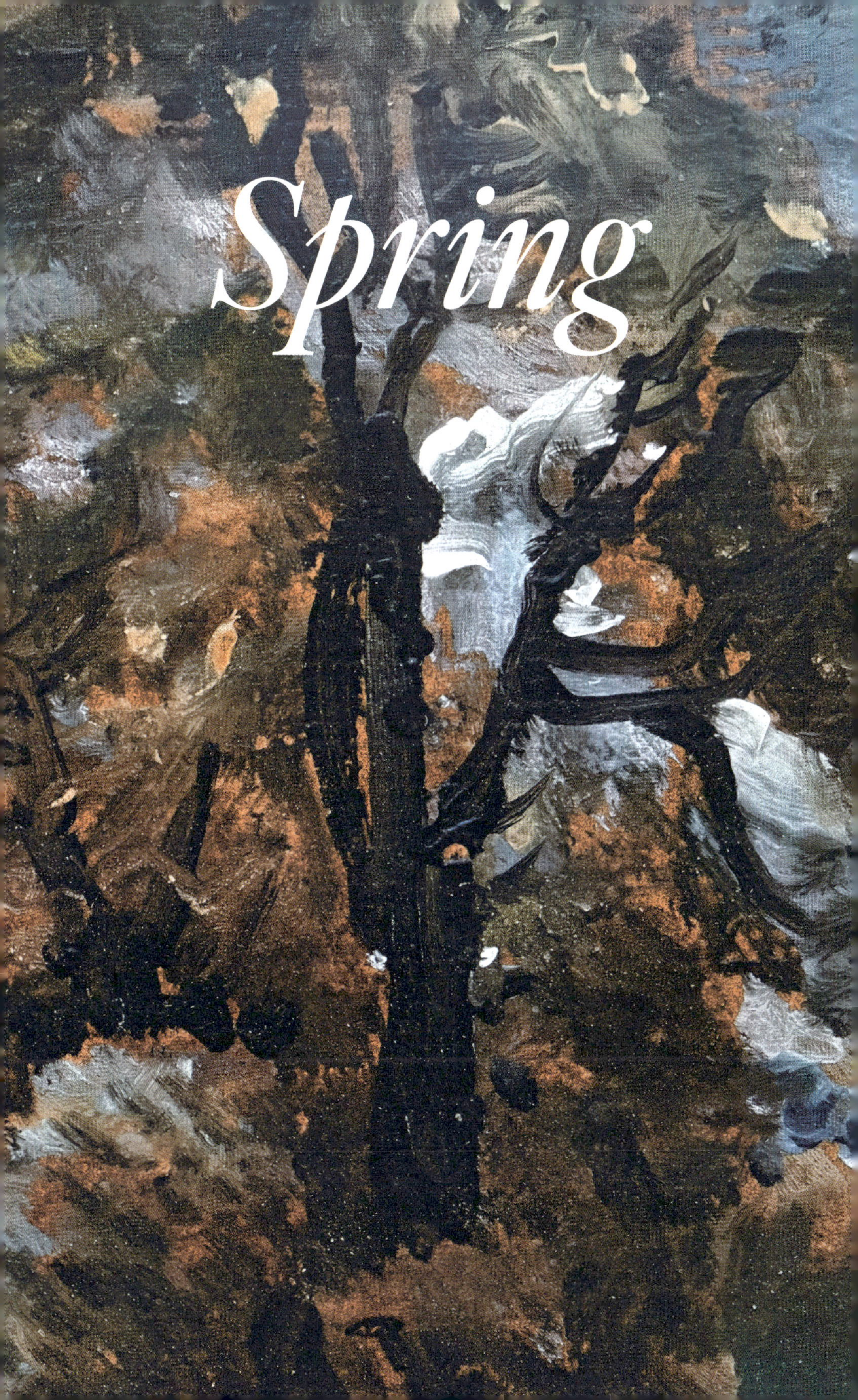
Spring

'I love the exhilarating freshness of spring'

A purl through burnt glass

The balance of John Constable's working year was all wrong. His favourite season was spring, when primroses and cowslips speckled the banks, trees frothed with flowers and bluebells scented the woods. Virtually every time he got out into the country in April or May, he would exclaim that it was the best year yet and he had never in his life seen such beauty. But unfortunately for him, this glorious season of budding and blossoming coincided precisely with the weeks he needed to be in London. The Royal Academy of Arts – the pivot around which the British art world revolved – opened its annual Summer Exhibition on the first Monday of May. Artists were obliged to spend the earliest months of the year in their studios, completing pictures and arranging transport for the appointed submission days at the beginning of April. The Academy's hanging committee would then make its selection and decide where each painting would be placed – positioning was all-important. Then there were the 'varnishing' days, when artists were invited into the galleries to make last-minute changes to their pictures before the Royal Family came in for their private view and the Royal Academicians gathered for their Annual Dinner. And once the exhibition had opened to the public it was politic for them to make themselves available to sweet-talk potential buyers. It was a busy and demanding time in every way – artistic, administrative, social. Hardly the moment to pack up and leave town.

Constable had lived through twenty-two springs when, in 1799, he first moved to London from East Bergholt in order to study art at the Royal Academy Schools. That made him slightly older than most of his

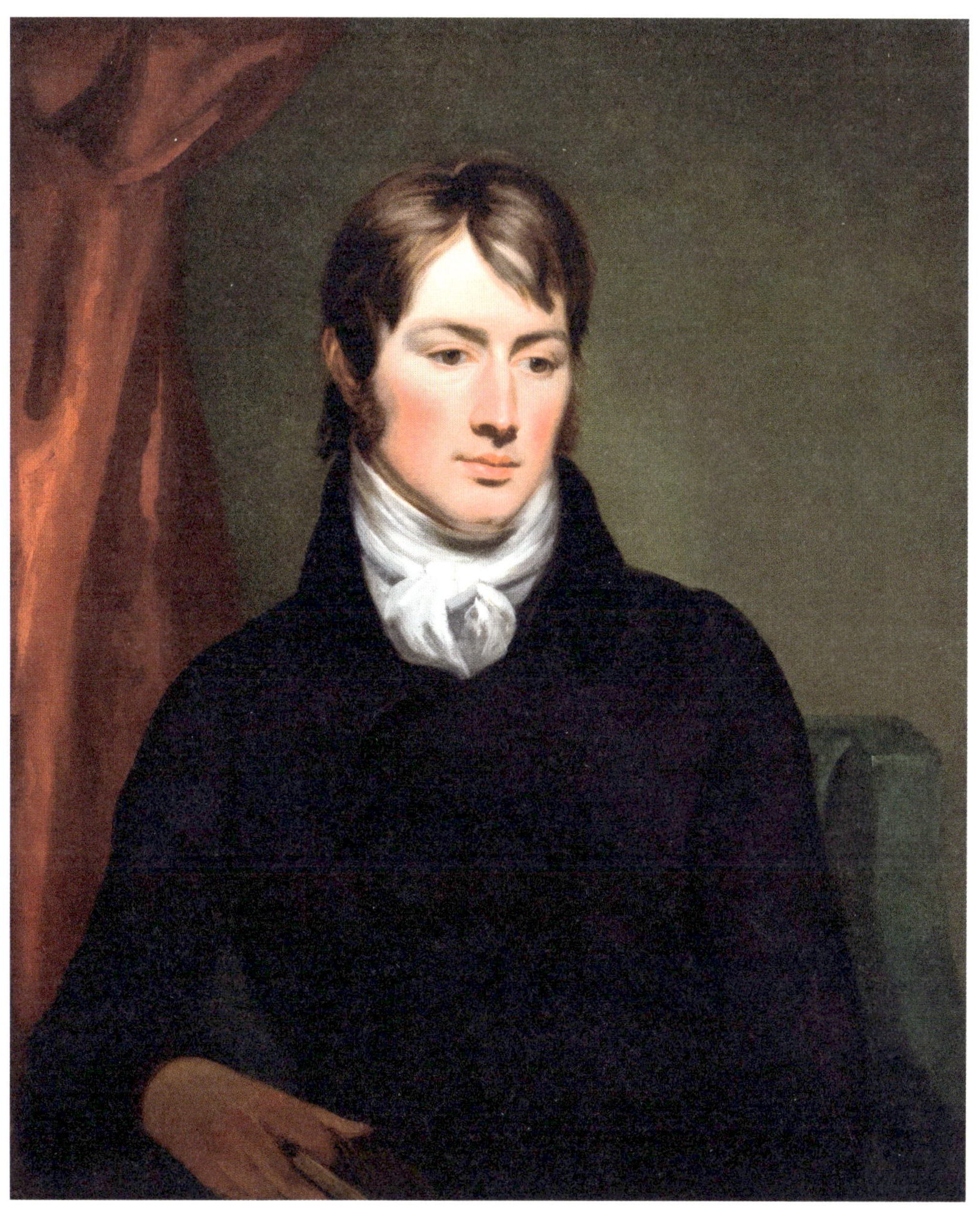

Ramsay Richard Reinagle, *Portrait of John Constable*, c. 1799. Oil on canvas.

contemporaries, young men who typically arrived in their late teens or on the cusp of their twenties. Of course, it was not uncommon for parents to put up opposition to a child who wanted to pursue a precarious career as an artist – it was the rare mother and father who encouraged their offspring to take this path – but even so, young John had faced a higher barrier and a longer delay than most. His father, Golding Constable, had inherited money and property, and from this basis had established a lucrative business milling and transporting grain. He had forty-odd acres of land in and around East Bergholt, a windmill on the heath, watermills at Flatford and Dedham, barges to work the navigable River Stour and a brig to take sacks of flour from the port at Mistley up the Thames estuary to London. Having built an imposing house for his family slap bang in the centre of East Bergholt on the profits, this well-to-do merchant may have acquired social status for his family, but he brought up his sons to work. Golding would no more have left the future of his business uncertain than he would have allowed his corn to go unharvested or his boats uncaulked. As far as he was concerned, John would be his successor and that was that. The circumstances were particularly unfortunate in light of John's inclinations: it was not even as though he were the eldest of the brothers. Golding, named for his father, was two years older; but this lovable, unreliable young man could not be persuaded to take responsibility, or in fact to interest himself in anything other than shooting game. He was also prone to fits, which were probably due to epilepsy. So when John reached the age of sixteen, he was sent down to his father's dry dock to learn how barges were made, and over to his windmill to grind grain into flour and to discover what the sky could tell him about the changing weather. He would have been instructed in the maintenance of watermills, windmills, barges, locks and towpaths, as well as in book-keeping and the managerial side of the business. It was only when Abram, the baby of the family, finally came of age and agreed to step into the role himself that John was free to make art his profession, rather than a passion to be followed in his spare time. But his experiences stood him in good stead: he would become the only landscape painter of his generation who knew how a windmill actually worked and could tell you the week of the year by the colour of ripening corn in a painting.

What was he like, this young man whose prayers had just been answered? Shortly after his arrival in London, his sometime friend and fellow art student Ramsay Richard Reinagle painted a portrait. He captured Constable's high-coloured complexion; the short sideburns that were fashionable at the time; hair the colour of a conker flopping youthfully over his forehead. His striking, rather wholesome good looks had turned heads in East Bergholt and earned him the nickname 'the handsome miller' (when a group of local girls called on him at home, saying they wished to see his paintings, his mother teased them by enquiring: well, young ladies, would you like to go up to my son all together – or one at a time?). Reinagle also captures a reflective expression in his eyes and a slight, self-possessed smile. Many of his fellow students at the Royal Academy would have been more worldly wise than this young man from Suffolk, but his experience of managing his father's business – as well as his few extra years – had given him an air of authority. The portrait exudes the quiet confidence of a man finally granted the life he always knew was his by right.

Getting used to life in London can be hard: Constable found this at the beginning of the nineteenth century as many young people have since. Back in Suffolk, his life had been an outdoors one regardless of the season, whether he was seeing goods in and out of the warehouses at Mistley Quay, checking the progress of crops in the fields, sketching in the lanes or out walking with the family dogs. Things were different in his new environment. 'I seldom go out as I am so much confined to work at present,' he reported in the early weeks of 1801 to John Dunthorne, a close friend and amateur artist from East Bergholt with whom Constable had spent many days companionably sketching. 'I paint by all the daylight we have, and that is little enough, less perhaps than you have by much, I sometimes however see the sky, but imagine to yourself how a purl must look through a burnt glass.' A bright day, when the spring sunshine lit up the London streets, only made things worse. 'This fine weather almost makes me melancholy,' he had told Dunthorne the previous year; 'it recalls so forcibly every scene we have visited and drawn together. I even love every stile and stump, and every lane in the village, so deep rooted are early impressions.'

In years to come, when John had long been accustomed to life in London, his siblings knew exactly what to say when they wanted to persuade him

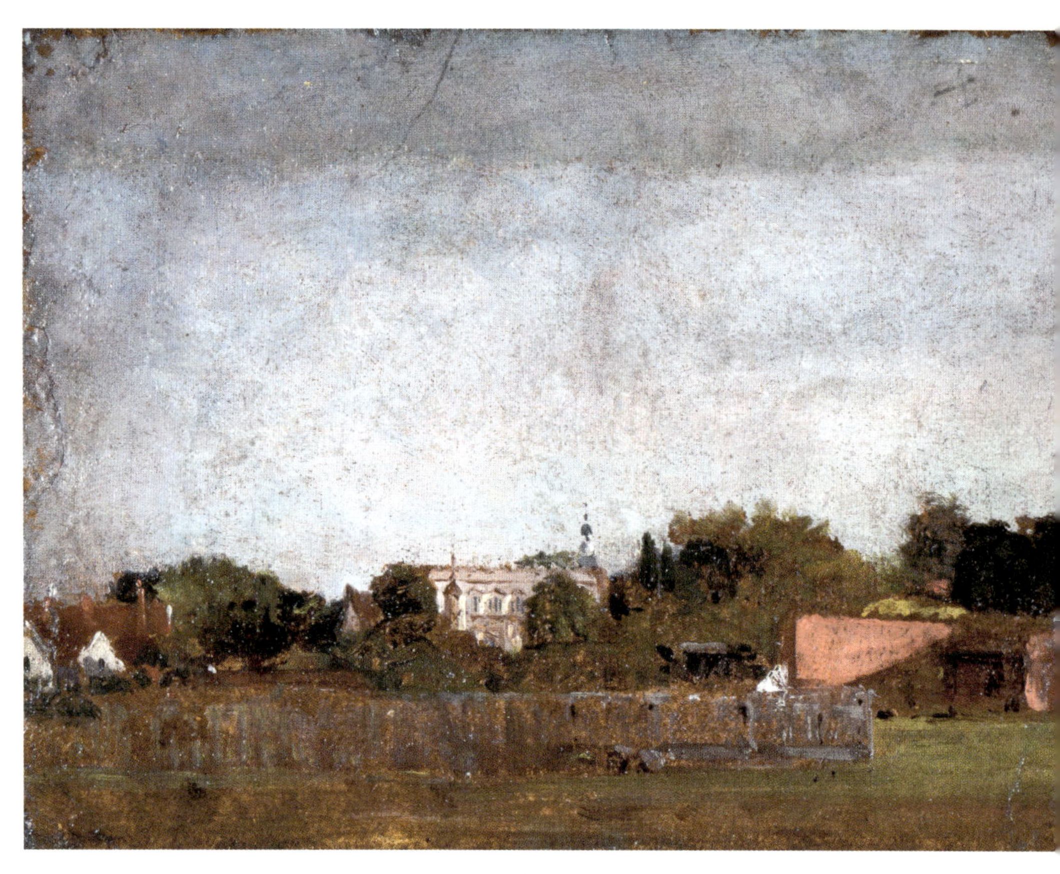

East Bergholt House, c. 1809–11. Oil on millboard. This view of the back of Constable's home in East Bergholt shows a fashionable three-storey house with five sash windows on each of the upper floors that framed views over the family farm. St Mary's church is on the left.

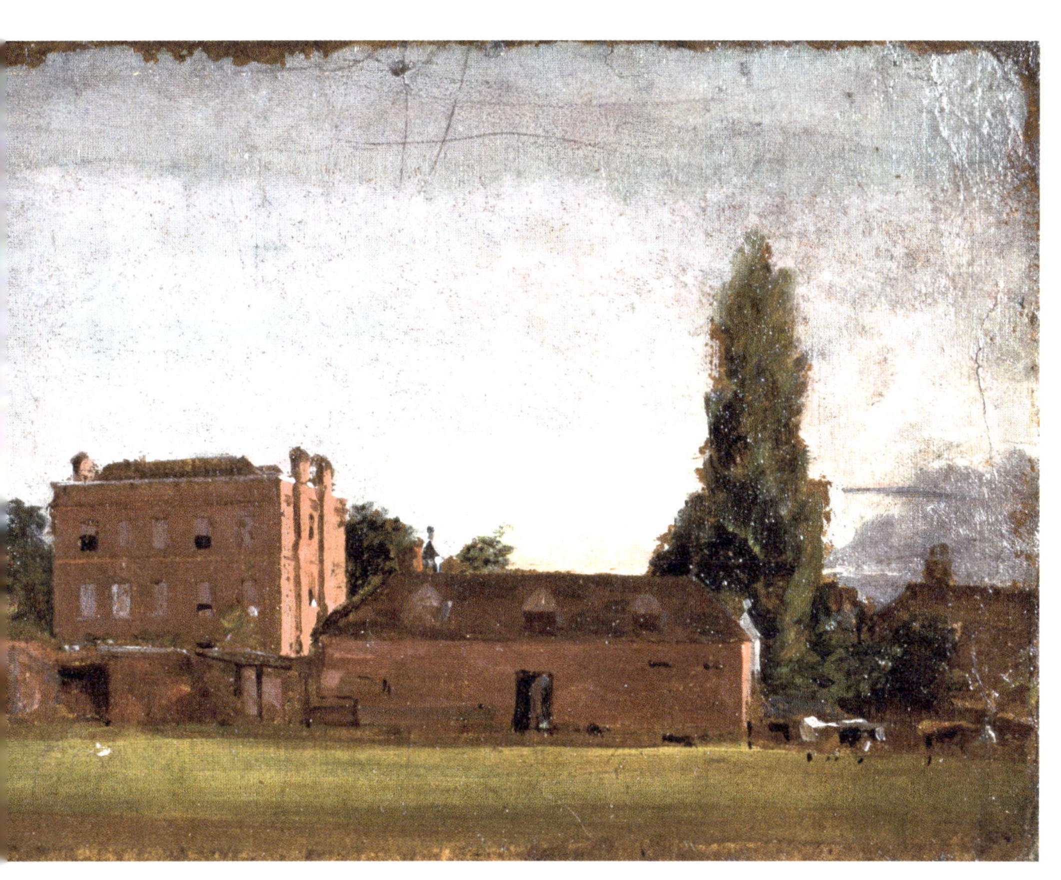

to visit. 'When you have arranged your plans would it not be a wise step in you to take a *snuff* of native air?', his sister Mary enquired; 'the country alone would charm you and the *song of early birds* and everything in Nature is delightful around this sweetest spot on all the earth'. On the occasion of this particular letter, however, he could not leave town. His wife Maria had given birth to a baby daughter, a fifth child in their growing brood, at the end of March 1825; that, along with moving everyone to Hampstead for the summer, kept him too busy for even a sniff of the Suffolk spring.

From 1799 until his marriage in 1816 – which is to say through most of his twenties and all of his thirties – Constable had lodgings in London but would normally spend several months of the year at the family home in East Bergholt, leaving London in June or July and often not returning until early November. This was when he roamed the fields and lanes with his sketch-books, storing up views and memories for the winter and spring to come. And yet even at this time Constable's relationship with the seasons was probably more complicated than his family realized. Look again at his let-ter to Dunthorne: his language is almost violent when he writes of the force of his recollections, the deep roots of his feelings and the love – not affec-tion, not liking, but *love* – of the ordinary things to be found in any village. Who but Constable would admit to loving a stump? The visceral quality to his feelings could only have come through his particular combination of artistic vision, practical knowledge and devotion. He had lavished time paying close attention to local trees, lanes and cottages with his sketchbook on his knee. But six and a half years in his father's business had required him to do more than look at his surroundings; this boy had had to develop a farmer's eye. He had learned to anticipate changes in the weather and the season, to feel them through his skin. He had had to study the quality of the till, the swelling of the navigable River Stour after rain, what the direction and strength of the breeze meant for the windmill's sails – and how to read the sky.

It was an unusual combination in an age in which most landscape paint-ers toured each summer in search of picturesque spots in the usual places – in Britain, Derbyshire, the Lake District and north Wales were the most fashionable – but it was to serve Constable well. He was obliged to paint the pictures that he hoped to exhibit at the Royal Academy in his London studio during the winter and early spring, when the days were shortest and lamps needed to be lit. And yet Constable came to be known in his time – as he is now – for making the weather and the season feel vividly present. In November 1825, he mentioned to a friend that he had just been visited by a neighbour in Hampstead, the actor Jack Bannister, who wanted to buy a painting. 'He has long desired one of me, in which, he says, he can feel the wind blowing on his face. He says my landscape has something in it beyond freshness, it's life, exhilaration &c.' (That '&c.' a typical eyebrow-raise in the face of gushing praise.) A picture such as *The Cornfield* is animated by the warm breeze of a summer's day, even though it was begun in London as 1826 got off to a chilly start. Constable performed imaginative acrobatics in order to project his mind to the Suffolk summer and recreate the experience of being in a place he loved. His roots in the places he painted, his knowledge of them at different times of year and his mental habit of picturing them gave him the ability not only to show people the appearance of a place in a particular season, but to make them feel it too. As he found his feet in London during these early years, however, all this lay ahead of him.

A fresh start

In the spring of 1802 Constable found himself at a turning point. For the first time, he had submitted a picture to the Royal Academy's annual exhibition. It was accepted by the Academicians who sat on the committee, and it appears in the catalogue as no. 19. As pictures were numbered according to their placement in the room, a look at that year's catalogue tells us that it hung between no. 18, *Tygers* by Sawrey Gilpin, and no. 20, *A Shipwreck on the Coast of Picardy* by François Louis Thomas Francia. In contrast to these titles, which in their different ways offer excitement and drama, Constable's submission was simply called *A Landscape* – with the result that to this day no-one can be entirely sure which one it was. It was a laconic, take-me-or-leave-me kind of title. But the fact that the picture was there at all was a distinct achievement. Constable had marched into territory policed by the most prestigious artistic establishment in Britain and planted his flag.

The exhibition open, Constable could prepare to leave for East Bergholt. At the end of May 1802, he wrote to Dunthorne announcing his imminent arrival in the village; but whatever he intended to say to his friend when he fetched paper, sat down at his desk and dipped his pen in the inkpot, what he actually wrote turned out to be not so much a letter as a manifesto for the future direction of his art. 'For these few weeks past', he announced, 'I beleive I have thought more seriously on my profession than at any other time of my life – that is, which is the shurest way to real excellence.' Describing the exhibition to Dunthorne as containing 'little or nothing … worth looking up to', he may have intended to give the impression of worldly wise disappointment, but really this is fighting talk. He had not only seen his work hung, for the first time, alongside that of other artists, many of them distinguished – he had also become aware that it measured up. Signs of weakness in others told him he was in the game. 'The great vice of the present day is *bravura*,' he continued, 'an attempt at something beyond the truth' – in other words, the walls were covered with slapdash bids for dazzling effect. In the face of this superficial, meretricious art, there was, he continued to his friend, 'room enough for a natural painture [a kind of Franglais for painting]'. He acknowledged that up until that point he had tried to shape his own style of landscape painting by looking at other artists' work and, as he put it, 'seeking the truth at second hand'. Now, he saw that that could only lead to stale and derivative pictures. He concludes: 'Nature is the fountain's head, the source from whence all originality must spring.' This young painter had found a door leading to territory he could make his own. He had thrust it open and stepped through.

Elevated talk of fountainheads, sources and originality was all very well. But what practical steps did Constable need to take to create the kind of art that he knew would not be fashionable, but that he felt passionately was needed? The answer lay back at home: from his rooms just north of Oxford Street, Constable was thinking of Suffolk and picturing the landscape in his mind's eye. 'I shall shortly return to Bergholt where I shall make some laborious studies from nature', he told Dunthorne, adding that he was aiming at 'a pure and unaffected representation' of scenes 'with respect to colour particularly'. But it wasn't just his art that he felt needed an overhaul; as he told his old friend, he had a new determination to manage his

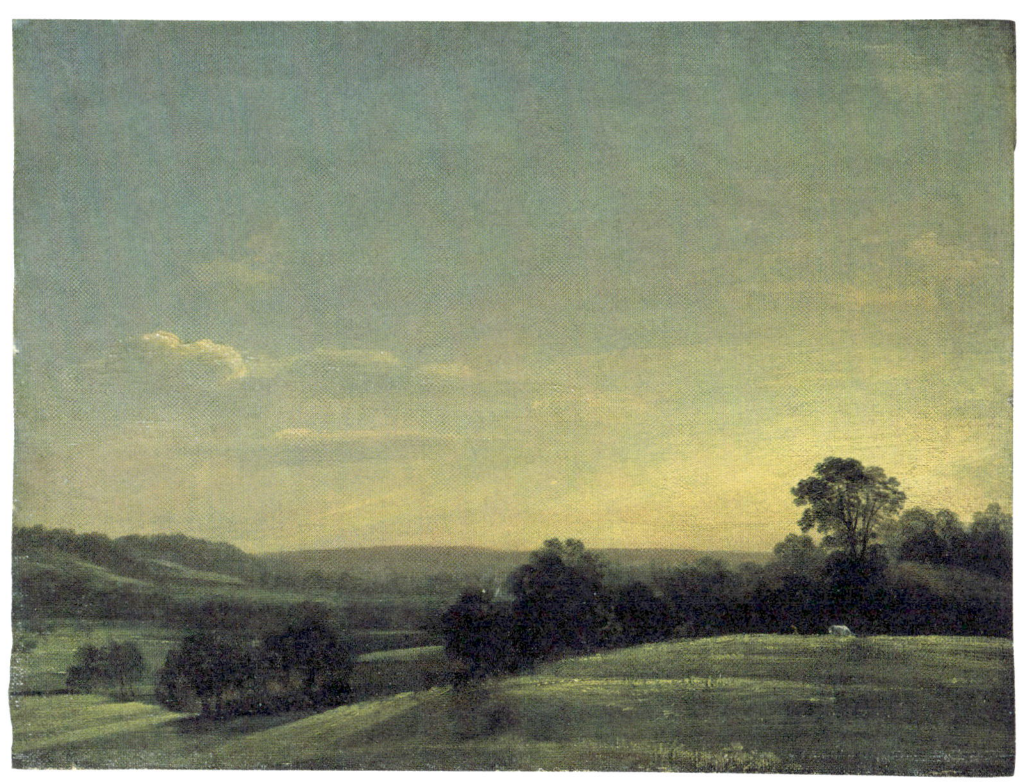

Dedham Vale, evening, July 1802. Oil on canvas. *Detail overleaf.*

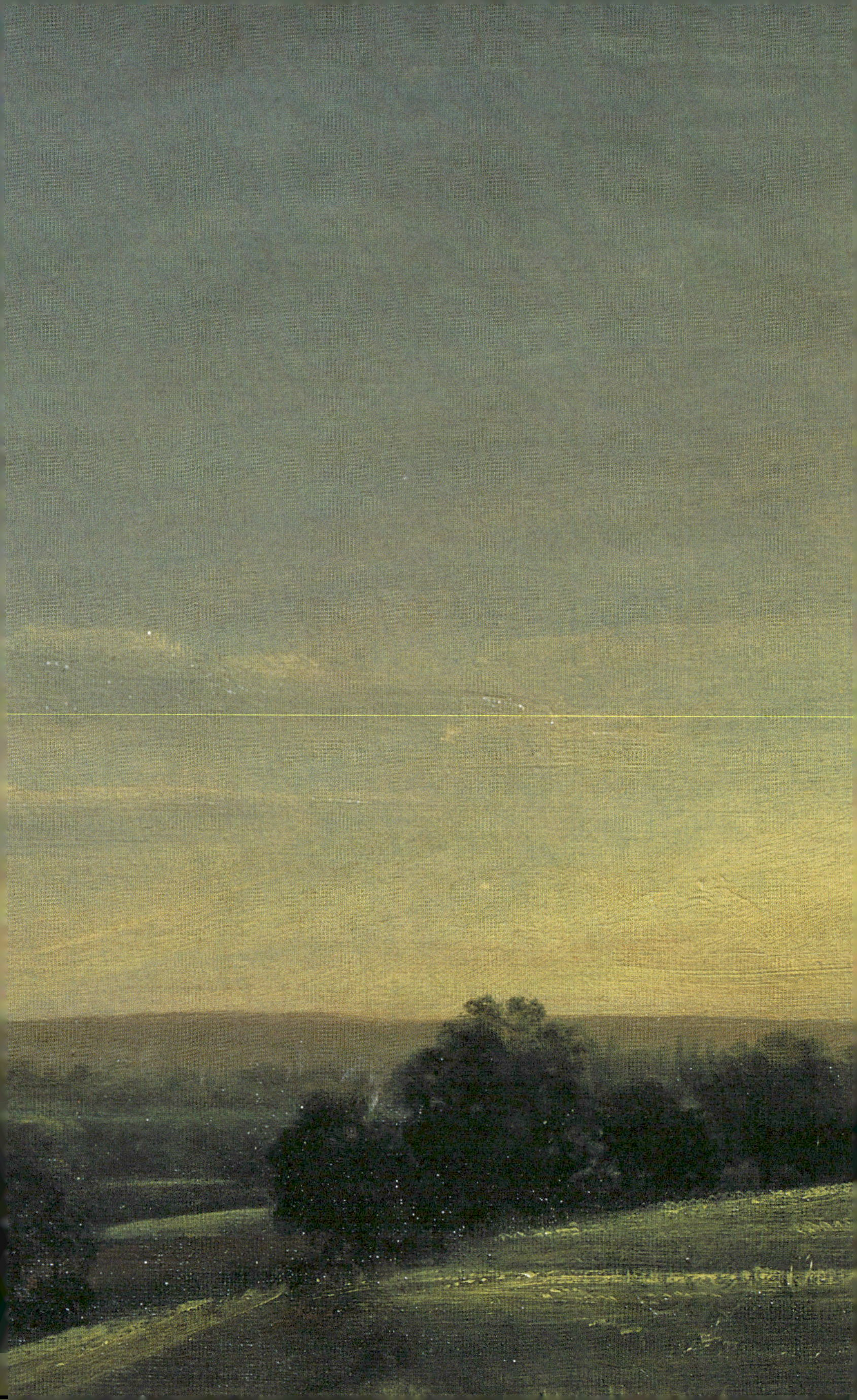

time better and to adopt a more single-minded approach to his work: 'I am come to a determination to make no idle visits this summer or to give up my time to common place people.'

All that summer and well into the autumn, as the mornings became misty and the light more golden, Constable remained in East Bergholt and focused on the woods and vales he had known all his life. But it was with a difference. For the first time, he tried hard to look at them as they appeared to his eye, without the filters of the landscape art he knew, loved and had stored away in his mind. It wasn't at all easy. Thomas Gainsborough in particular often got in the way. Constable's earliest drawings of the lanes and cottages around East Bergholt reveal the influence of his illustrious Suffolk predecessor in every line. 'I fancy I see Gainsborough in every hedge and hollow tree', he had reported excitedly in 1799 during a campaign of sketching around Ipswich, where Gainsborough himself had lived in the 1750s before his move to fashionable Bath. Constable's beloved Claude Lorrain, the celebrated French artist of the seventeenth century, whose paintings he had seen in the collection of his friend and mentor Sir George Beaumont, kept beguiling him with glorious visions of Italianate landscapes framed by lofty trees and fading into blue distances. These were challenges Constable would face throughout his career. 'When I sit down to make a sketch from nature,' he confessed years later, 'the first thing I try to do is, *to forget that I have ever seen a picture*'. It is ironic that today many of us find it hard to look at Dedham Vale, East Bergholt and Flatford without thinking of Constable's own paintings. Artists have a way of getting between us and a view, however objectively we try to look.

Back in 1802, after May's resolution, he was trying as hard as he could. Some of the evenings he had resolved not to fritter away were spent outdoors, trying to capture the subtle changes the evening light made to the colour and atmosphere of the landscape. One July evening he took his canvas and set up an easel in a meadow that lay behind West Lodge, the house of his accommodating neighbour Mrs Roberts, which commanded a magnificent view up the Stour Valley towards Stoke-by-Nayland. The resulting composition, among the first Constable made under his rigorous new regime, is a study of raking light and long shadows. He may not have been able to suppress Claude entirely – the old artist seems in particular to have whispered in his ear about the elegant tree on the right – but an East Anglian spirit of place is tangible. Turf sparkles with the last rays of a setting sun and the sky, the colour of ripe wheat near the horizon, is washed with teal, while down in the valley smoke from kitchen fires rises in the windless air.

The turning year

The seasons mattered to Constable in ways that are hard to imagine now. He was born on the cusp; had he belonged to a younger generation, his mind would have been shaped by different pressures. There are a few historical events that divide time into a 'before' and an 'after': the English Reformation is one, as are the English Civil Wars and the World Wars of the twentieth century. Among the most thoroughly transformative was the industrial revolution, which brought irrevocable change in the space of Constable's lifetime. In 1776, the year of his birth and the commercial introduction of the Watt steam engine, England's economy was largely rural. By the time of his death in 1837 – the year Queen Victoria came to the throne – blast furnaces were churning smoke into the skies, factories and textile mills were drawing huge numbers of people into towns and steam power was radically changing the distance and the ease with which people and goods could travel.

But the places Constable knew best – Suffolk, Essex, Sussex, Wiltshire – remained predominantly rural. Of course there were signs of what was to come, often right there in the familiar landscapes he drew and painted: great pits, for instance, where sand was being quarried from Hampstead Heath by speculative builders to fuel London's rapid expansion; or the impressive new chain pier in Brighton, completed in 1823, that served as a landing stage for steam packet boats to Dieppe (Constable didn't approve, calling it a 'dandy jetty'). Signs were present in small things too: in 1831, his sister Ann wrote to him with one of the newly patented steel-nibbed pens ('I am writing this with a Metallic Pen, Cousin Mary gave me') that were swiftly to replace the quills people had used for hundreds of years. And yet the pattern of the farming year that underpinned it all, the ploughing, sowing, haymaking and harvesting, remained woven into the fabric of rural life. Letters from Constable's brother Abram, keeping him up to date with business matters, are full of anxious observations about the spring being early or late that year, the weather unusually wet or dry. The pages of the sketchbooks Constable kept in the 1810s are densely populated with the ploughmen, reapers and gleaners he observed at different times of year at work in the fields around East Bergholt – some of whom would have been employed on the family's arable land. He would have known their names. This rootedness made him attentive to the smallest details of the natural world as the year unfolded. On one of the last days of January 1816 he was a few miles east of Bergholt, in the village of Harkstead on the Orwell estuary, when, on sitting down with his sketchbook to make a drawing of the church, he heard a wryneck's call – a sign of the coming spring. It was significant enough for him not only to note it on his drawing with the date, but also to add that on 12 January he had heard a thrush's song. These things mattered enough for him to remember them, to write them down. Constable's precision was driven both by business and art, the former bringing methodical rigour, the latter providing an unusually intense capacity for observation.

The pattern of the seasons was also stamped on Constable's cultural landscape. On several occasions when his paintings were exhibited, he quoted short extracts from poems in the catalogue to illustrate his theme. When *The Cornfield* was shown at the British Institution in 1827, for example, he chose lines from 'Summer' in *The Seasons*, a lengthy poem cycle by the Scottish writer James Thomson: 'A fresher gale / Begins to wave the woods and stir the stream, / *Sweeping with shadowy gust the fields of corn*' (he ignored the fact that they actually describe the evening, not noon as represented in the picture). *The Seasons* was among the most famous poems of its day, one that shaped people's currents of thought for generations. First published in 1730, it became so wildly popular with the reading public that it went on to be printed in more than four hundred editions. Until the later Victorian period, when tastes changed and it finally fell out of fashion, there would have been few middle-class homes without a copy on their bookshelves. '*That* is true fame!' reflected Samuel Taylor Coleridge as he picked up a battered and much-read copy one day in the parlour of a country inn. The poem describes the progress of the year from earliest spring to winter, and the changes the seasons bring to the landscape, from spring flowers and summer rains through to the harvests of late summer and the fogs and snowstorms of November and December. There was even a children's version, of a sort: as a boy growing up in a wealthy and aspirational household, Constable is likely to have read John Aikin's *Calendar of Nature: Designed for the Instruction and Entertainment of Young Persons* (1784), a book that introduces its readers to each month with descriptions of its agricultural activities and the changes to be seen in flowers and trees, punctuated with copious quotations from Thomson and other authors. Given the choice, many adult readers of today would probably prefer Aikin: Thomson's verse can be hard work. It teems with allegorical representations of the Seasons, the Months, Nature, mythical figures and classical gods: May blushes, Zephyrs drift and the King of Day rejoices. Theatrical, exclamatory and artificial, it is exactly the kind of poem that reminds us how much we owe to Coleridge, William Wordsworth and the other Romantic nature poets, who dispensed with classical paraphernalia and sought instead to express how it felt to be out in the natural world with the kind of language you or I might use. Who were doing with words, in fact, what Constable did with paint.

But in its heyday, *The Seasons* answered a profound need. It was, in a way, a sophisticated contemporary version of the medieval Labours of the Months, the once-ubiquitous rhymes and pictures that divided the year into an unchanging cycle of pruning, ploughing, sowing, tending, harvesting, fruit-gathering, slaughtering and Christmas feasting. Depicted everywhere from calendars to stained-glass roundels, these monthly tasks were once so ubiquitous that everyone would have had them by heart. The year of hard work begins and ends with warmth and home comforts: 'By this fire I warme my hands; / And with my spade I delve my lands,' announce January and February, while all is neatly tied up with November's preparations for December's celebrations. 'At Martinmasse I kille my swine; / And at Christemasse I drinke redde wine.' The convention might gradually have become old fashioned, but when Thomson revived it for a new, educated audience – readers like Mr and Mrs Constable and their children – it still danced through the predictable course of the year to the rhythm of unchanging human experience. For Constable, *The Seasons* cast a validatory glamour over the agricultural year, endorsing it as a suitable subject for art.

Thomson's poem set the agenda for others. Among the most important for Constable was *The Farmer's Boy* (1800) by the Suffolk poet Robert Bloomfield, which he mined for extracts to embellish the titles of his paintings when they were listed in exhibition catalogues. Bloomfield had grown up in rural poverty in Honington, a village that lies between Bury St Edmunds and Thetford, and had been sent to labour on his uncle's farm at the age of about twelve. Though coloured by nostalgia, *The Farmer's Boy* draws on Bloomfield's boyhood experiences of working on the land, expressed through the figure of the young farm labourer Giles, 'meek, fatherless and poor'. While Bloomfield occasionally emulates Thomson's grandiloquence – 'Fled now the sullen murmurs of the North, / The splendid raiment of the Spring peeps forth' – the prominence given to humble Giles's tasks grounds the poem in the earthiness of the agricultural year. Balancing an acknowledgment of the physical toll of labour with a wider perspective, Bloomfield offered a farmer's-eye view that was closer to Constable's own experience than Thomson's orotund rhetoric. In 1814 he used Bloomfield's couplet 'But unassisted through each toilsome day, / With smiling brow the ploughman cleaves his way' in the Royal Academy catalogue to accompany his painting *Landscape: Ploughing Scene in Suffolk* – the smile refers not, as it might first strike the reader, to rural contentment, but to the shape of the furrows in the straining labourer's forehead.

The seasons themselves were not only felt out there, in the fields and the streets: their effects were subtler than that. They were at work inside Constable's body, affecting his muscles, nerves, glands and brain. That, at least, was the opinion of his greatest friend, John Fisher, who wrote to him at the beginning of September of 1829 setting out his own view of the year:

> I yearn to see you tranquilly & collectedly at work on your next
> great picture; undisturbed by gossips good and ill natured; at a
> season of the year, when the glands of the body are unobstructed
> by cold, & the nerves in a state of quiescence. You choose February
> & March for composition; when the strongest men get irritable

& uncomfortable; during the prevalence of the NE: winds, the great distraction of the frame, & the gradual cause in England of old-age. Then at such a season, can your poetical sensitiveness have its free and open play? Sep: Oct: & Nov: are our healthiest months in England. Recollect, Milton had his favourite seasons for composition. The season you select for composition is the chief reason for the unfinished, *abandoned* state of your surface on the first of May.

Fisher's vision of equivalences between the human frame and the year's cycle had been widespread in the Middle Ages and lingered on throughout the eighteenth and into the nineteenth century. It was based on a system initially devised in ancient Greece by Hippocrates and later advanced by the Roman physician Galen, which proposed that the human body, with its four humours of blood, choler (yellow bile), melancholy (black bile) and phlegm, was a microcosm of the wider world, corresponding both to the four elements of earth, air, fire and water and to the four seasons. As such, the body was powerless against the effects of climate and temperature – its humours simply rose and fell like mercury in a thermometer. Spring, being hot and moist, summoned up the blood and encouraged an optimistic outlook; summer was hot and dry and made people irritable; autumn was naturally the season for melancholy feelings; while the chill and damp of winter resulted in a phlegmatic attitude and placid, unruffled behaviour. Vestiges of these ideas lingered on for a surprisingly long time, before eventually being absorbed into new theories of the weather's effects on physical and psychological health founded on evidence-based medical research. Seasonal Affective Disorder is estimated to affect around three people in every hundred in the UK – though we now put it down to a paucity of sunlight rather than an excess of phlegm.

For Constable, Fisher's remarks, however well meant, were not particularly helpful. His own view of the weather was a practical one. He was solicitous of his beloved Maria, whose health was delicate. 'I need not tell you,' he wrote to her at the end of February 1816, 'that you must take all the care possible of yourself this horrid season – the spring is the most dangerous of all the seasons, and is only loved by the poets, who are another race of beings.' And yet, like every other artist with ambitions to succeed at the Royal Academy, he had to work on his canvases in the months and weeks leading up to May's exhibition opening whether the March wind was blowing or not. And what Fisher interpreted as the 'unfinished, abandoned' look of his pictures was not evidence of hurry – or not always – but of Constable's attempt to replicate the flickering appearance of foliage as it was blown by the breeze and caught by the light (he was often criticized for this by reviewers, and made sporadic attempts to create a greater effect of conventional 'finish').

In common with a great deal of proffered advice, Fisher's was more applicable to the giver than the receiver. He imagined himself to be highly susceptible to atmospheric conditions. The previous April, for instance, he had felt obliged to apologize to Constable for rushing home to Dorset with no warning after he had promised to stay with him in London. He blamed his erratic behaviour on the weather and its alarming effect on his nerves:

> I beg your pardon for using you so ill when in London. But the cold, bitter, North-East winds kept me in such a state of irritation, the whole of my stay in London, that I should have been a most unpleasant inmate to you, & have disturbed your serenity … I gave you all of my company that I *dare*: & at last suddenly left London & its damp windy streets in a precipitate fit of desperation.

'I have not yet recovered it', he goes on rather histrionically. 'There is a deep cellar in the infernal regions which is reserved for the most desperate. London in March is a type of it. See Miltons *cold* Hell.'

Constable's reply, if he made one, has not survived. He did, however, express his own more robust attitude to the English climate to Fisher a couple of months later, when he wrote: 'The weather may be more settled by the time I come to you, but the fine effects of such a season make ample amends for their inconvenience'. Whether or not this was a gentle rebuff to Fisher's neuroses, it echoes the feelings about rain he had shared with Dunthorne back in 1803, when he described a voyage along the Kent coast made in April and May (the furthest Constable ever travelled beyond English shores): 'I saw all sorts of weather. Some the most delightfull, and some as melancholy. But such is the enviable state of a painter that he finds delight in every dress nature can possibly assume.' Either way, Constable was determined to assert how necessary it was for him to respond immediately to natural and aesthetic phenomena, come rain or shine. Both were part of the story he needed to tell about the landscape. And though expressed mildly, his words also revealed an entrenched habit of mind: back in East Bergholt, during his years of training in his father's business, it would have been ridiculous to bewail the havoc the weather was wreaking on his nerves and rush indoors. For now, he could smile at his younger friend's valetudinarian anxieties – although as he got older, he, too, would come to worry about March winds and the perilous chill of winter.

A bend in the road

Constable's life was divided into a 'before' and an 'after'. In the autumn of 1809, during a visit to East Bergholt, he fell in love. Maria Bicknell was a clever, lively and attractive young woman, twenty-one to Constable's thirty-three, who was visiting Suffolk to see her maternal grandfather, Dr Rhudde, the wealthy and influential rector of East Bergholt. If the couple had expected encouragement all round, however, they were to be disappointed. Dr Rhudde turned out to be implacably opposed to their marriage, and over the next seven years put every obstacle he could in their way, announcing at one point that he no longer considered Maria to be his granddaughter – a threat to disinherit her. There is something of the pantomime villain about this cruel and obdurate man, who would not be out of place in a novel by Charles Dickens. No doubt social class accounted largely for his passionate disapproval: though Constable's father was a wealthy and well-respected individual in the local community, he was a merchant through and through, well below the level of the gentry; Maria's, as solicitor to the Admiralty and to the Prince Regent, moved in the highest professional circles. Dr Rhudde himself was a Royal Chaplain, a role attained by only the most distinguished of clergy. Money must also have been a serious issue; Constable was not enjoying conspicuous success in his career. It would be a full decade before he was elected an Associate of the Royal Academy – a mark of recognition from his peers, but a considerable distance from the coveted rank of Academician – and he was chronically impecunious. Worse, he showed no signs of even attempting to get a proper job. In 1802, for instance, when he was considered for the post of drawing master at the new Military Academy at Marlow, he shrank from employment with something approaching horror, explaining to Dunthorne that 'had I accepted the situation offered it would have been a death blow to all my prospects of perfection in the Art I love.' Even the most sympathetic supporter would have been hard pressed to agree that Constable was in a financial position to marry a woman whose upbringing had prepared her for a comfortable standard of living.

So the 'before' part of Constable's life did not entirely end, as it might otherwise have done, in 1809, but stretched out for seven long summers; the dial only moved to 'after' in the autumn of 1816, when the couple finally married. The delay caused immense pain to them both. In the middle of December 1811 Maria was so discouraged that she attempted to break off their relationship, but Constable rushed to visit her and persuaded her to take heart. Even so, his own spirits were so low at the beginning of the new year that his youngest sister Mary was dispatched to London to stay with him at his lodgings in Charlotte Street; she remained by his side as winter turned into spring. Her brother recorded her presence in a sketch-book: there she is on a chilly April day, keeping warm with a thick fur wrap around her shoulders and reading a letter. But although these years of protracted courtship were emotionally fraught, they turned out to be crucial ones in Constable's development as an artist. In the sketches he made from the summer of 1810 onwards it is as though his vision of a future with Maria has jolted him into working with new energy and purpose. They exude a sense of urgency, a drive for success. He also knew that when he eventually married Maria, he was likely to be separated from his beloved Suffolk scenes, his cottages, stumps and millponds, more decisively than ever before. This focused his mind.

In the second week in May of 1811 Constable accompanied his mother, who had been visiting family near London, back home to Suffolk, where he stayed for three weeks. It was a rare chance for him to see the country-side in spring. On 17 May, a bright, windy Friday, he took his sketching kit

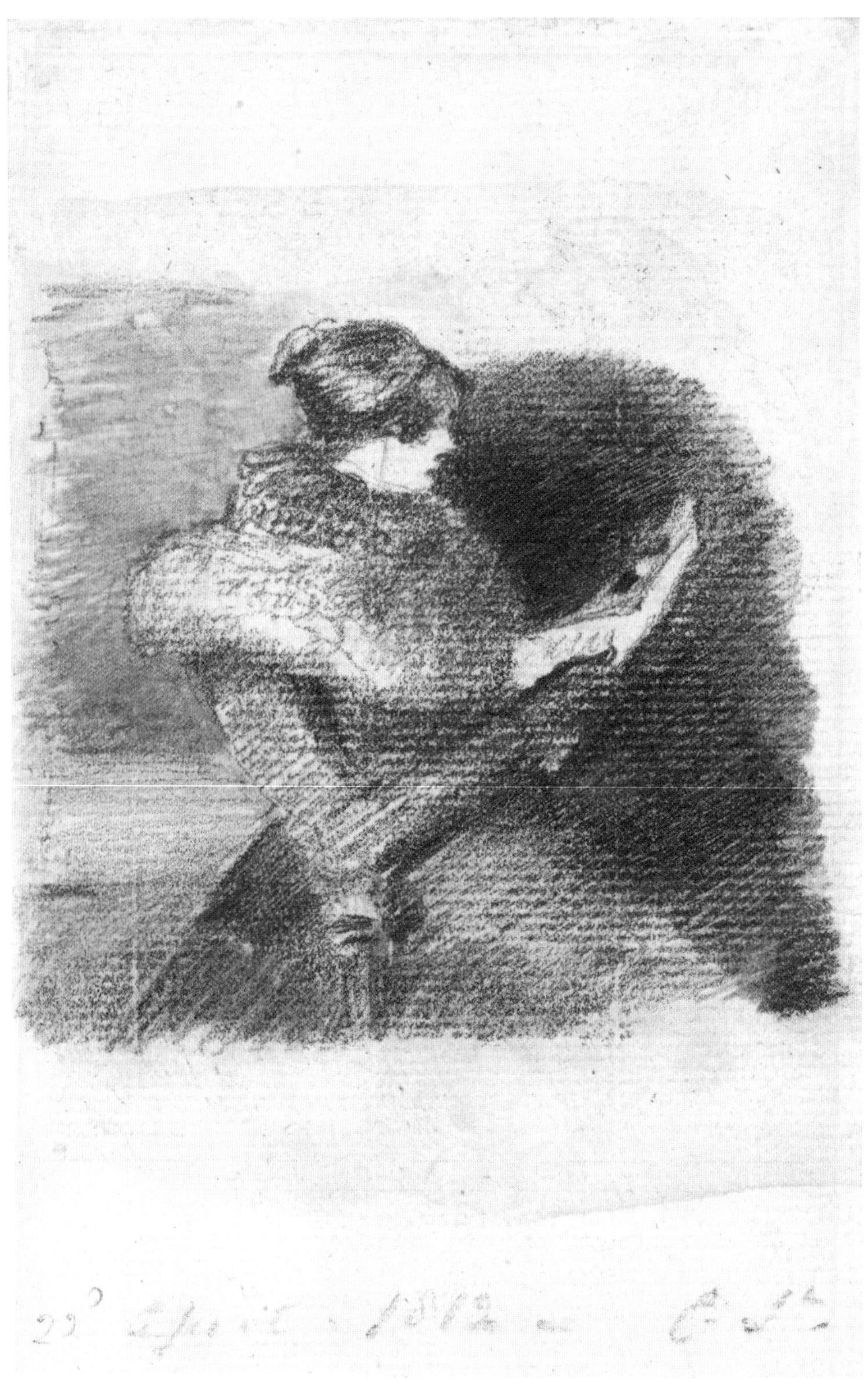

Mary Constable reading, 22 April 1812. Graphite on paper.

and walked along the familiar lane that opened off the main street opposite his house and led downhill towards Flatford and his father's watermill.
He stopped just before it made a sharp turn and settled himself on the
grassy bank with his paintbox on his knee. From his vantage point he
could see over the backs of grazing cattle to the fields of Flatford beyond;
rising smoke suggests the presence of a farmhouse, or even the mill itself.
He pinned a piece of paper to the inside of the lid – you can see the pin-
holes in the corners – and rummaged in the box for his paints. Although
Constable's default position was still to use pencil for sketching out of
doors – it was a versatile medium, perfect both for silvery lines and for rich,
deep shadows – for about three years now he had also been using oils. This
was less efficient and messier, yes – metal tubes were yet to be introduced,
so he would have been squeezing paints onto his palette from the rubbery
pigs' bladders that were traditionally used to keep them moist and worka-
ble – but the world was in colour, and he wanted to do it justice. However
skilfully pencil was used (and Constable was a master of the medium), grey
tones could only go so far to suggest the rippling chromatic variations of
a single tree, let alone the subtle changes to ripening crops in a patchwork
of fields or the hues of the sky over the course of a day. Constable wanted
to capture what happened to the landscape second by second, as the light
changed and the wind ruffled the foliage. He had already primed the sheet
of paper he was using that day with paint the warm brown of a cow's coat,
so he was applying his colours onto a mid-toned ground. He let this show
through in areas where it adds to a sense of changeable light, or reveals
his efforts to record the clouds as they were stretched and thinned by the
breeze. He painted the new spring leaves of the elm on the right, blown
back to expose its dark branches. Then he dabbed in three rooks riding the
wind, one nothing more than two lozenge-shaped strokes.

This fast-paced, barely finished response to nature was for him, and him
alone – he never intended to exhibit it and would probably be baffled at the
interest shown in his oil sketches today. They were, however, the lifeblood
of his art. Using a characteristically agricultural metaphor, he once said
that he would happily 'part with the corn but not with the field that grew it'.
He made the sketch that day so that when he was back in his London studio, he would be able to remember not just the familiar shapes of the fields

he had known all his life and the bend in the lane that carts always had to slow down for, but a deeper sense of place that acknowledged how swiftly its appearance changed. The minutes and hours of that blustery Friday in May might never come again, but with his brush and a few squeezes of the pigs' bladders he could at least record them on the wing.

Messenger clouds

The oil sketches Constable made out of doors vividly record the here-and-now of his experience, the breeze on his skin, the smell of woodsmoke drifting from farmhouse chimneys and the sudden brightening of the landscape that struck his eye when the clouds broke. In many cases he turned them over and wrote on the back; in time he took to recording not only the date, but the time of day, the precise weather conditions during his sketching and even what happened after he had packed up his painting box and walked home, whether there was a fine sunset or a shower overnight. Together they form a weather diary, a record of phenomena that would otherwise be forgotten as quickly as the shape of a cloud. (An observation made by his mother might have lodged in his mind and prompted this; she wrote to him one January of intensely cold weather and higher snow drifts than she could ever recall, then adds 'tho' without keeping a diary, I know of scarcely any occurrence sooner forgot than the weather'.) When Constable came to sum up what he had been trying to do, he lifted a line from a poem by Lord Byron: he said he wanted to use painting 'so as to note "the day, the hour, the sunshine and the shade"'.

But for all his ability to catch transience on the wing, Constable was no camera, primed to record the appearance of one brief moment. The landscape he knew was too complicated for that; the lanes, trees and fields of his corner of Suffolk bristled with memories and emotions. These were places where, as his sister Martha put it, he had 'hung a thought on every thorn'. He kept returning to them because they always had more to offer him. 'But I should paint my own places best', he wrote to his friend Fisher in 1821, ' – Painting is but another word for feeling.' As a statement, this is so heartfelt, so far from what any of his ambitious contemporaries might have said, that it is like finding a love letter in a bundle of bills. Now, in

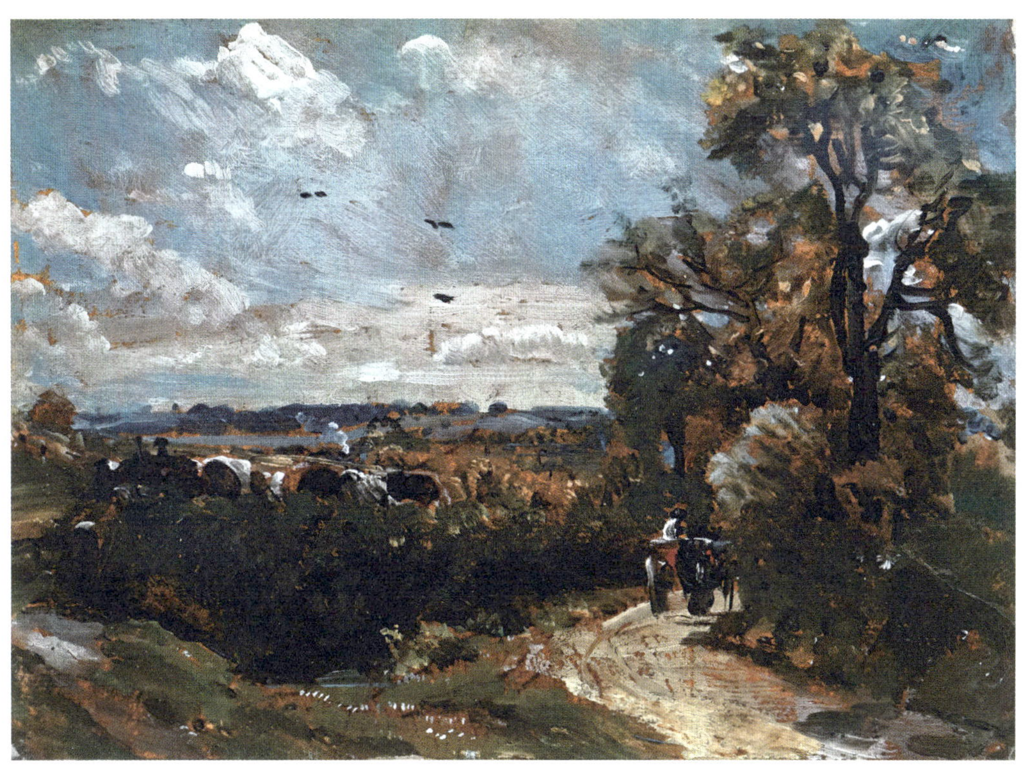

A cart on a lane at Flatford, 17 May 1811. Oil on paper laid on canvas. *Detail overleaf.*

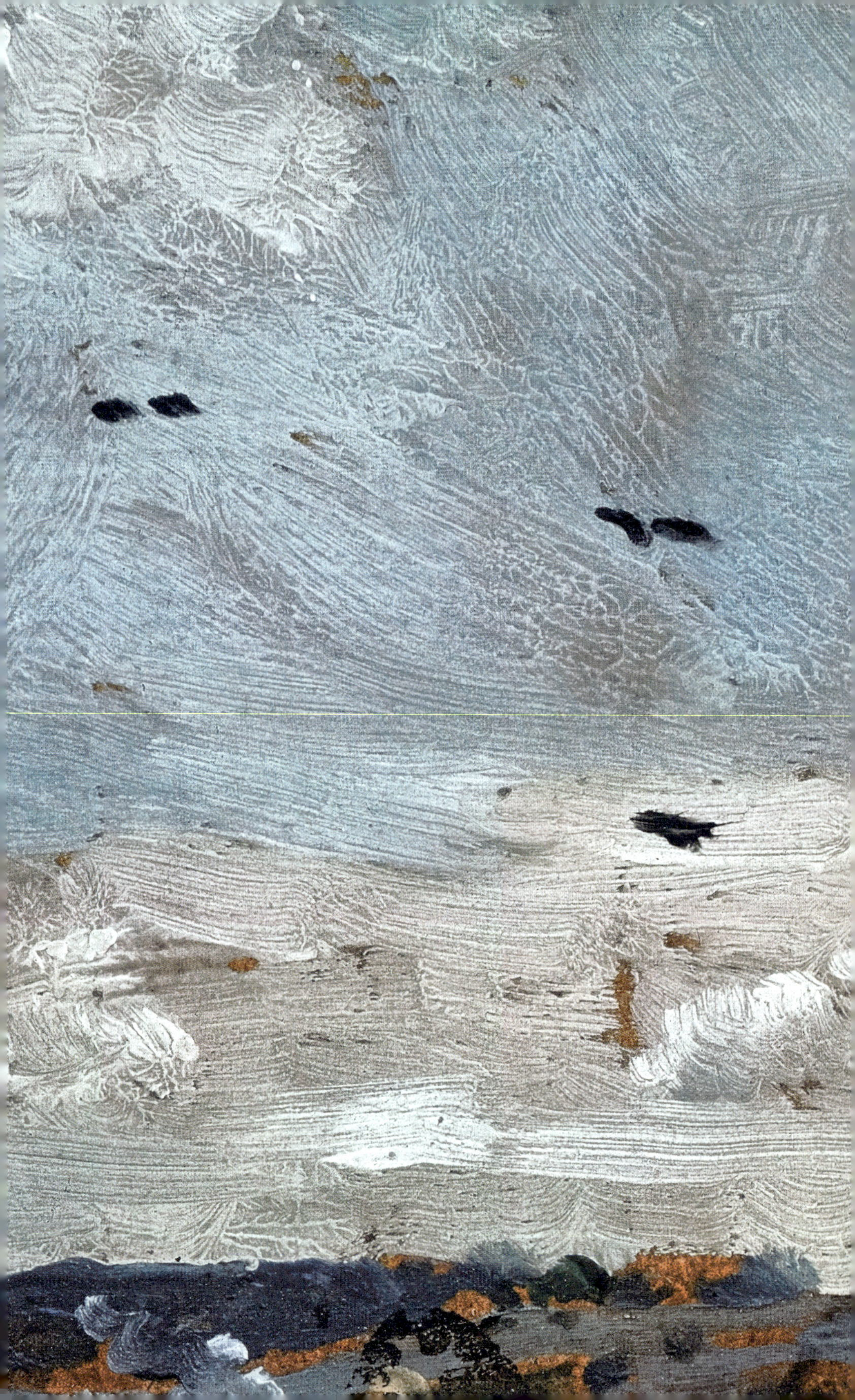

these in-between years of courtship, in the times when he was away from the East Bergholt landscape, Constable's thoughts were occupied with it. *Pre*occupied, perhaps. Maria, who had grown as astutely familiar with his habits of mind as with his annual pattern of work, wrote to him in April 1812 asking if he would soon be visiting Suffolk. 'You are as fond of the country as I am,' she observed, 'how beautiful it will soon be, you have given this place a higher interest to me than it ever had before. I am sure your thoughts are often directed there, are they not?' It was a bold declaration of emotional commitment, and not just to the landscape: he and the country had begun to be mixed up. If John and Maria could not actually walk arm-in-arm down its quiet lanes, then at least their thoughts could meet there.

Constable was also sensitive to a spiritual dimension in nature. It is easy to underestimate the importance to him of Christian faith, partly because it does not correspond to the mores of our increasingly secular age – and partly for the simple reason that he rarely mentions it. On one occasion in which he does, however, his words brim with such spiritual ecstasy it makes you pause to wonder whether you knew him as well as you thought. The new life brought by spring evidently delighted not just his eye and his heart but his soul, too. Walking through a blooming landscape in May 1819, on a brief visit to East Bergholt to see the conclusion of the sale of his family home, following the death of both parents, he wrote to Maria of finding it supercharged with significance:

> I have been this morning a walk up the Langham Hills, and through
> a number of beautifull feilds & by the side of the river – and in
> my life I never saw Nature more lovely … Every tree seems full
> of blossom of some kind & the surface of the ground seems quite
> lovely – every step I take & on whatever object I turn my eye that
> sublime expression in the Scripture 'I am the resurrection & the life'
> &c, seems verified about me.

Just then, Constable's mind was on death as well as new life: that of Dr Rhudde, who had died three days previously. 'Was it not singular', he asked Maria, 'that I should arrive in the village just as the bell was tolling for the

Doctor?' The rector had long since ceased to exercise his malevolent control over the couple, but whether Constable was conscious of it or not, the news that they were finally free of him appears to have made his own spirit soar.

Another brief springtime visit to Suffolk, in April 1821, found Constable in a particularly reflective and nostalgic mood, even for him. 'I have called on most of the neighbours – drank tea at Ann's last evening – had a stormy walk home over the heath', he wrote to Maria.

> How sweet and beautifull is every place & I visit my old haunts with renewed delight but filled with many regrets & not without many sad & melancholy reflections on the various and solemn changes since the days of my youth. Nothing can exceed the beautiful green of the meadows, which are beginning to fill with buttercups, & various flowers – the birds are singing from morning till night but most of all the sky larks. How delightfull is the country, but I long to get back to what is still more dear to me.

Among the 'old haunts' he visited that day, 19 April, was East Bergholt Common. It was being ploughed to prepare it for sowing, which prompted him to make two rapid pencil drawings of the scene, one of which stretches across both pages of a sketchbook opening to form a panoramic view. He also made a small, sketchy oil that is thought to have been painted in his London studio rather than on the spot, because it is so similar in detail to the double-page drawing. Instead of his more usual paper, he has used an oak panel – the grain is clearly visible through the paint – and has left patches of the wood untouched in some areas where it could serve to represent earth. (Or rather, he thriftily re-used the panel: he had already painted one side with a night scene of Church Street in East Bergholt.) The result is a picture of not much happening in a flat and relatively featureless landscape. There is a tree on the left and a ploughman with two horses on the right, with a prominent windmill and, on the distant horizon, a church and village. What drama there is comes from the great billowing cumulus clouds in the wide sky. And yet Constable valued this little sketch so highly that he chose to include it when, in 1830, he began to publish a series of prints reproducing his paintings called *Various Subjects*

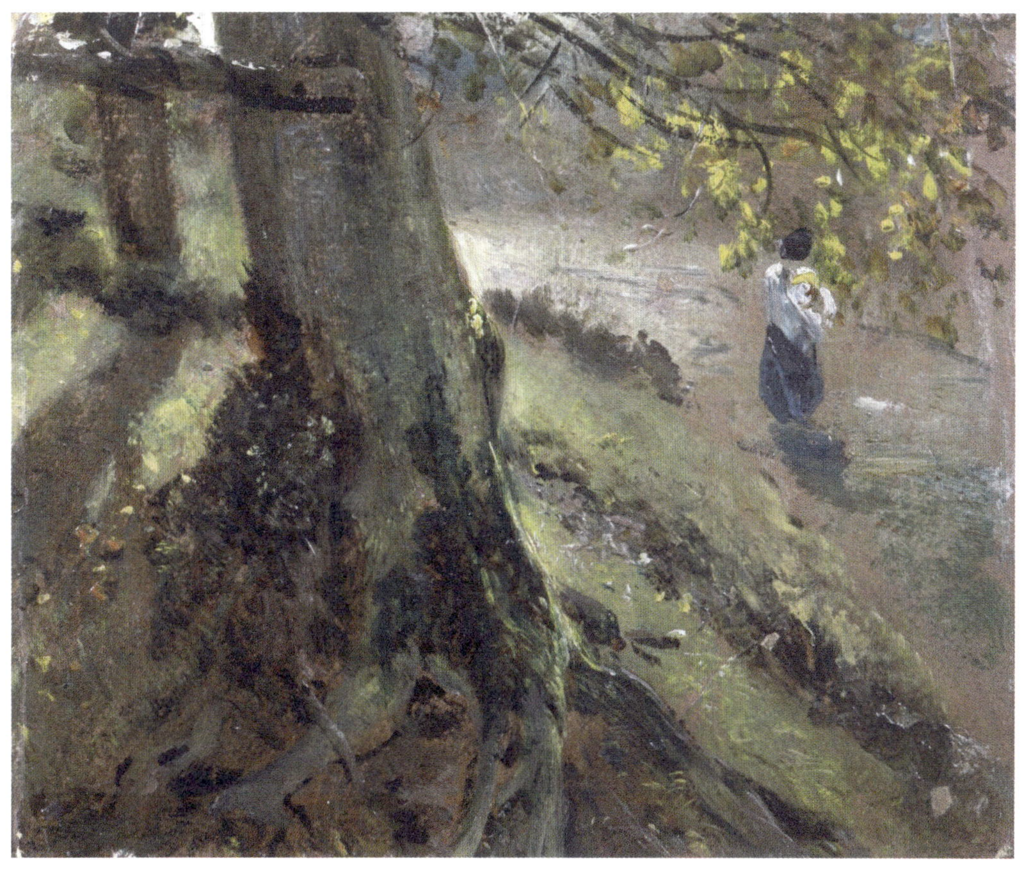

Study of tree trunks, *c.* 1821. Oil on paper.
On the rare occasions Constable visited
the country in springtime, he always
exclaimed at its beauty. 'Every day brings
out the trees & blossom', he wrote to Maria
from Dedham on Easter Sunday 1821.

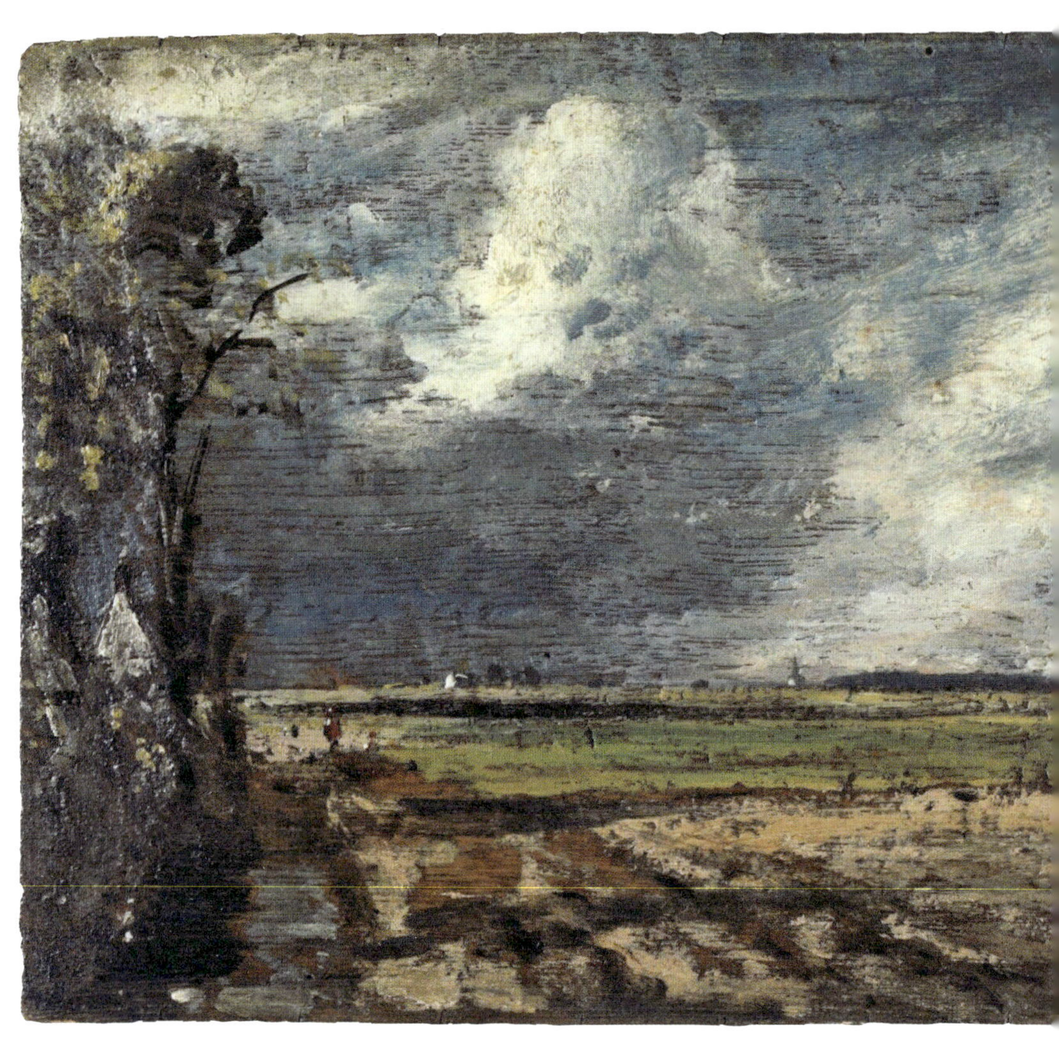

Spring: East Bergholt Common, 1821. Oil on panel.

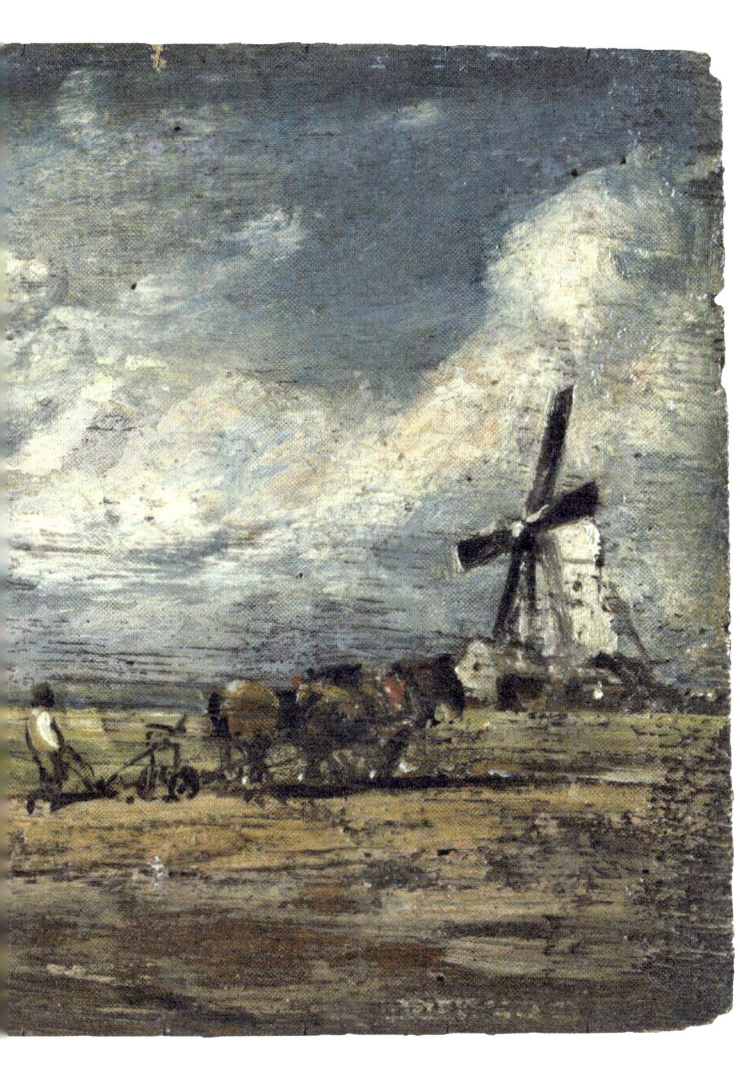

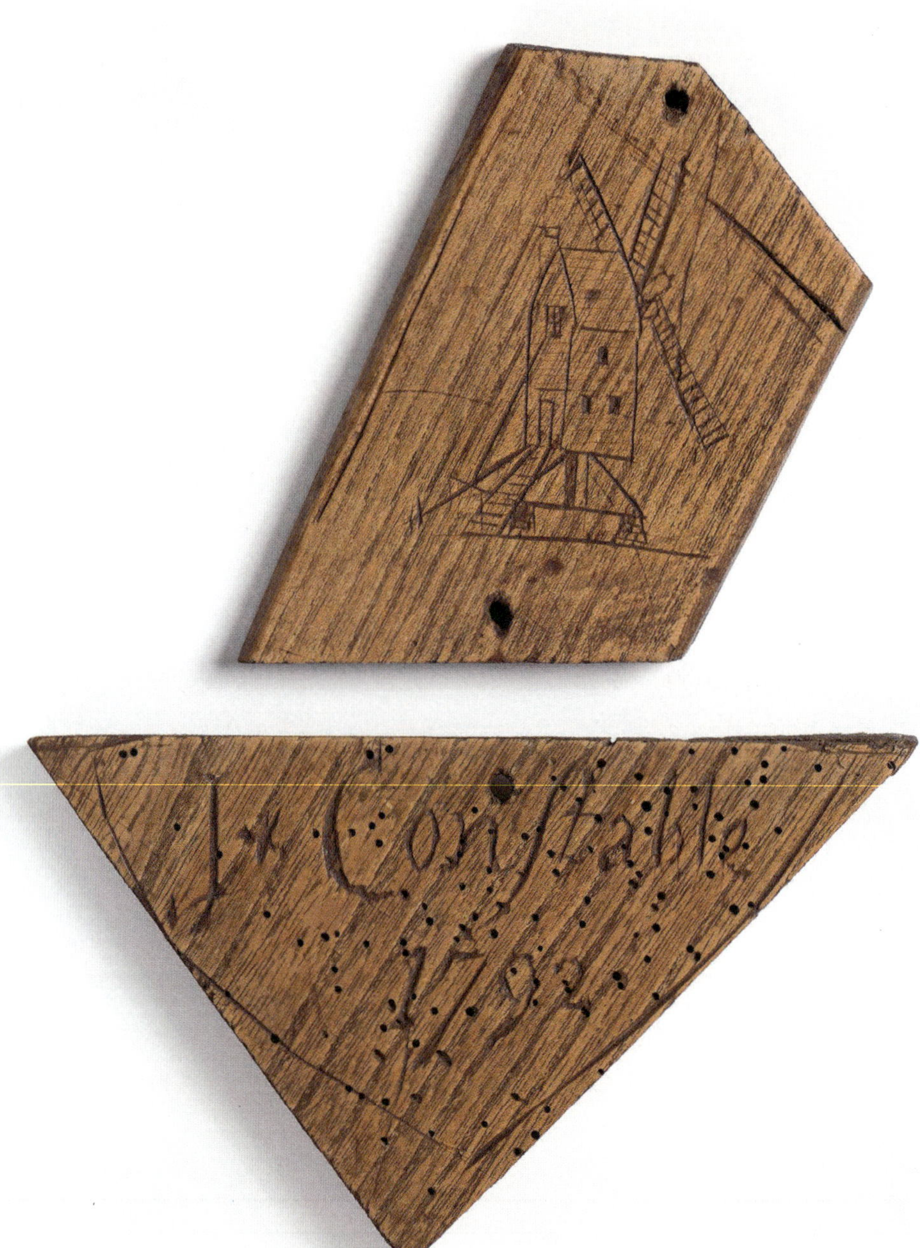

Windmill, signature and date incised
on fragments of wood panelling once
lining the interior of the windmill
on East Bergholt Common, 1792.
Pen knife and ink on wood.

of Landscape, Characteristic of English Scenery (generally known as *English Landscape*), an emotionally charged project with which he presented his vision to the world.

Look closely at *Spring*, and at what it represents, and it becomes clear that the apparently simple picture is charged with meaning and nostalgia, with 'delight' as well as 'melancholy reflections'. Part of East Bergholt common had been acquired by Golding Constable in 1816, the year of his death, and was ploughed for the first time the following year. The windmill in the background is Pitt's Mill, in which Constable had worked for his father; when he was about sixteen and beginning his training, he had incised a neat drawing of a windmill on the wooden walls of its interior, signed it 'J. Constable' with the literary flourish of a long 's' and dated it 1792. This ambiguous commitment both to windmills and to depictions of them was still in situ in 1840, when it was seen by his old friend and biographer C. R. Leslie. The rough wooden panel upon which *Spring* is painted recalls his act of teenage graffiti.

Spring opens up a wider perspective, too. The windmill in the background may be a part of Constable's own life story, but it also represents the cycle of the seasons: the destination, later in the year, of the crop which is about to be sown in the freshly turned earth. Within this modest picture is a story of youth, maturity and family; of work, tradition and continuity. There he was, all those years later, on the same spot, still drawing windmills.

Constable's *English Landscape* project allowed him to put into words what some of his paintings meant to him. He singled out just seven of the twenty-two prints for this particular treatment. *Spring* was one, so we know it was special to him. He chose, however, not to reveal its profound emotional significance, but instead began his essay with a typically flowery quotation from Thomson's *Seasons* describing a frolicking Zephyr gently awakening Spring, who comes forth from her bower to 'clothe in gladsome-glistening green / The genial earth'. He takes a paragraph-long sentence to get out from the poet's shadow. 'This plate', he begins,

> may perhaps give some idea of one of those bright and animated
> days of the early year, when all nature bears so exhilarating an
> aspect; when at noon large garish clouds, surcharged with hail or

sleet, sweep with their broad cool shadows the fields, woods, and hills; and by the contrast of their depths and bloom enhance the value of the vivid greens and yellows, so peculiar to the season;

He sounds a little self-conscious about addressing his audience. This was, after all, a rare opportunity to explain his art; he made a number of drafts of his essays and kept starting again, revealing his anxiety about getting it *right*. But after another fortifying burst of poetry, his pace suddenly quickens. He finds himself writing about clouds, and is suddenly absorbed in a subject that fascinates him. They accumulate, he goes on,

in very large and dense masses, and from their loftiness seem to move but slowly; immediately upon these large clouds appear numerous opaque patches, which, however, are only small clouds passing rapidly before them, and consisting of isolated pieces, detached probably from the larger cloud.

These floating much nearer the earth, may perhaps fall in with a much stronger current of wind, which as well as their comparative lightness, causes them to move with greater rapidity; hence they are called by wind-millers and sailors 'messengers', being also the forerunners of bad weather. They float about midway in what may be termed the *lanes* of the clouds; and from being so situated, are almost uniformly in shadow, receiving only a reflected light from the clear blue sky immediately above, and which descends perpendicularly upon them into these lanes. In passing over the bright parts of the large clouds they appear as darks; but in passing the shadowed parts they assume a gray, a pale, or lurid hue.

We are no longer listening to the orator deliver carefully polished sentences, but to the passionate observer who, by this time in his career, had made a sustained and groundbreaking study of skies and who kept abreast of the most up-to-date meteorological treatises on the subject. He has got down from his lectern to touch our arm and direct our attention to the sky, pointing out this or that detail. We are also listening to the experienced windmiller, who grew up in a household in which there would have been daily conference about the strength of the wind, the clouds and the weather they promised for the coming hours and days. Constable may be asking us to look up at the sky and at great impersonal clouds, but they are as much a part of his life story as the windmill and the common itself.

Constable ends his essay with a passionate argument in favour of spring, pitting it against its opposite number. 'The Autumn only is called the painter's season', he writes, 'from the great richness of the colours of the *dead* and decaying foliage, and the peculiar tone and beauty of the skies'. Atmospheric autumnal scenes represented the artistic conventions he had spent his career determinedly pushing against. Why paint *dying* nature, he asked with scornful emphasis, when you could paint it bursting with life? Focus instead on the 'great variety of the tints and colours of the *living* foliage' that delight the eye with their contrast to the 'russet browns' and other 'drear remains of the season that is past'. The elegiac mood of autumn had little to do with his vision of the landscape. For Constable, the country was a site of busy agricultural work – any pause is only one in which labour is about to recommence. *Spring: East Bergholt Common* may be about his own past, but it also looks forward, thrumming with the energy of industry and the great agricultural cycle, the year's activity from ploughing to milling, set in motion by the new season. Even his clouds carry news about the future.

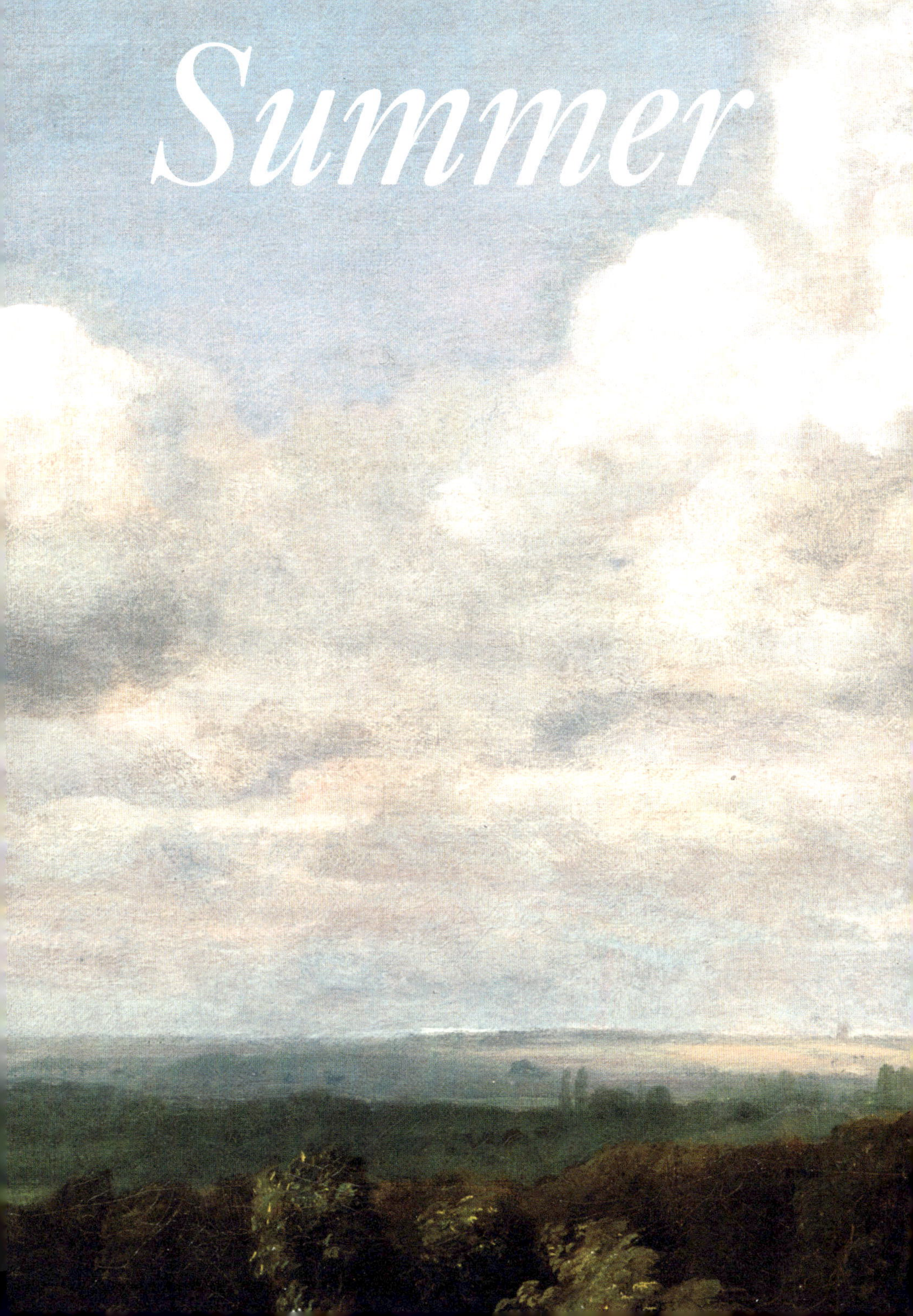

Summer

'I took several beautifull walks in search of food for my pencil this summer when I hope to do a great deal in landscape'

My beloved Bergholt

East Bergholt was to Constable what the Alps were to J. M. W. Turner. During the summer months, Constable's near-contemporary – born the previous year to him – travelled regularly in France, Italy and Switzerland when the French Revolutionary and later Napoleonic wars permitted, and throughout England, Scotland and Wales when they didn't. To choose a single year, 1819, when the continent had reopened to British tourists following the Battle of Waterloo, Turner travelled to Turin, Como, Venice, Rome and Naples, returning via Florence and the Mont Cenis pass; Constable rented a cottage in Hampstead for his young family and on one occasion popped back to East Bergholt. It was not that he was inherently averse to such trips – he had, after all, toured the Peak District in 1801 and in 1806 had spent seven weeks sketching in the Lake District, a highly productive visit that gave him enough material for several exhibition pictures. It was just that the more he drew and painted the buildings, lanes and fields around East Bergholt, the more interesting they became. The tenant farmer Willy Lott's house may have been a familiar part of the scene, but Constable found it no less absorbing for that: a different viewpoint could change everything. Moment by moment the light and weather altered its colour and form and kept drawing him back. If he took just a few steps down the towpath, the trees, river, bridge and buildings reconfigured themselves. He could sketch the lock on the Stour near his father's mill at Flatford on a stormy afternoon, under clouds the colour of a pewter plate; and he could paint it again on a fine day, feeling the warmth of the sun on his back, a shaft of sunlight slicing

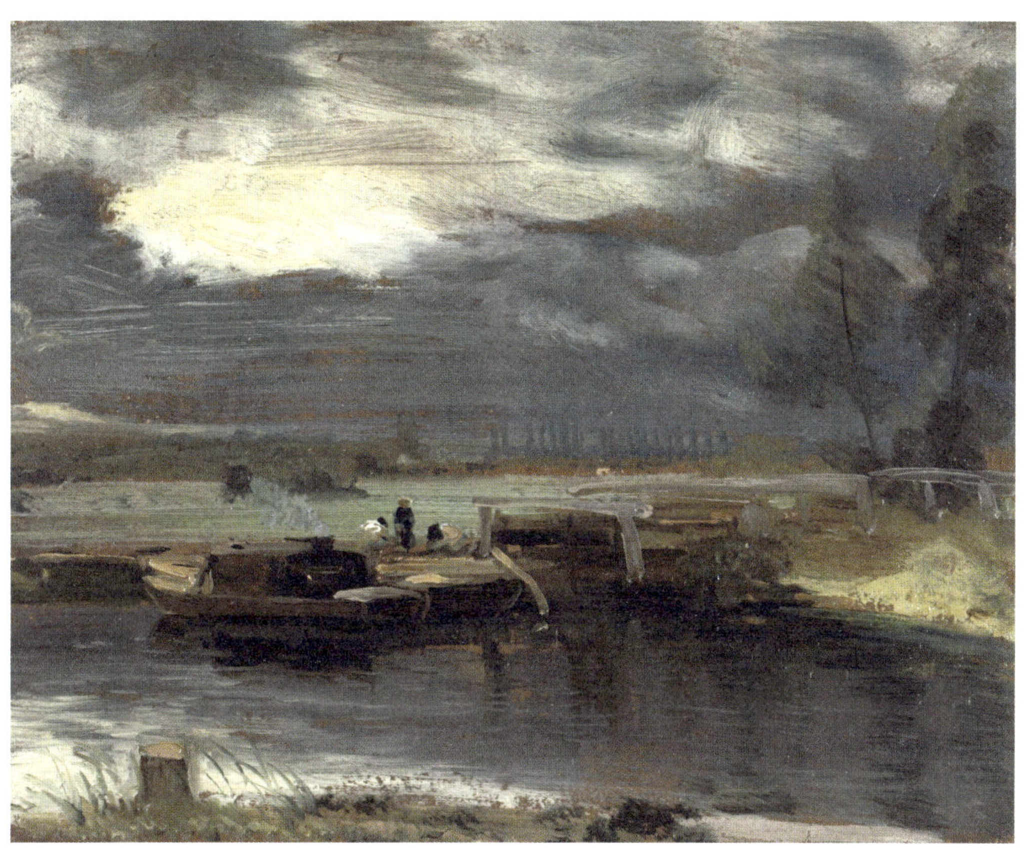

A barge on the Stour at Flatford Lock,
c. 1811. Oil on paper. A barge is waiting
to enter the lock, on the right. The
stormy light is reflected in the water.

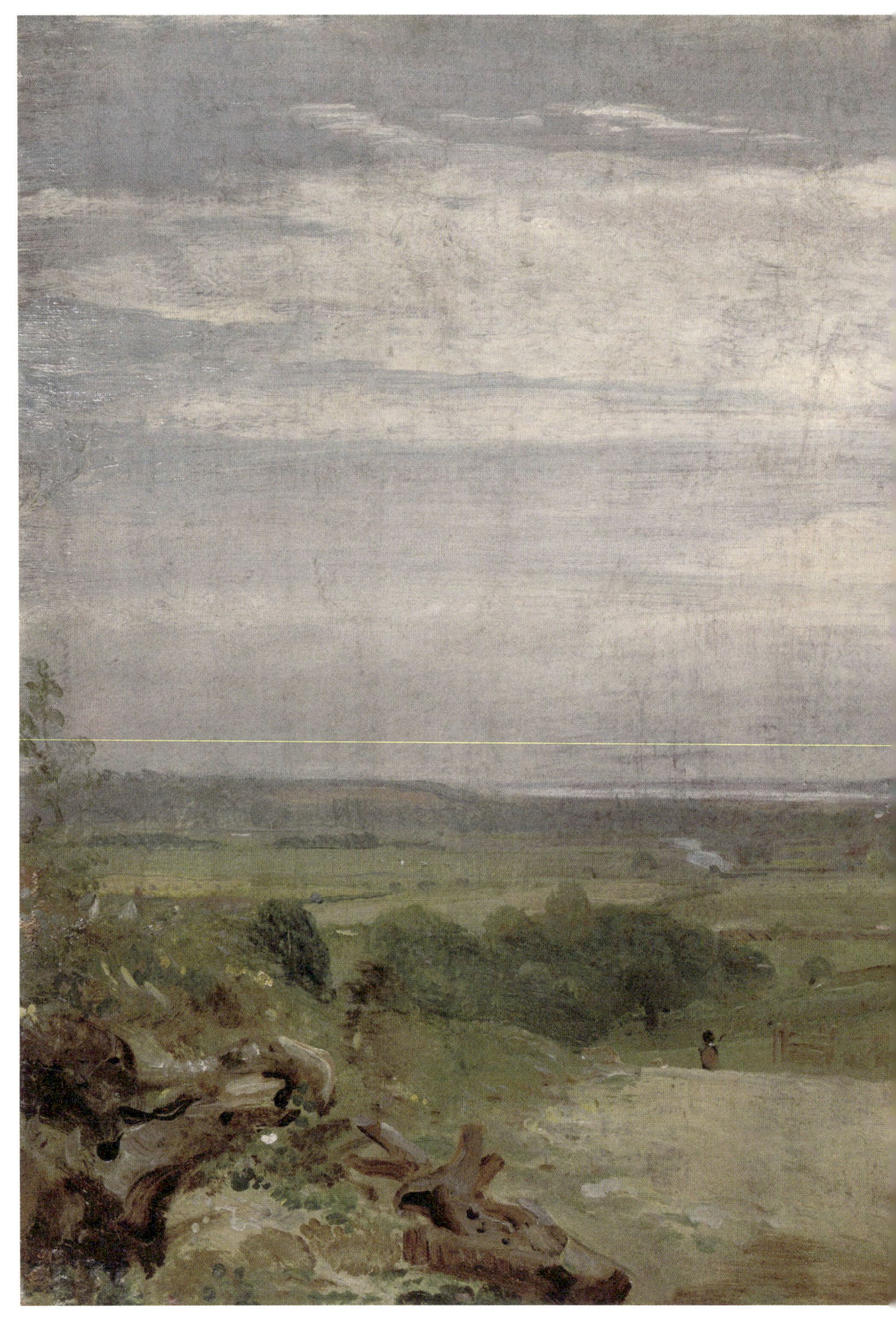

Summer morning, Dedham from Langham, 1812. Oil on canvas.

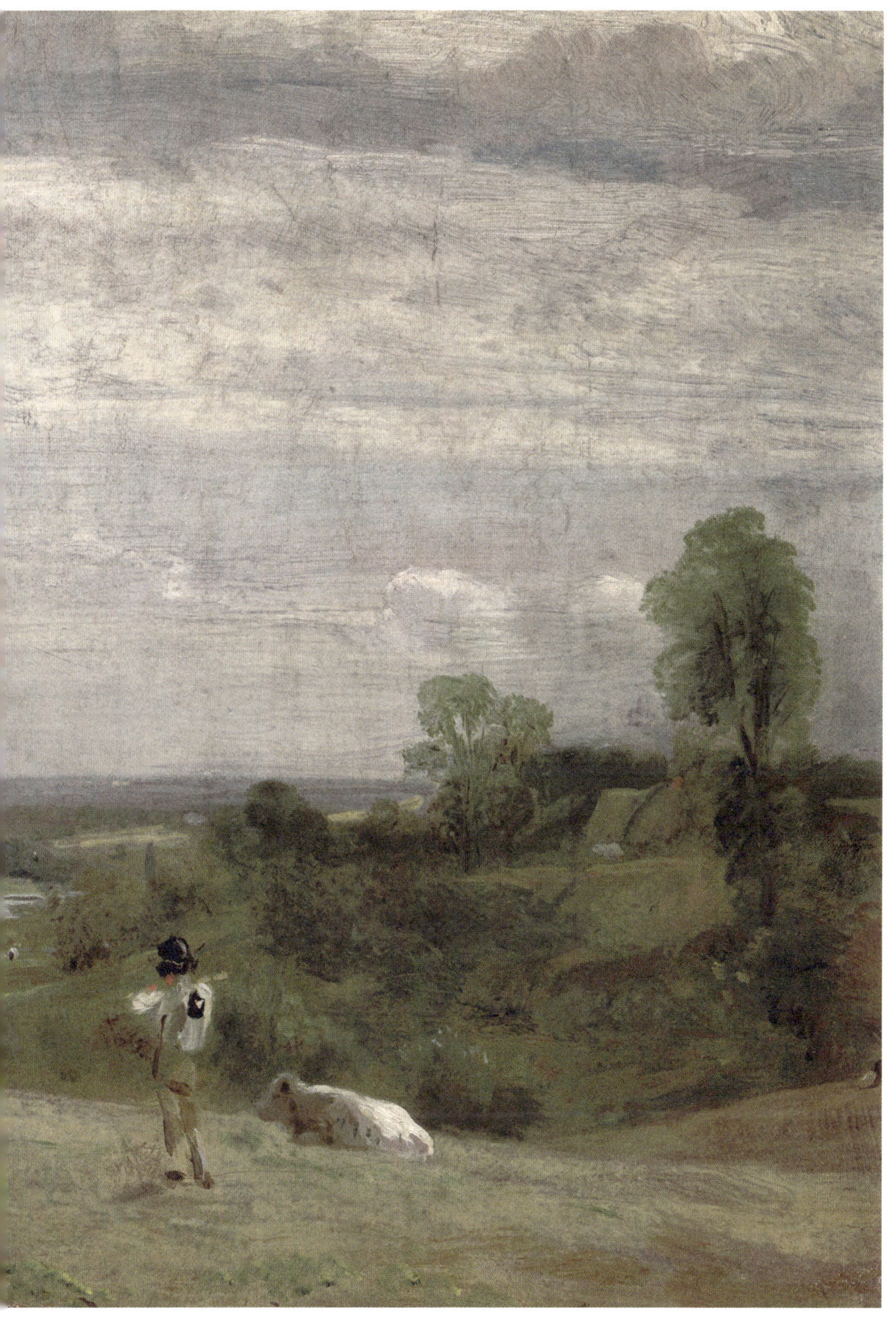

through the green water. The knapped flints of St Mary's church in East Bergholt always had more to tell him, no matter how many times he studied their cloudy depths. While Turner was seeking sublimity in mountain gorges, Constable was finding profound inspiration in a millpond.

Constable was not unaware of the problems his chosen subjects posed. His pictures could look unambitious: Turner could make Devon resemble the Italian campagna and mix Richmond up with Arcadia; Constable painted East Anglian landscapes in which it looked as though it might rain. Turner had been honoured by the artistic establishment by being made a Royal Academician in 1802, the same year that found Constable standing tentatively at the threshold of his career. Ten years later, however, just before returning to East Bergholt for the summer months, his confidence had grown. He wrote to Maria explaining the reason for his dogged determination to stick to local subjects:

> I am still looking towards Suffolk where I hope to pass the greater part of the summer, as much for the sake of pursueing my favourite study as for any other account. You know I have succeeded most with my native scenes. They have always charmed me & I hope they always will – I wish not to forget early impressions. I have now very distinctly marked out a path for myself, and I am desirous of pursuing it uninterruptedly.

By July he was joking about what seemed like an obsessive attachment to the local places he loved. 'I am sure you will laugh', he told Maria, 'when I tell you I have found another very promising subject at *Flatford Mill*.'

Long weeks of summer in East Bergholt gave Constable the leisure and freedom to wander and draw the places he loved. It was a time of deep happiness, tainted only by Maria's absence. 'Nothing can exceed the beautifull appearance of the country at this time,' he wrote to her, having taken the coach from London three days before; 'its freshness, its amenity – the very breeze that passes the window is delightfull, it has the voice of Nature.' Among the 'native scenes' he sketched that summer of 1812 was one made from the village of Langham, which gave him a raised vantage point over the vale towards Dedham with its church tower, the River Stour appearing here and there in fat bends and opening up at the horizon into a silvery estuary. It was early morning when he began, the fair-weather cloud creating an opalescent haze that turned the fields sagey shades of pastel green and the river milky white. The painting, made on the prickling grass with the buzz of insects in his ears, seems to shimmer with the rising temperature of the morning.

As well as solitude and the chance to work undisturbed – he was once so absorbed that a field mouse hid in his pocket while he was painting – the summer also brought noisy, boisterous entertainment. At the end of July the annual fair took place, filling the village green with stalls, sideshows and milling crowds. For several years running, Constable seized upon this interesting transformation of the familiar scene, sketching the to-ing and fro-ing from the windows of his parents' house and describing to Maria 'a tumult of drums & trumpets & buffoonery of all sorts'. Drawings of the fair appear in a tiny sketchbook – just 8.9 × 12 cm (3½ × 4¾ in.) – that is now one of the treasures of the Victoria and Albert Museum. He put it in his pocket between July and October of 1813 when he went out walking, often accompanied by the family's dogs, including his favourite, a pug called Yorick. He mostly stayed close to East Bergholt but occasionally ventured further afield to Chelmsford, Colchester and Mistley. He modestly mentioned this sketchbook to Maria. If she looked through its pages, he wrote, she would see how he 'amused [his] leisure walks, picking up little scraps of trees, plants, ferns, distances &c &c'. This unassuming little book is so tightly packed with drawings, sometimes three, four or even more to the page, that it feels like a conjuring trick: the wide vista of Dedham Vale unfolds before our eyes, despite being the third of the size of a playing card; views of churches, cottages and mills are so fully realized it is possible to forget you are looking at a drawing the width of two postage stamps. Taking a pencil, on a single page he drew a view over a wide, sunny landscape with cows sheltering under a tree and a church in the distance; then he turned the sketchbook around through ninety degrees and drew a lane with trees leading to the gable end of a cottage, with a figure walking towards it; he drew a man with a scythe slung over his work-weary shoulders; then turned the book again and deftly outlined two supervisors in tall hats, one with arms folded and chin tucked in, as though ruminating over

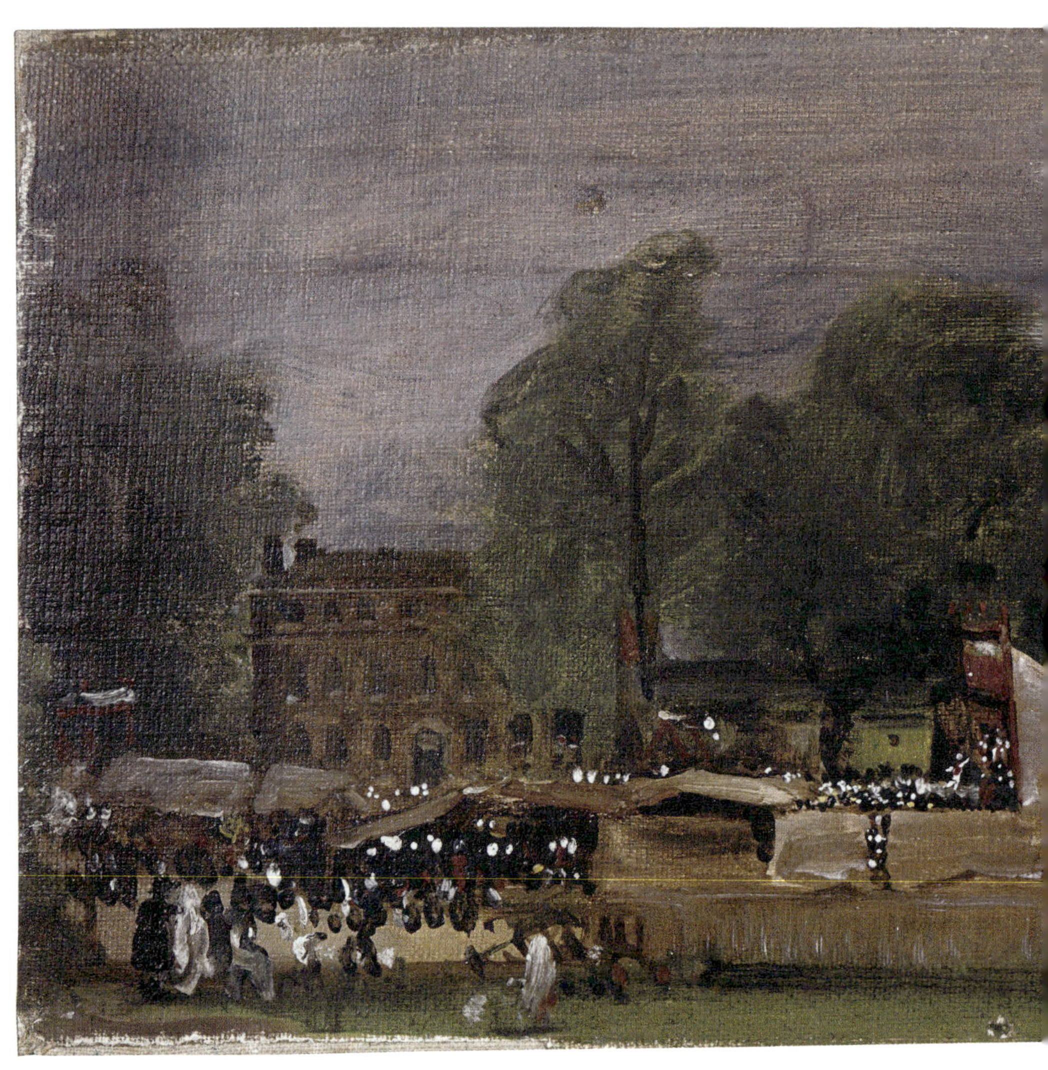

East Bergholt fair, 1811. Oil on canvas.

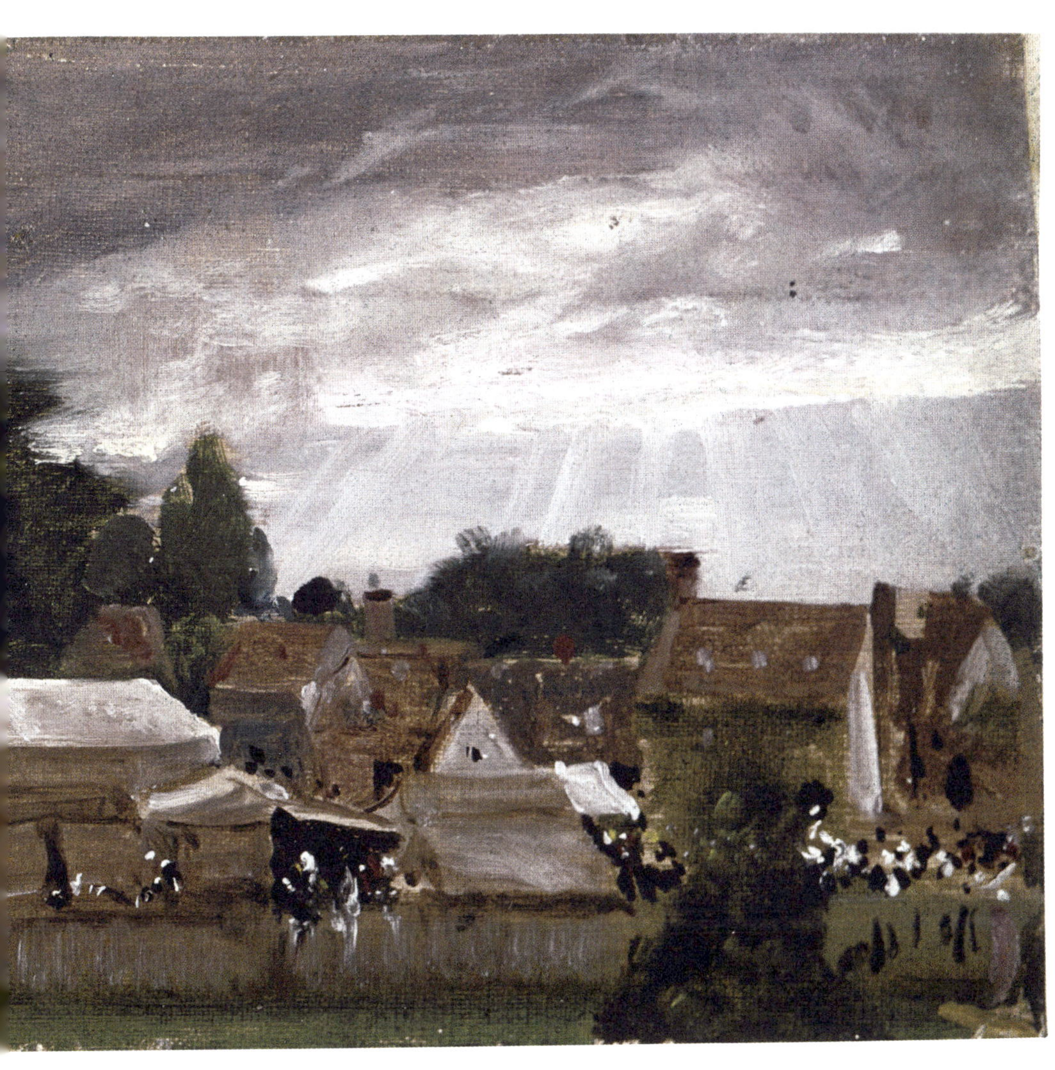

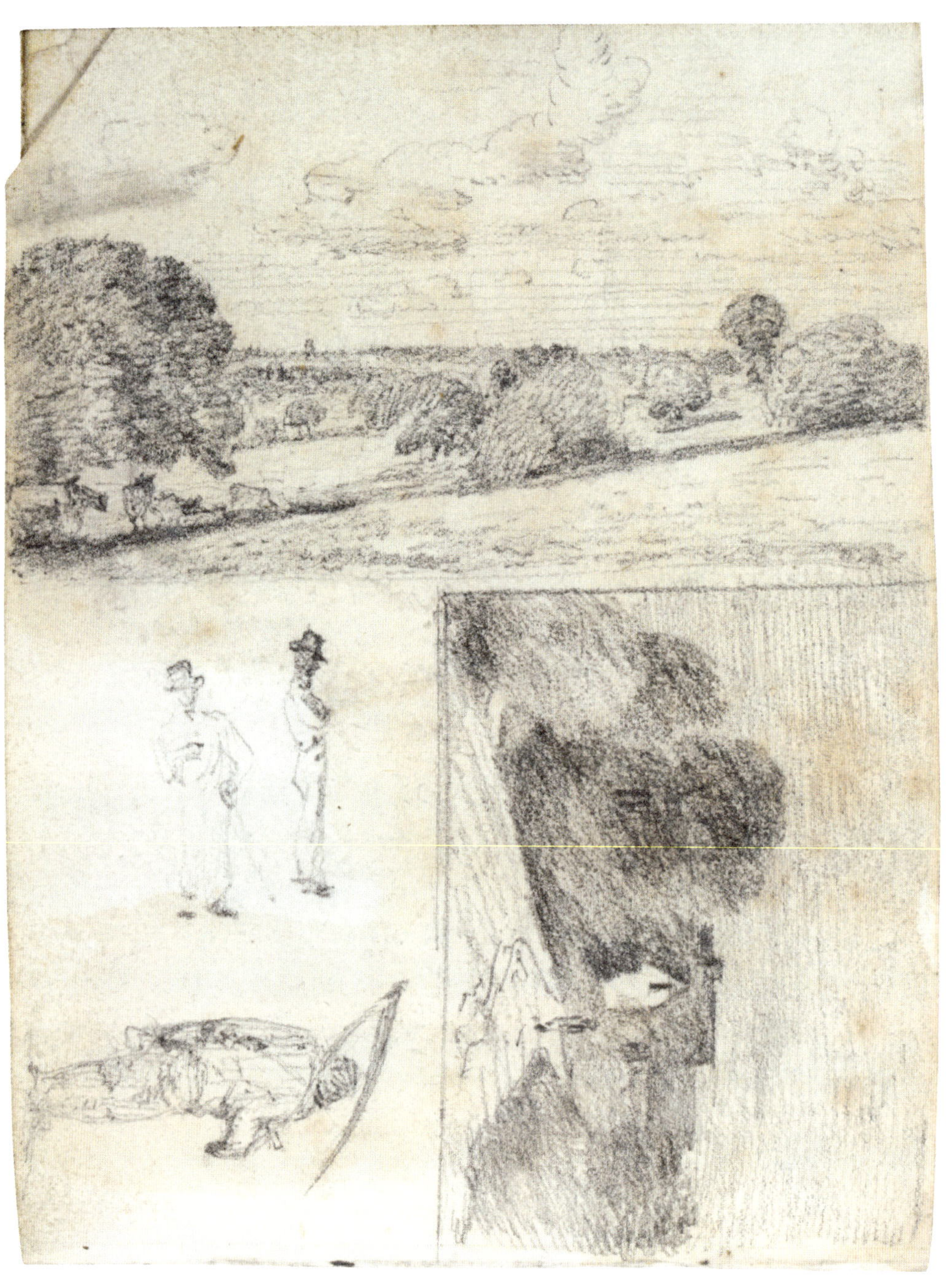

Dedham Vale, a lane and farm workers;
a threshing yard and a house by a church
in Colchester, pages 46 and 69 from a
sketchbook used in Suffolk, 1813.
Graphite on paper.

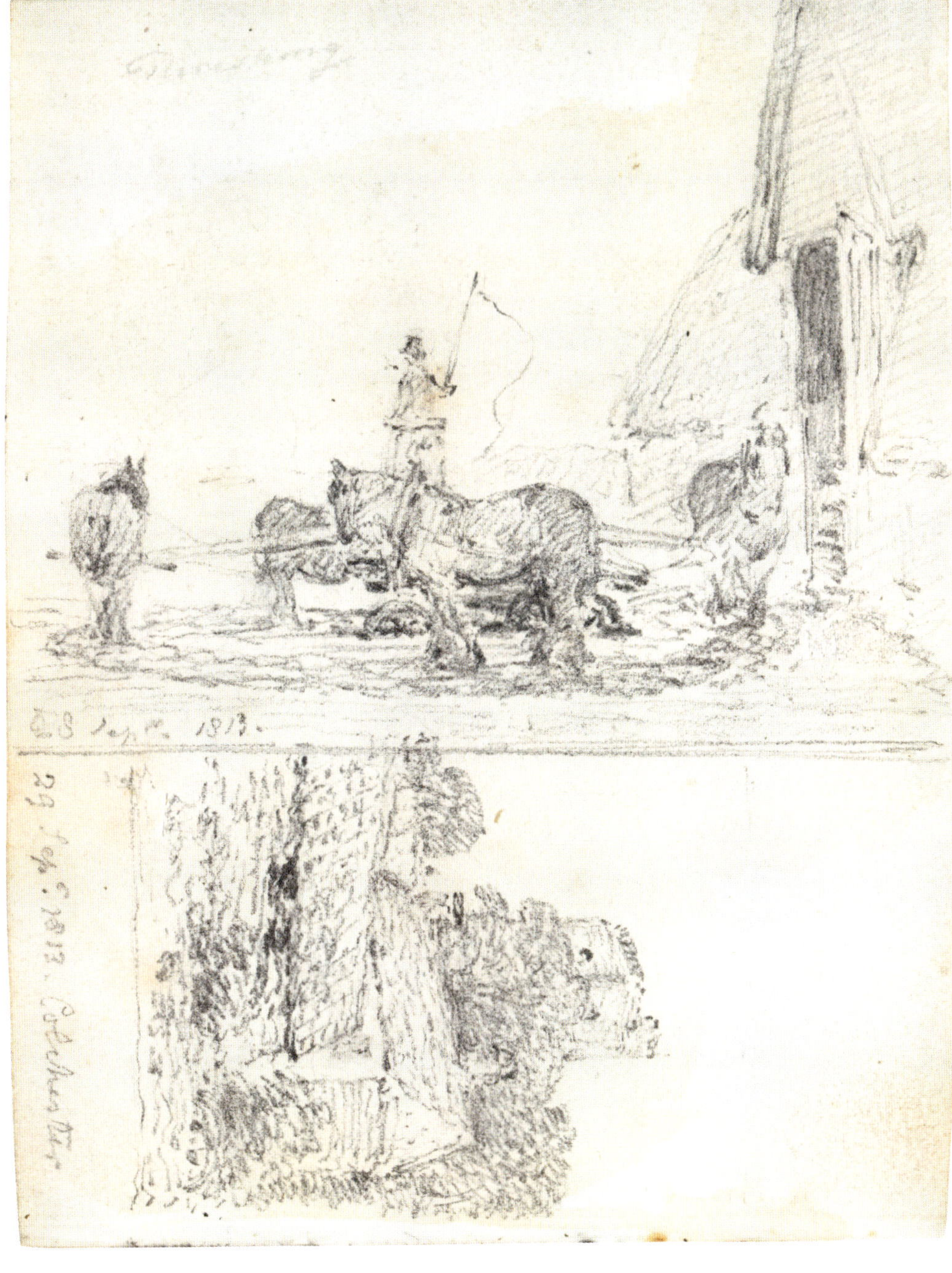

Strasbourg
8 Sepr. 1813.
29. Sep. 1813. Strasbourg

a difficult job. No-one but Constable could draw with such conviction on such a small scale. Years later he would take this sketchbook in his hands when he was working on a painting and wanted a precise record of a view, a figure, a stump or a stile.

Turn the pages of this unassuming book and we can keep pace with him as he walked, pausing where he paused and seeing views through his eyes. On 10 July he stopped to draw a mill or barn on the far side of a pool; three days later, he drew a narrow path through a field tall with standing corn, with a view of Dedham Vale in the distance. On 19 July he sketched a lane in the village next to his father's house, which he marked with a cross and noted: 'House in which I was born'. The following day he sat in the churchyard of St Mary's in East Bergholt and sketched its ruined tower twice over. He wasn't always alone on his walks: another artist – his friend Dunthorne? – sits on a folding stool in one drawing, hunched over his own sketch. As the season turned and the corn was harvested, Constable's subjects reflected the shift in activities. On 28 September he was in a farmyard sketching four horses working a threshing pit, controlled by a man with a whip; turn to the next page, and there is a man ploughing with two horses, preparing the field for winter wheat.

Landscape is my mistress

'What charming weather you have for sketching', wrote Maria on 25 August 1813 – a day during which he had drawn a thatched cottage beside a lane and part of the church in East Bergholt, squeezing them onto the same page. 'I wonder which you have thought of most this summer, landscape or me (am I not a sad jealous creature?).' For Constable, though, how could two things that were so closely associated with each other be separated? Although outwardly objective, the scenes he was drawing had deep emotional resonance for him. The word he would use to describe that summer's sketchbook to Maria when he wrote of 'picking up little scraps' is telling: he called it a 'journal'. A sketchbook contains records of things seen; a journal, on the other hand, is a more personal account of days and experiences, a form of diary.

The following summer, back in 'my beloved Bergholt' again, he filled another sketchbook, even smaller than the previous year's. Early one evening in the middle of September 1814 he sat down by the window in his room upstairs, took out a sheet of writing paper and began a letter to Maria. He tried to express how he felt when he looked at the landscape that had become their place, in which every turn of a lane, every path by a field, every view, reminded him of her:

> I can hardly tell you what I feel at the sight from the window where I am now writing of the feilds in which we have so often walked. A beautifull calm autumnal setting sun is glowing upon the gardens of the Rectory and on adjacent feilds where some of the happiest hours of my life were passed.

Later that evening, in the growing dusk, he left the house to breathe the cool evening air and stroll through the quiet village before going to bed. A huge crescent moon caught his eye: it was rising above trees next to a cottage. Stopping and taking a soft pencil – chosen because it was suitable for richly atmospheric shadows – he made a sketch by the moonlight and inscribed it 'Sunday. eveng. Sepr. 18th. 8 o'clock'. There is a hushed quality to his drawing, a saturation of feeling and sense of place; we could be by his side in the dark lane, looking up and watching the moon as it rises above the trees like a sign of hope. If paper conservators ever devise a test for the density of emotion captured in strokes of graphite, this little drawing would register near the top of the scale.

If there was a downside to spending a protracted period at home, it was being in the way of the kind of parental advice that in the winter months could only arrive in small, controlled doses. During the summer and autumn of 1812 Constable came under considerable pressure from his father. Golding may have been reconciled to his son's chosen career, but he was still opposed to the kind of artist John wished to be. Why, he asked, did his son persist in being a landscape painter when he was getting prestigious commissions for portraits from local gentry such as William Godfrey, younger son of Peter Godfrey of Old Hall, the grandest house in East Bergholt? As a businessman, Golding understood portraiture: in the sphere of art, it was a safe bet. Wealthy people would always be prepared to

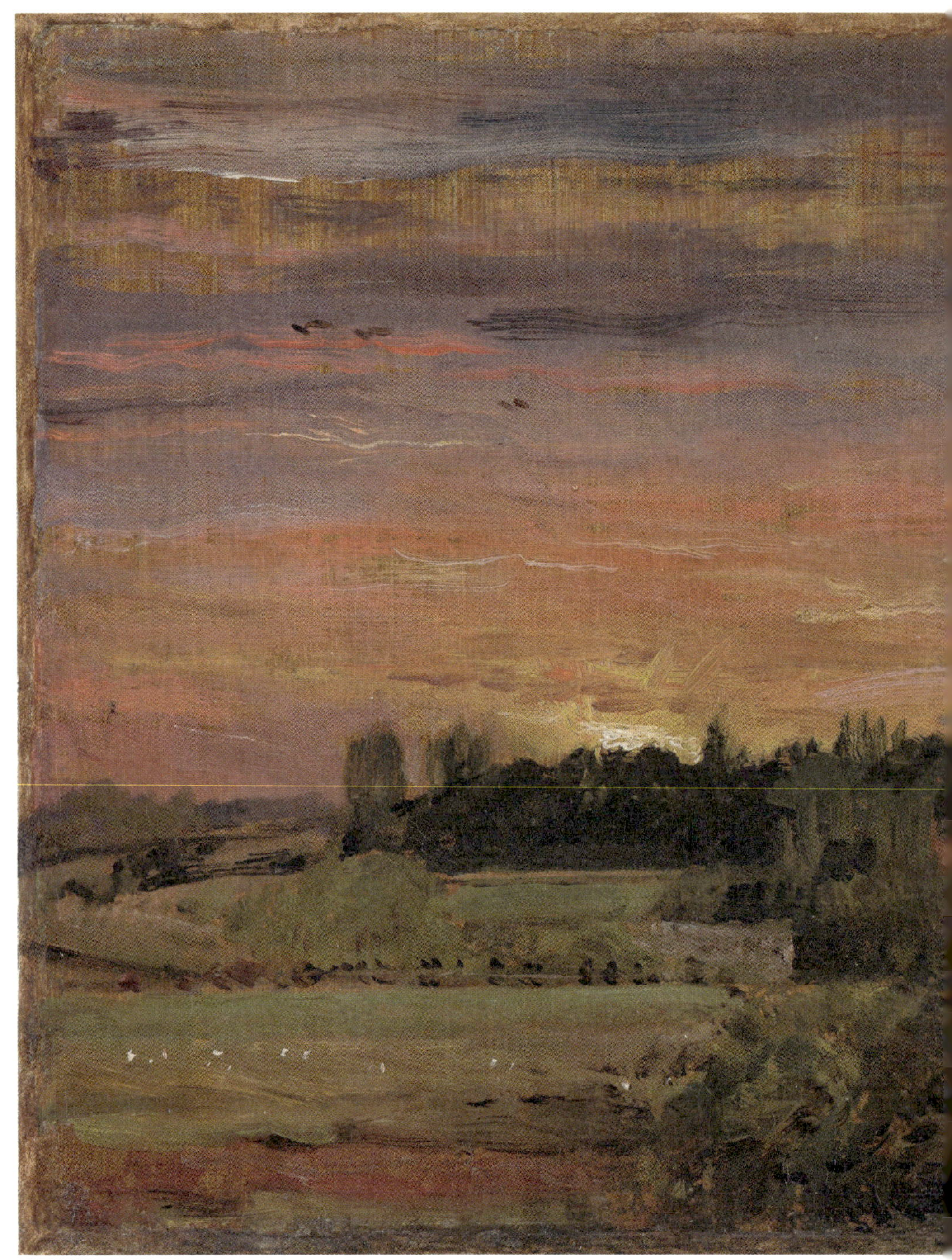

The rectory from East Bergholt House, 30 September 1810. Oil on canvas laid on panel. Constable painted this view at dawn, from a back window of his family home. His focus was the rectory, with its distinctive grove of trees. As the place Maria Bicknell stayed when she visited her grandfather, it had particular emotional resonance for the artist.

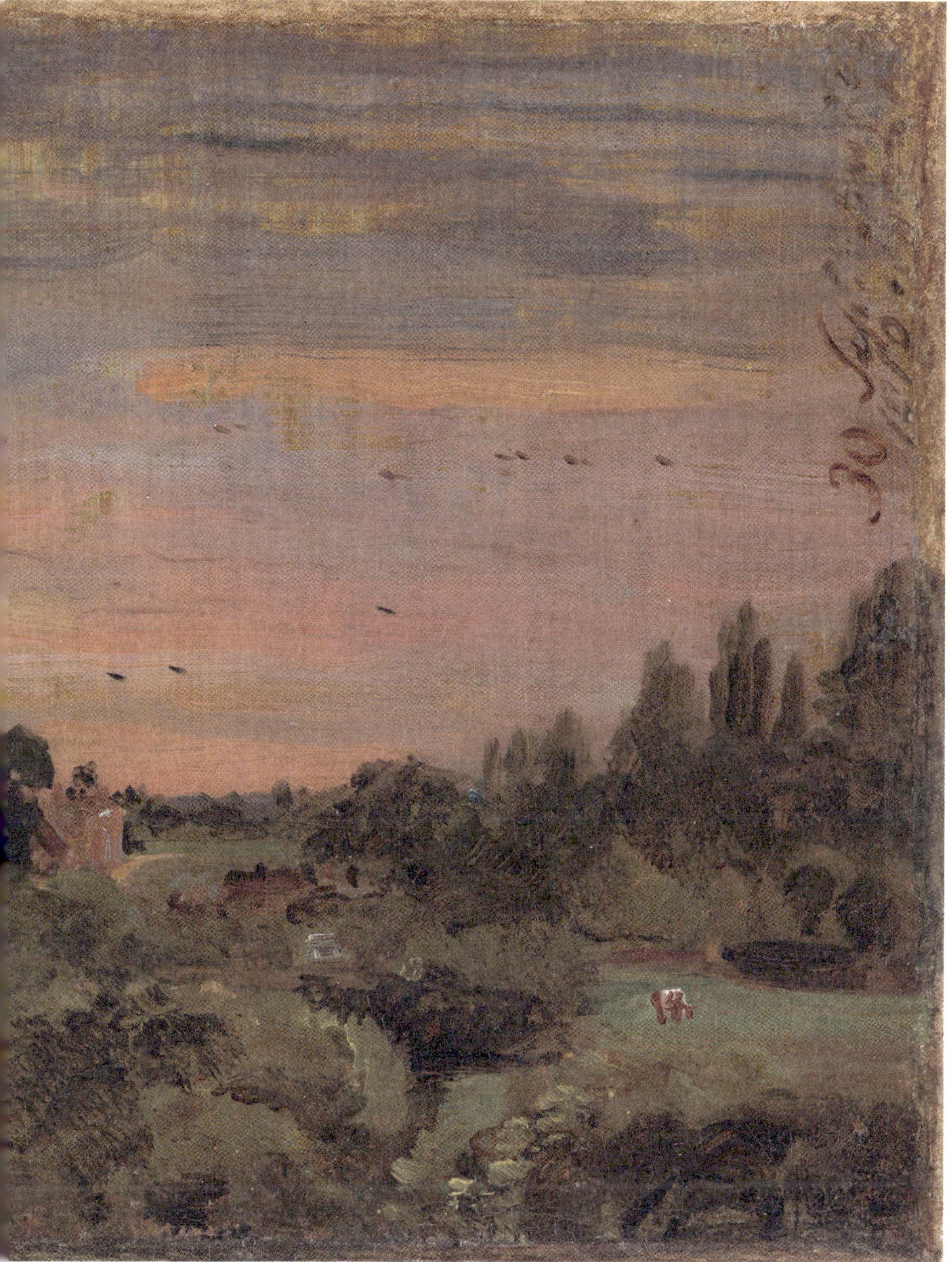

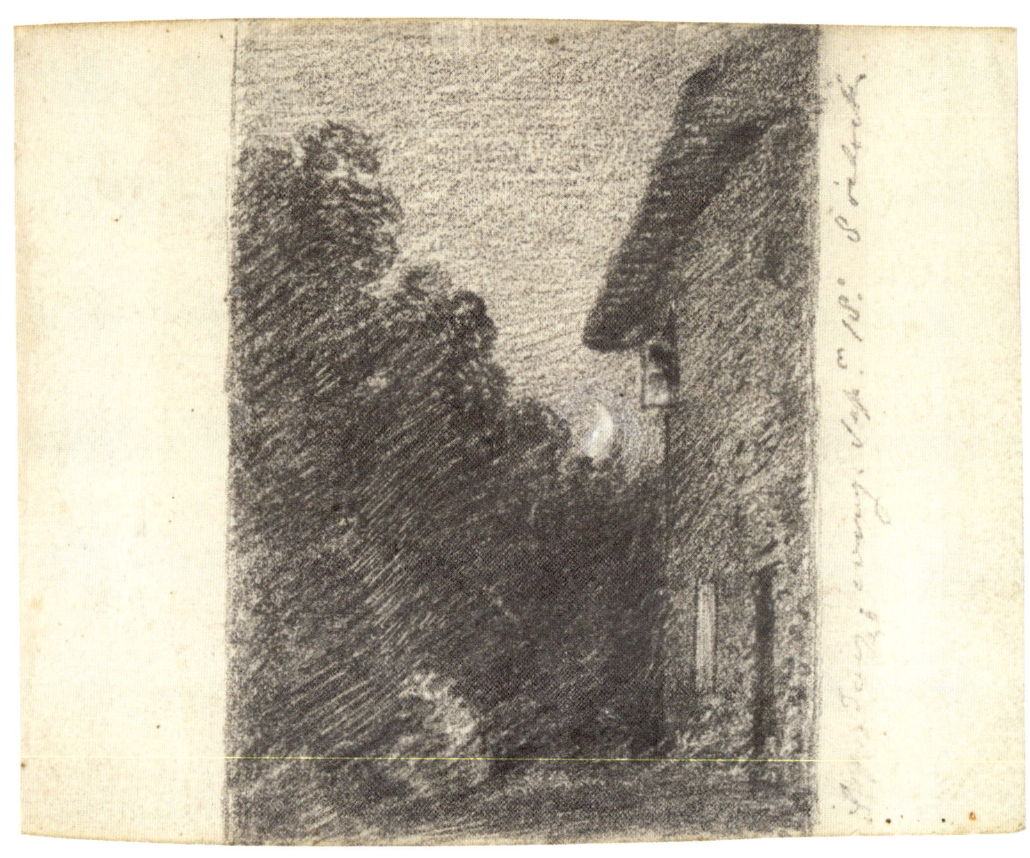

East Bergholt street by moonlight, page 67
from a sketchbook used in Suffolk,
18 September 1814. Graphite on paper.

commission portraits – the English, indeed, were famously keen to have their likenesses recorded – and the transaction was a straightforward one. After a portrait commission was proposed and a fee agreed, the painting was executed, delivered and paid for. With landscapes, the situation was far less clear-cut. In most cases it was a riskily speculative venture: the artist painted a picture which would be submitted to an exhibition venue such as the Royal Academy or the British Institution. If accepted – and there was no guarantee it would be – it would hang there, competing with the other paintings for a buyer. It might very well not find one, and instead have to return to the artist's studio – an unrealized investment of time and materials, taking up much-needed space ('lumber' was Golding's word for it). This was, unfortunately, a situation in which John had all too often found himself over the last decade. From Golding's point of view, it was not a sensible way of doing business and, quite naturally, he was agitating for his son to make portraiture his career. He was, John noted, 'uncommonly affectionate' at that time – a warning sign if ever there was one. He even dangled the gift of 'a pretty little house at Dedham' if John would only give up his London life along with his dream of becoming a successful landscape painter.

Some bracing conversations must have taken place in the drawing room of East Bergholt House during the summer evenings of 1812. As his parents worried about his future, John complained about the irksome time he was having painting a little girl's portrait at Wivenhoe Park in Essex, a commission that had come as a result of his successful portrait of William Godfrey (he particularly disliked 'being so shut up during the fine weather'). Were other inducements put in John's way? Were there threats as well as promises? We know from his letters to Maria that he continued to honour his father. 'I am hourly receiving every kindness from the best of parents', he wrote in July. And yet, for all this, he would not be diverted from his chosen path. John knew his father well; he respected his views and acknowledged the good sense of them. But it was no good. He would not – could not, even – compromise. Perhaps things would have been different if he and Maria had already been married, but in her prolonged absence landscape had become like a lover to him; whatever mood he was in, he could go to it and find joy, or comfort, or solace (*which have you*

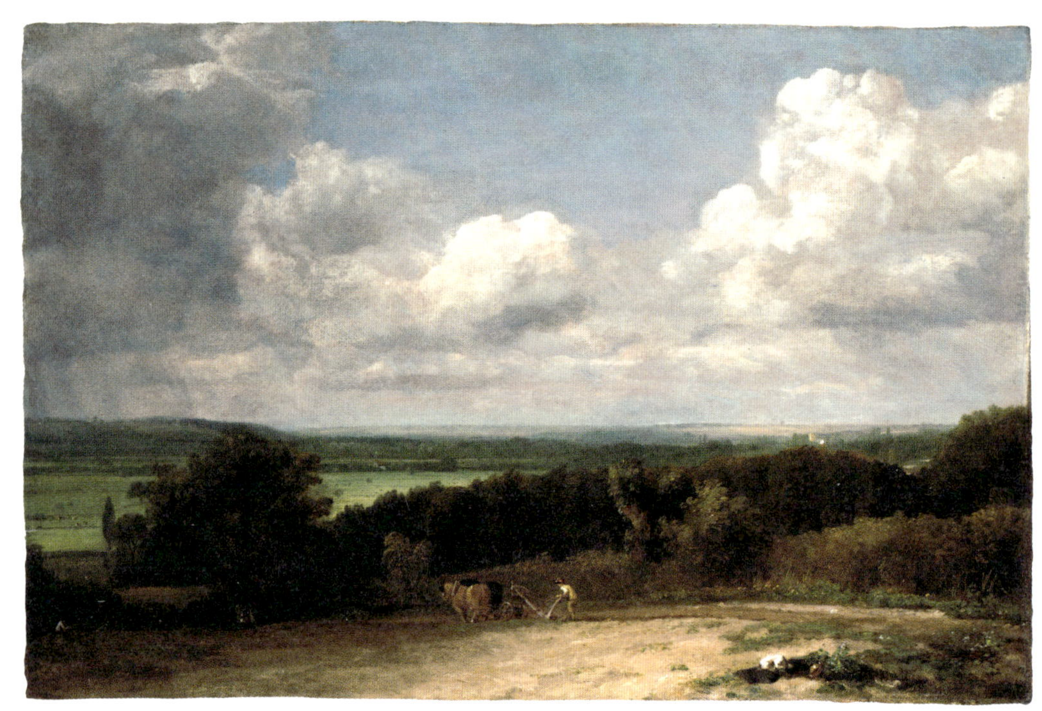

Landscape: Ploughing Scene in Suffolk
(*A Summerland*), 1814. Oil on canvas.
When Constable produced another
version of this composition in 1824–25
(now in the Yale Center for British Art),
he chose to paint the foliage in autumnal
colours rather than the summer greens
shown here, perhaps wishing to give
the impression of a more conventional
season for ploughing.

thought of most this summer, landscape or me?). He could not separate himself from it any more than he could relinquish his beloved Maria. 'My father is always anxious to see me engaged in Portrait,' he explained to her on 28 September, 'and his ideas are most rational, but you know Landscape is my mistress – 'tis to her I look for fame'. One wonders how well Golding knew his son. Was he frustrated at finding him as unresponsive as a stump, not even the pretty little house at Dedham capable of breaking his resolve? Or did he, in his heart of hearts, know that it was useless?

A summerland

Constable may have downplayed the value of his little 'scraps' to Maria, but a current of ambition runs through his sketchbooks. During the successive summers he was out walking with the dogs from East Bergholt House, oil sketching at Flatford Mill or drawing at the edge of a cornfield – 'living a hermit-like life', he said, 'though always with my pencil in my hand' – he was searching for scenes that he could transform into compositions fit to hang on the walls of the Royal Academy. He thought there was potential in a pencil sketch he had made at noon on 25 July 1813, from a vantage point at the edge of the park of Old Hall, home of the Godfreys. With his back to the fence he could see a view that divided itself in two: in the foreground were fields bordered by trees, and beyond the deep green foliage was a sweeping view over Dedham Vale under a huge East Anglian sky. He decided to use it as the basis for a picture he exhibited there the following summer, to which he eventually gave the title *Landscape: Ploughing Scene in Suffolk*.

The drawing he made in his sketchbook has no ploughmen in it. Neither, until February 1814, did the painting. But at that point Constable must have lost confidence and begun to feel that, when worked up to a larger scale, it was too empty to make a successful composition. Farmers' fields, trees, the river and Dedham village with its square church tower were enough for *him*, but he might have begun to worry that the picture-buying public would expect more animation – what Gainsborough had once called 'a little business for the Eye'. Turning over the pages of his sketchbook, he found drawings he had made of men ploughing with horses and decided to make use of them. 'I have added some ploughmen to the landscape from the park pales which is a great help', he wrote to Dunthorne. But a ploughing scene in high summer, with the trees in their full foliage? The subject itself was popular, harking back to the age-old tradition of the Labours of the Months; but scenes like this were invariably set in the ploughing seasons of spring or autumn. Constable, however, chose to depict an anomaly in the farming calendar, peculiar to certain areas of East Anglia. Tracts of particularly heavy clay land that were too difficult to work in the earlier months of the year were ploughed instead in June or July, then wheat was sown well ahead of the normal time. No-one would choose this: it was hard work for both horses and men because the earth dried in great clods, and the heat of the day made it more gruelling still. But farmers were forced into it by the nature of the land. A field treated in this way was called a 'summer-tilth' or a 'summerland' – the title, more specific than it sounded, that Constable later gave to the mezzotint of the painting in *English Landscape*. A local farmer would have recognized exactly what was going on – but most people would have been puzzled. Another artist, keener on the symbolism of ploughing, would no doubt have avoided the subject. For Constable, though, this practice was of particular interest because it was a practical solution to a local problem. And because he knew that field and he knew who owned it. 'I dread those feilds falling into Coleman's hands', he continued to Dunthorne, 'as he will clear them a good deal and cut the trees'. Constable saw the landscape in multiple dimensions: it was not just an aesthetic spectacle but land to be farmed and managed in ways specific to its qualities. It had a past and a future; it was part of the cycle of the seasons.

How well, though, did his painting evoke the atmosphere of a summer's day? In his London studio, Constable worried. Try as he might, he struggled to recreate on a large canvas the noonday heat of late July, the memory of which rose up to meet him whenever he opened his sketchbook. 'I must try and warm the picture a little more if I can', he continued to Dunthorne. 'But it will be difficult as 'tis now all of a peice – it is bleak and looks as if there would be a shower of sleet.'

Arriving back in East Bergholt in early June 1814, his picture hanging on the Royal Academy's wall, Constable was, as ever, struck afresh by the

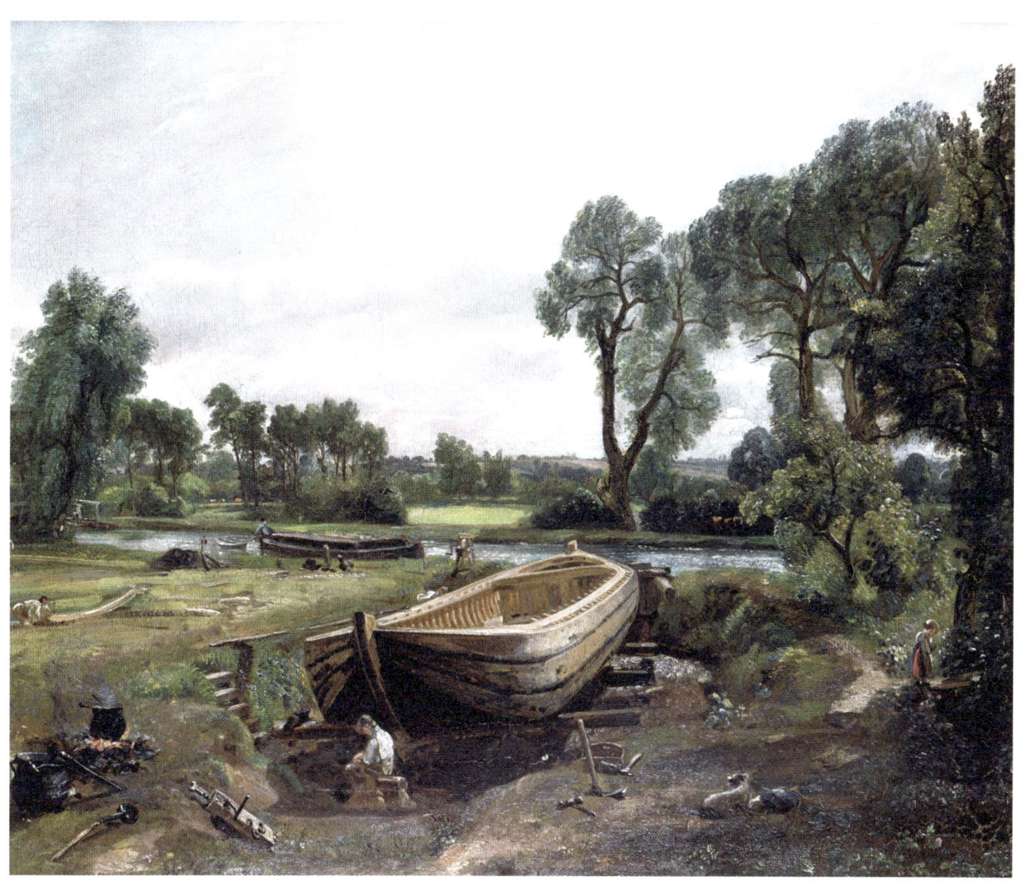

Boat-Building near Flatford Mill, 1815. Oil on canvas. *Detail overleaf.*

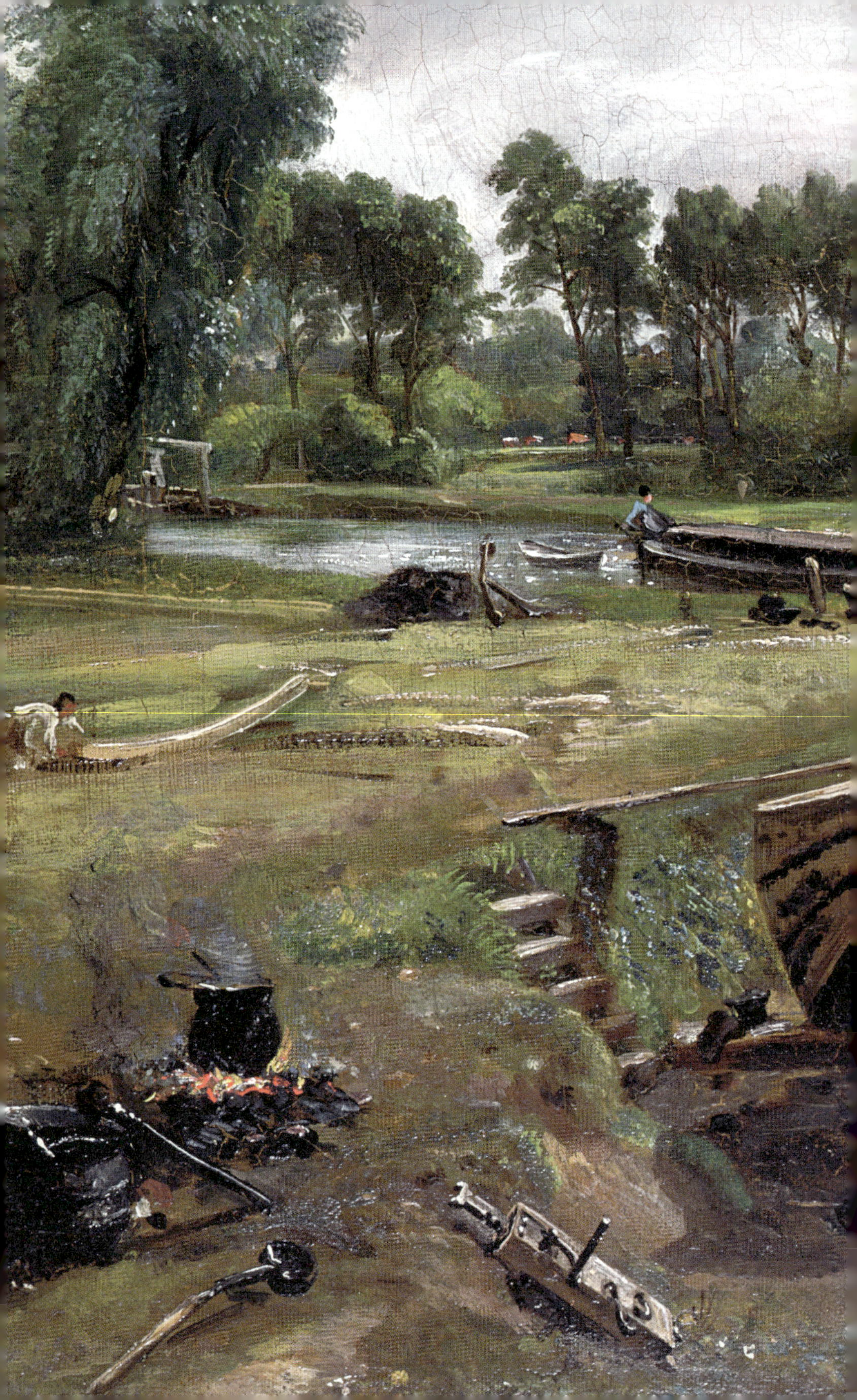

loveliness of the place. 'The village is now in great beauty', he told Maria. 'I think I never saw the foliage more promising – and as I love the trees, and feilds, better than I do the people, I can tell you [little] about our "new neighbours"'. This summer, however, he would take a different approach to his work. *Ploughing Scene in Suffolk* had shown him the problems that came from scaling up from a tiny panorama, made not even in landscape format but on the short edge of the sketchbook page. He had leaned too heavily on his imagination, and his picture had failed to sell. This summer he tried a more direct strategy.

Although he was used to making small oil sketches out of doors, now, in order to capture the atmosphere, the light and the weather – the landscape as it appeared under a Suffolk sky – he started to work on full-scale canvases in the open air. One early September day, as late summer began to shade into autumn, he put his sketchbook in his pocket and walked down the lane to Flatford Mill, where there was a dry dock for the maintenance of his father's barges. He was drawn there by industrious activity: taking advantage of the fine weather and long days, Golding had commissioned a new barge, or 'lighter', to be constructed to carry his cargoes along the Stour between Sudbury and the quay at Mistley. Work was nearing completion. To Constable, familiar as he was with the nuts and bolts of his father's business, the spectacle of this skilled labour was irresistible. He began to sketch the men at work in the dock and the cauldron in which they were heating pitch to caulk the barge's seams. Turning to a fresh page, he began a more formal drawing of the scene. Figures busy in the dry dock. Timbers in various stages of preparedness and all the tools of the barge-makers' trade scattered about. And behind it all, the river, a cornfield and the tall elms. As with *Ploughing Scene in Suffolk*, he knew he had captured an entire composition in miniature; now he could start work on canvas. This time, he would paint on the spot. He was in luck, as the weather was unusually fine that month. 'This charming season as you will guess occupies me entirely in the feilds', he wrote to Maria on 18 September. Over the following days and weeks he carried his easel to the dry dock, fastened his canvas to it and painted the scene in front of him as the men worked, the barge took shape, the light changed and the wind whispered in the leaves. According to his first biographer, he painted *Boat-Building* entirely in the open air. When

Constable saw smoke from a particular chimney begin to rise in the early evening air he knew it was time to take down his canvas, fold up his easel for the day and walk back to East Bergholt House for supper.

Two funerals

Thursday 9 March 1815. A cold day. After breakfast, John's mother Ann went outdoors to do a little gardening. While she was busy – perhaps pruning and tidying after the winter, perhaps inspecting the new circular flowerbeds she had created in place of overgrown shrubs – she felt giddy and stumbled once or twice. She went indoors and lay on the sofa, but became weaker as the day went on. Eventually, she took to her bed. It was almost certainly a stroke: her left side was paralysed and her speech slightly affected. Her children kept hoping, eagerly seizing on every little rally as a sign of recovery, but it was no good. Within three weeks this loving, energetic woman was dead.

John appears to have rushed back to East Bergholt to be at his mother's bedside in the middle of the month, after Abram wrote urgently to tell him that her condition was growing worse; but she lingered on day after day, and in due course he could no longer delay going back to London. There was considerable family pressure for him to return for her funeral on 4 April; 'all here seem to think it would be by all means right that you should attend, both with regard to yourself, & the appearance of neglect to the last outward duty, due to a deceas'd parent', wrote Abram two days beforehand; 'enough has been said to induce you at the moment to resolve to throw yourself into the Mail on Monday night to be with us on Tuesday, to pay the last rites'. But John could not be persuaded. It was, he told his brother, a critical period and he had urgent business that made it impossible for him to leave London. In a stroke of extraordinary misfortune, that year the two appointed days in which pictures could be taken to Somerset House, the home of the Royal Academy, to be considered for the annual exhibition were 3 and 4 April. Constable had prepared a record number that year – five oils, including *Boat-Building*, his experiment in outdoors painting, as well as three drawings. There was much at stake for him professionally, and he had been forced to make an agonizingly difficult choice.

Constable returned to Suffolk in early July for his customary long stay – though this time, for his father's sake, he resolved to remain as autumn turned to winter, making only short trips back to London. Another fine, hot summer unfolded, each day brimming with all the possibilities his corner of the county could offer; 'I live almost wholly in the feilds and see nobody but the harvest men', he reported to Maria. But things were different that year. His mother had been the soft power at the heart of the household; the woman that emerges from her surviving letters is capable, shrewd and warm. She was a born diplomat, a little garrulous, inclined to fret over matters such as warm socks and her children's lungs and always ready with a fitting adage or a Christian moral. Her absence brought about a sad change in the emotional weather at East Bergholt House. With the decline in his father's health exacerbated by his wife's death – 'My late loss brought me almost to the grave', Golding had told his son in May – a chilly apprehension that the life of the family home was drawing to a close cut through the summer's warmth.

During July and August, Constable painted two pictures that he never tried to exhibit or sell. Suffering being 'shut up during the fine weather', he used the first and second floors of the east-facing back of East Bergholt House as vantage points, pushing up the sash windows to get clear views over the grounds and the familiar landscape beyond. The first, *Golding Constable's Kitchen Garden*, was probably painted in July, because it shows unripe wheat in the field; the second, *Golding Constable's Flower Garden*, in August: the crop's richer colour suggests it was ready to be harvested. Sitting at the windows hearing the hum of insects from the garden and snatches of conversation between his sisters as they came and went, he recorded a panorama of the scenes he loved and suspected he was shortly to lose, those that told his life story. There is the village itself, with its friends and neighbours, its fairs and festivals; his father's red-brick threshing barn, busy and noisy at this time of year; the windmill on the heath, near the horizon. And, shadowed by its gloomy grove of trees, the rectory, home of the obdurate Dr Rhudde. The surrounding fields – Constable land – were the site of his courtship with Maria. In the foreground of the later painting is the newly laid-out flower garden, now blooming brightly with little plants, with its poignant associations with his mother. In both pictures he has given a peculiar quality to

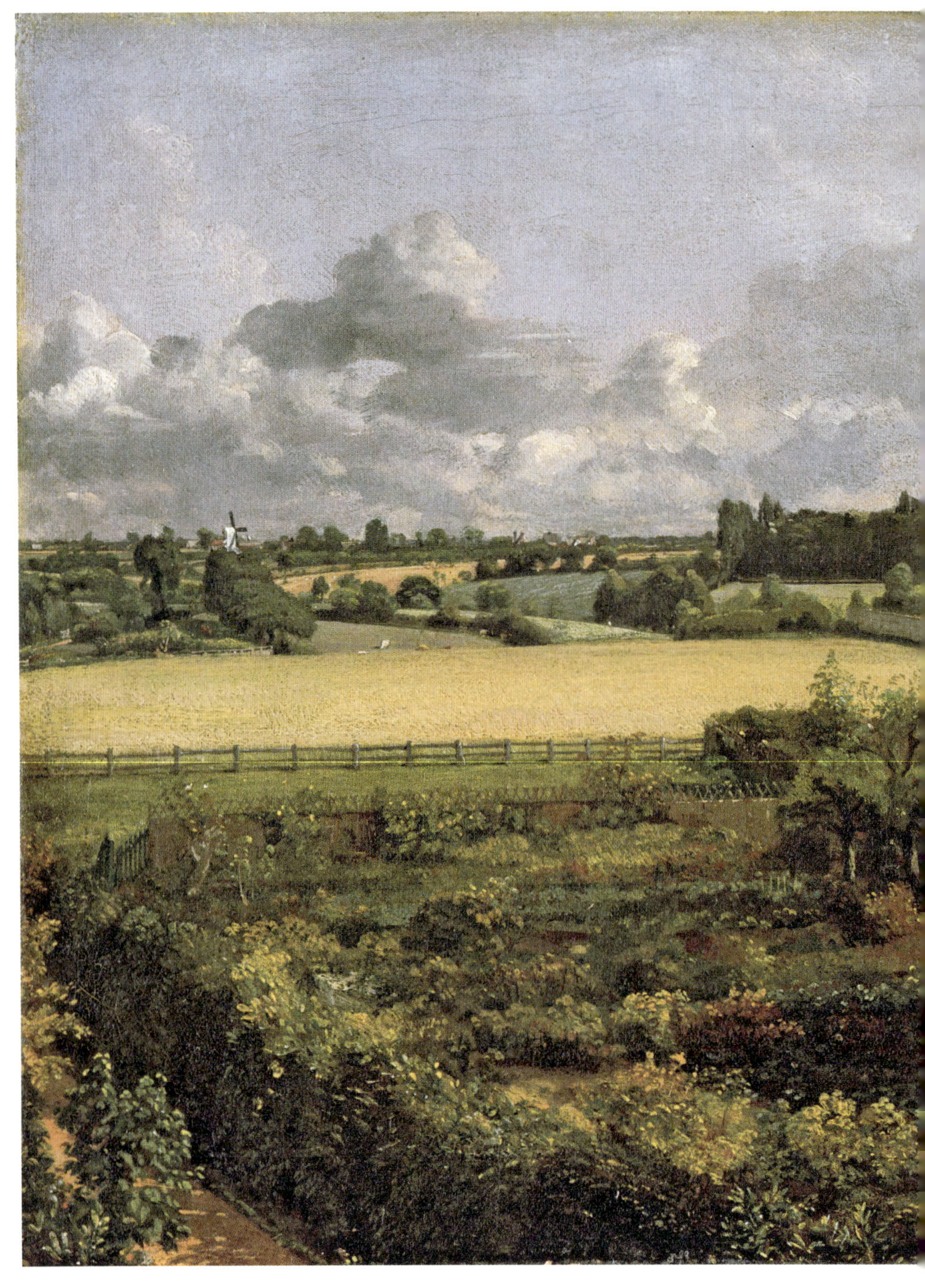

Golding Constable's Kitchen Garden, 1815. Oil on canvas.

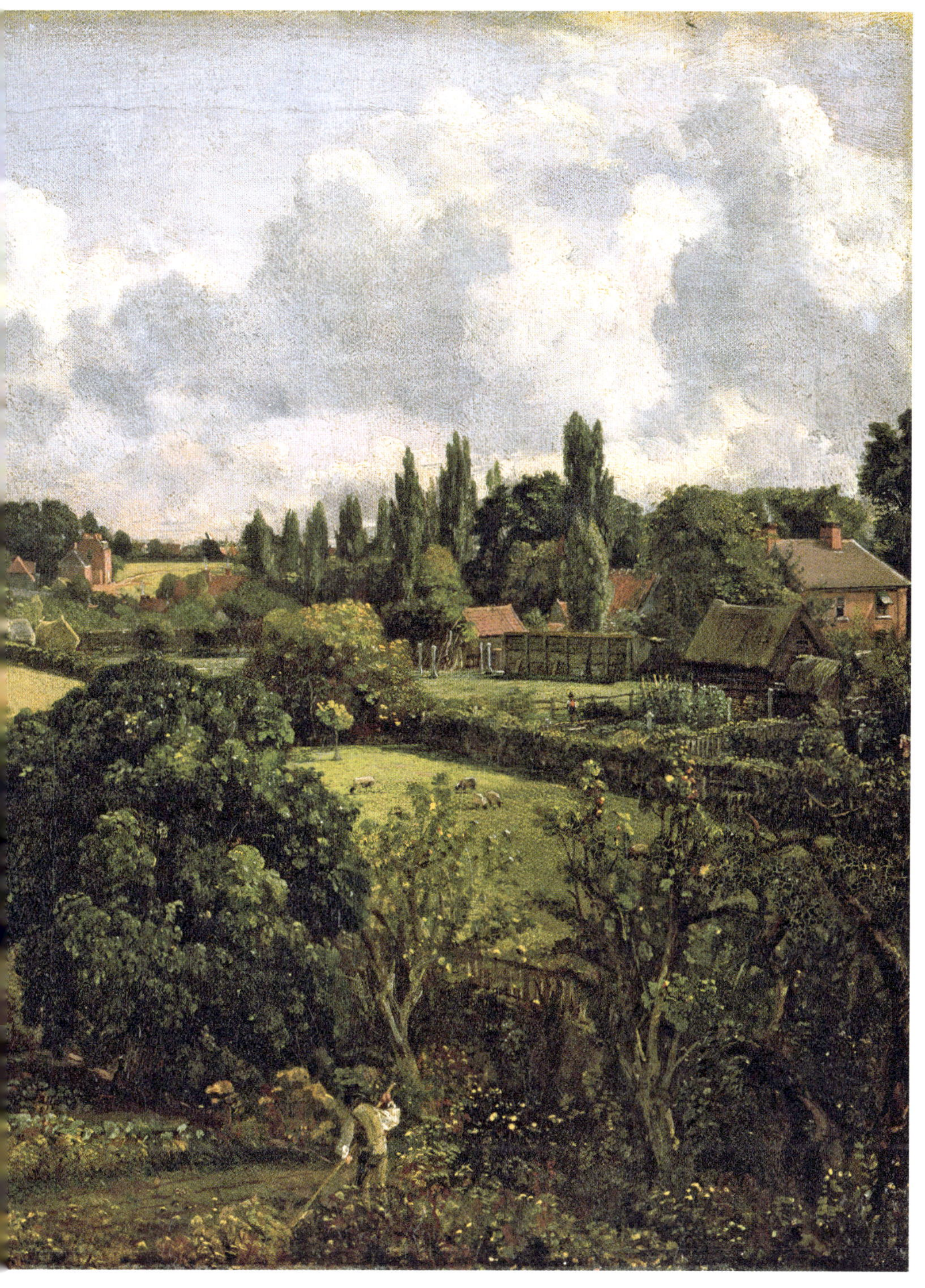

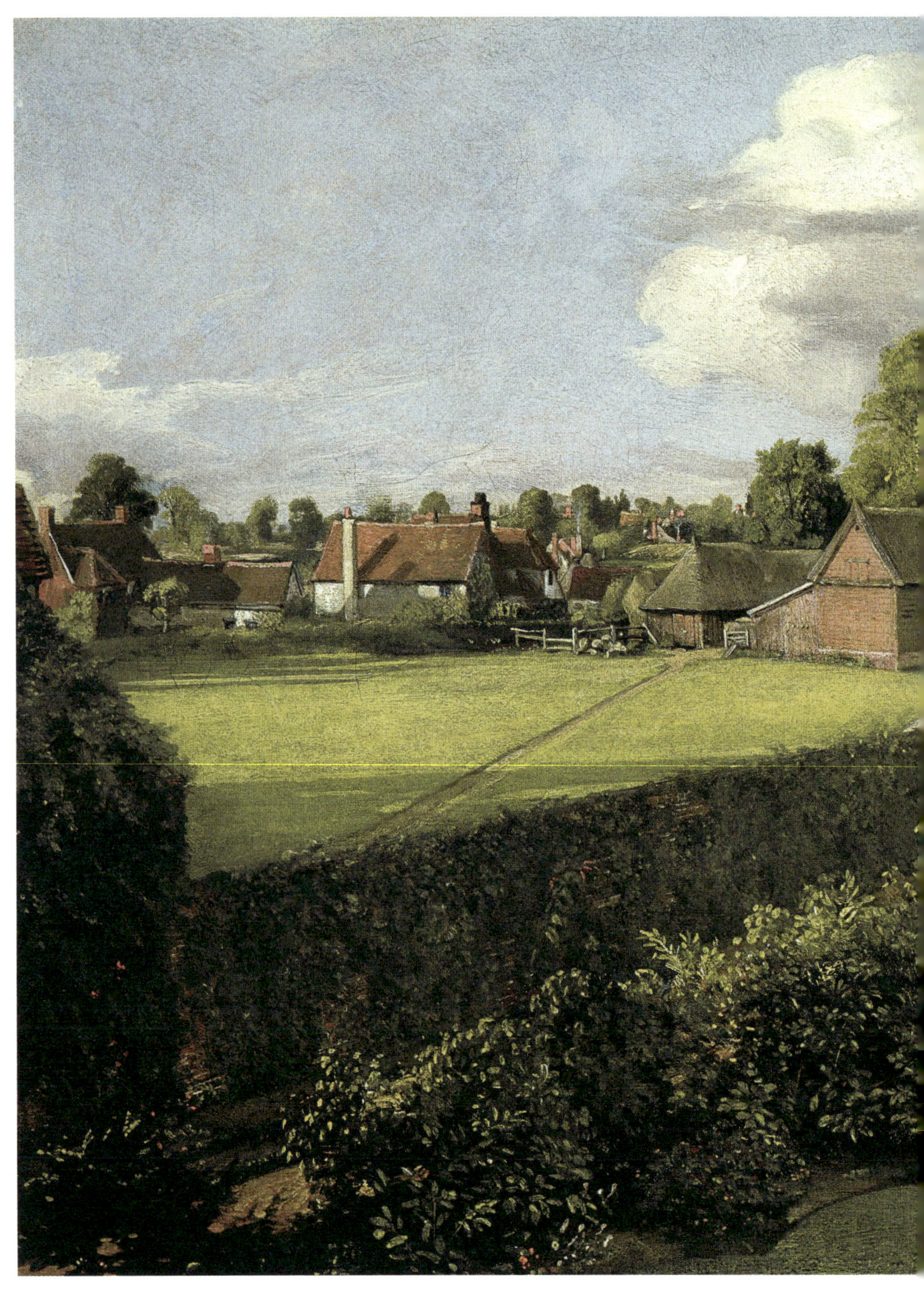

Golding Constable's Flower Garden, 1815.
Oil on canvas. The shrubbery borders
and flowerbed are laid out in the newest
fashion. A man can be seen threshing in
the central brick barn.

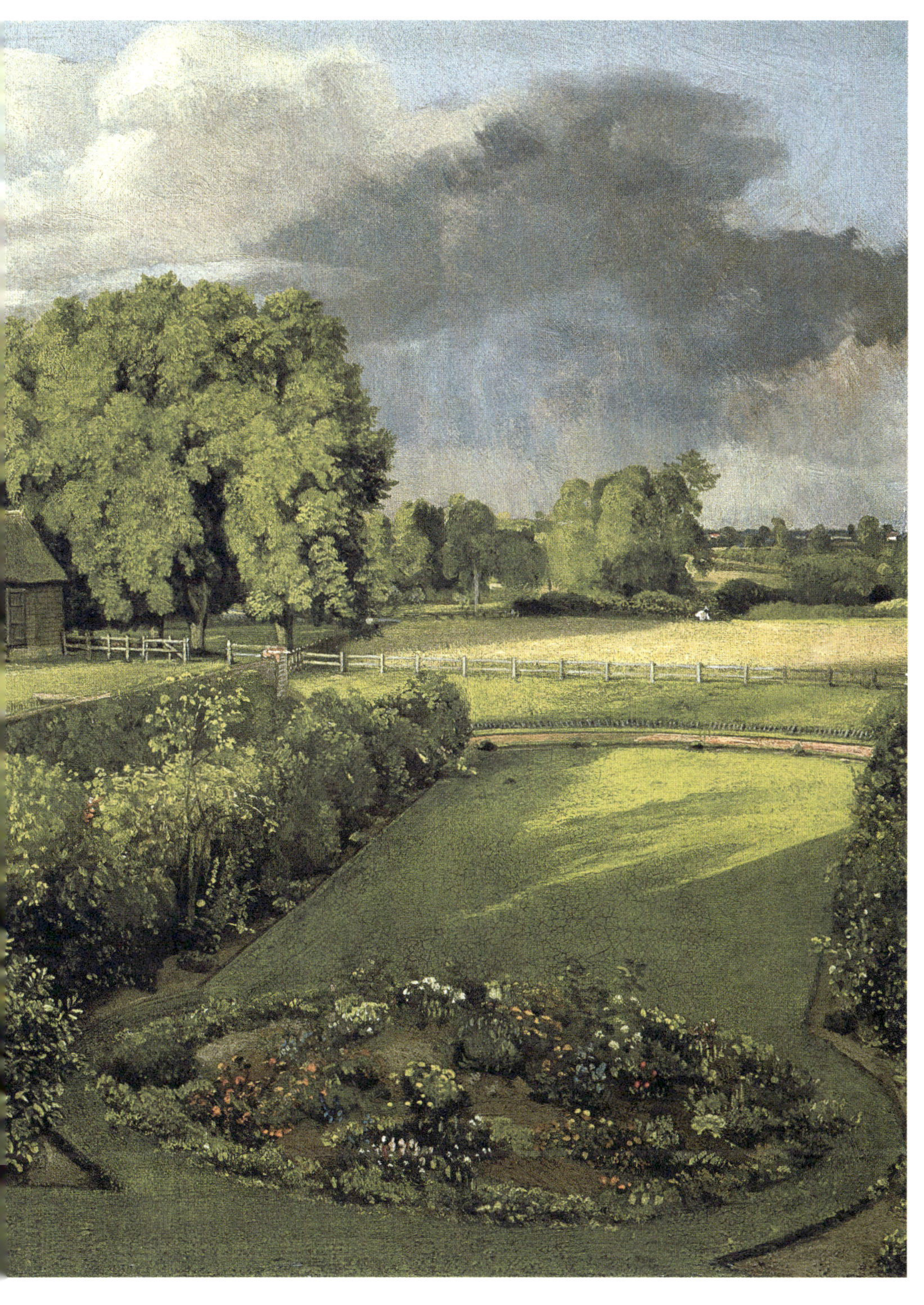

the light that he would never have got away with in works made with selling in mind: while the surrounding landscape is lit by bright summer sunlight, the gardens are drained of colour by deep shadows cast by the house and trees, as though they are in mourning. He could so easily have painted earlier in the day, before the sun moved round to the other side of the house, but he didn't. With immense care and meticulous clarity Constable committed these beloved scenes to canvas, shadows and sunshine alike, capturing for himself alone a slow accumulation of memory and emotion. The pictures were his way of saying goodbye – to his mother, his home and his past. To a part of himself. Perhaps they were also his way of paying the tribute that he had been prevented from doing at his mother's grave.

Constable stayed on at East Bergholt through the winter of 1815–16's snowfalls and severe frosts, making only short trips to London. It was March when he finally went back to the city to make final preparations for the exhibition. Two months later, his father was dead. This time, Constable was able to attend the funeral. Three days afterwards, early in the morning of 23 May, he was out walking when he stopped on a hillside to make a quick pencil sketch of a vast fallen tree and two men using ropes to manoeuvre it. One wonders how deeply he felt the symbolism. Now that his father was gone, the house – Constable's emotional centre of gravity for thirty-nine years – was to be sold and the funds divided between the siblings. With careful management of the income this would bring, Constable and Maria would finally be able to marry – whether Dr Rhudde, who would live for another three years, liked it or not.

A year without summer
The summer of 1816 was a summer like no other. On a personal level, the siblings knew that their long-settled habits of life would be broken. Decisions would have to be made about pieces of furniture that had stood on the same spot for as long as any of them could remember, about china, plate and linen. The knowledge unsettled the atmosphere like the slight thickening of the air that warns you of a coming storm. On a national level, it hardly felt like summer at all. In April of the previous year, the very day after Ann Constable's funeral service, a volcano called Mount Tambora on

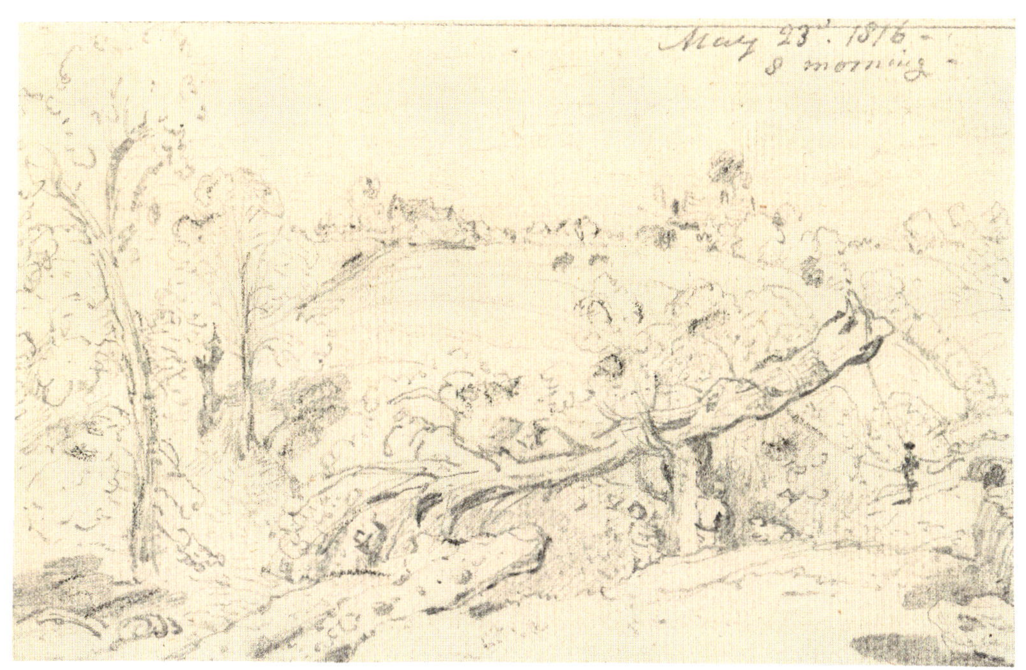

Landscape with a fallen tree, 23 May 1816. Graphite on paper.

the Indonesian island of Sumbawa had started to erupt. Volcanic ash rained down as far away as Borneo, Sulawesi and Java. The sulphur released into the air created a dry fog that had devastating consequences for the global climate. It took time for it to drift its way westwards, but eventually it reached England. On 3 November 1815, a day on which the temperature had dropped to near freezing, Constable wrote to Maria.

> I now fear there is at length an end to this beautifull season –
> but I cannot complain – there has been much bad weather on
> the Continent. Mary Constable has just had a letter from Miss
> Savile at Berlin – they have had no summer there – nothing but
> continual rains.

The bad weather dragged on and on, hollowing out the seasons as months came and went with so few of their normal features that 1816 came to be known as 'the year without summer'. In June, at the gloomy Villa Diodati in Geneva, Lord Byron, Mary Shelley, Percy Bysshe Shelley and Dr Polidori spent the cold evenings in a fashion more suited to December: writing gothic horror stories, one of which became Mary Shelley's *Frankenstein*. England had been shocked by a heavy fall of snow in the second week in May, and the situation did not improve much into the summer months. 'The weather has been uncommonly bad for hay,' reported Abram on 9 July, '& is now very uncertain … we have scarcely been without fires.' Both hay and corn were over a month later than usual. 'This has been a charming day and it will do a good deal of good to the corn which stands in much need of it', noted Constable with considerable optimism on a day in August when the sun finally made an appearance.

Despite the string of dark and chilly days that distinguished that summer from every other, Constable set up an easel at Flatford Mill and painted out of doors, as he had done before. He had found another subject every bit as technical and workaday as *Boat-Building*. Choosing a viewpoint on the riverbank, he focused on what happened when a barge being pulled by a horse along the towpath reached a bridge: how one boy unties the horse and another prepares to ride it around to the other side; and how a third boy – his whole body straining with the effort – uses a long pole to propel the

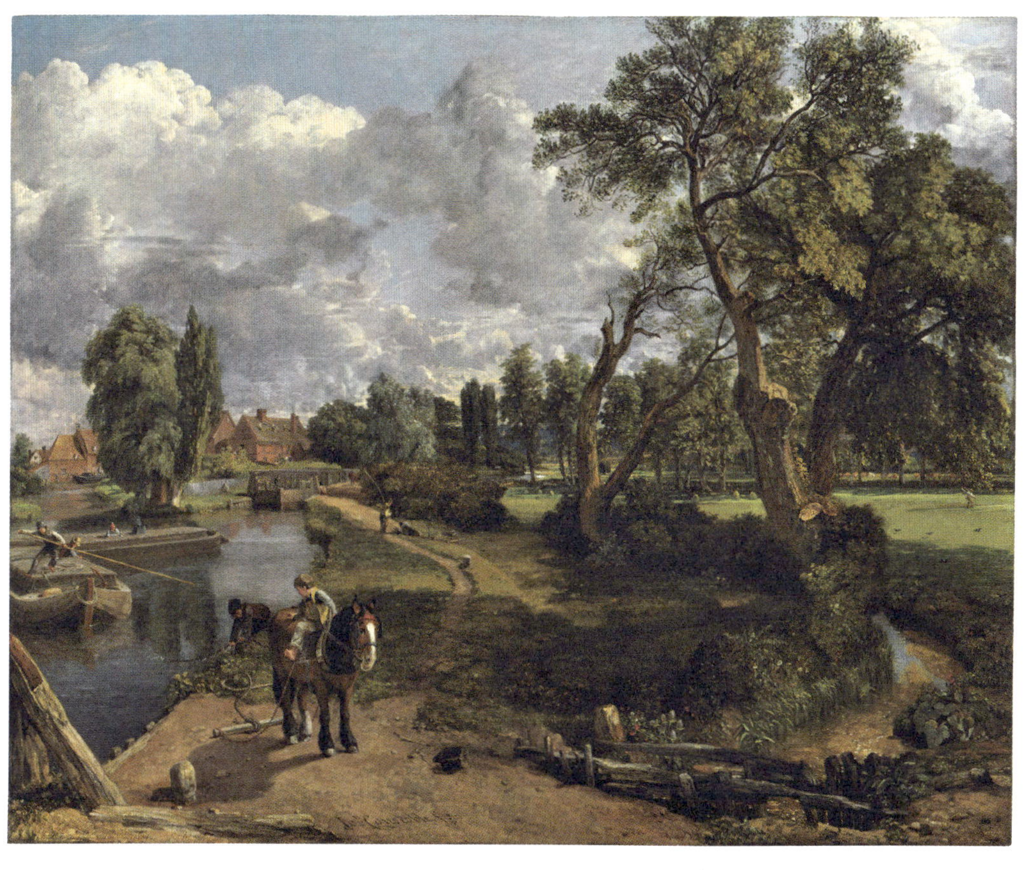

Flatford Mill: Scene on a Navigable River, 1816–17. Oil on canvas. *Detail overleaf.*

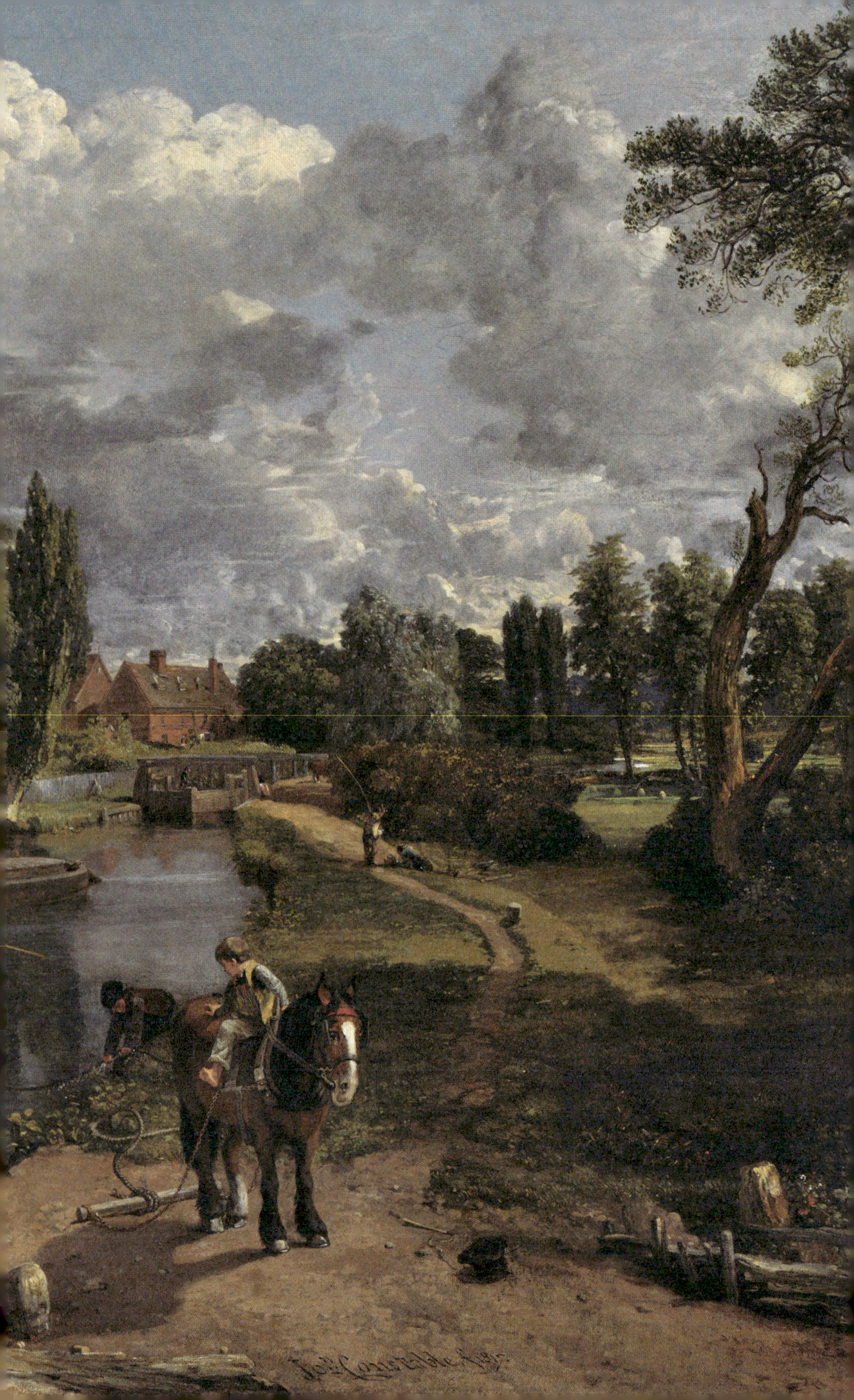

immensely heavy barge under the bridge, like an industrial-sized punt. But unlike *Boat-Building*, in *Flatford Mill: Scene on a Navigable River*, this work is confined to the bottom left-hand quarter of the painting. In the other three-quarters is an altogether less eccentric riverine landscape under the bright, animated sky of a late summer's day: tall trees, a clear stream, brick mill buildings, a lock. In the field to the right, a reaper has just finished cutting the hay, which is stacked in mounds. Rolling cumulus clouds alternatively brighten and darken the scene: it looks as though there might be a shower later. Although it was largely painted on the spot, it conveys little of the warmth of summer – which was perhaps accurate for that strangest of seasons. 'I think you must find it very cold being so much in the open air', remarked Maria on 5 September.

This is the picture Constable was working on in the weeks leading up to his wedding, which would be conducted by his friend John Fisher in London. It was to be followed by a honeymoon spent with Fisher and his wife Mary – newly married themselves – at their vicarage in Dorset. But as the time drew closer, Constable worried that he would not have time to finish his painting. He was also working on a view of Wivenhoe Park in Essex for General Rebow, and – as commissions always did – it ate irritatingly into the time he wanted to devote to his own work. With the planned wedding just days away, he wrote to Maria complaining that his Flatford picture was not 'forwarder' and making the unfortunate remark that 'the visit to [the Fishers] later in the season would have done as well'. Her reply was in a letter that Constable, understandably, did not keep; having endured years of delay, Maria was evidently not amused by this hint that their wedding might be shunted further into the autumn merely because he wanted to have more time at his easel on the riverbank, and had said so. After a flurry of explanations and apologies, however, things were patched up. The couple were married on 2 October at St Martin-in-the-Fields and set off from London. After short stays in Salisbury and Southampton, in the middle of October they arrived at Osmington, a village near the coast a few miles south of Dorchester, where they would stay until autumn turned to winter.

When he finally finished *Flatford Mill* – not until the early weeks of 1817 – Constable signed his name in the foreground. Rather than a conventional signature, however, it is a visual joke: 'Jon Constable' is written

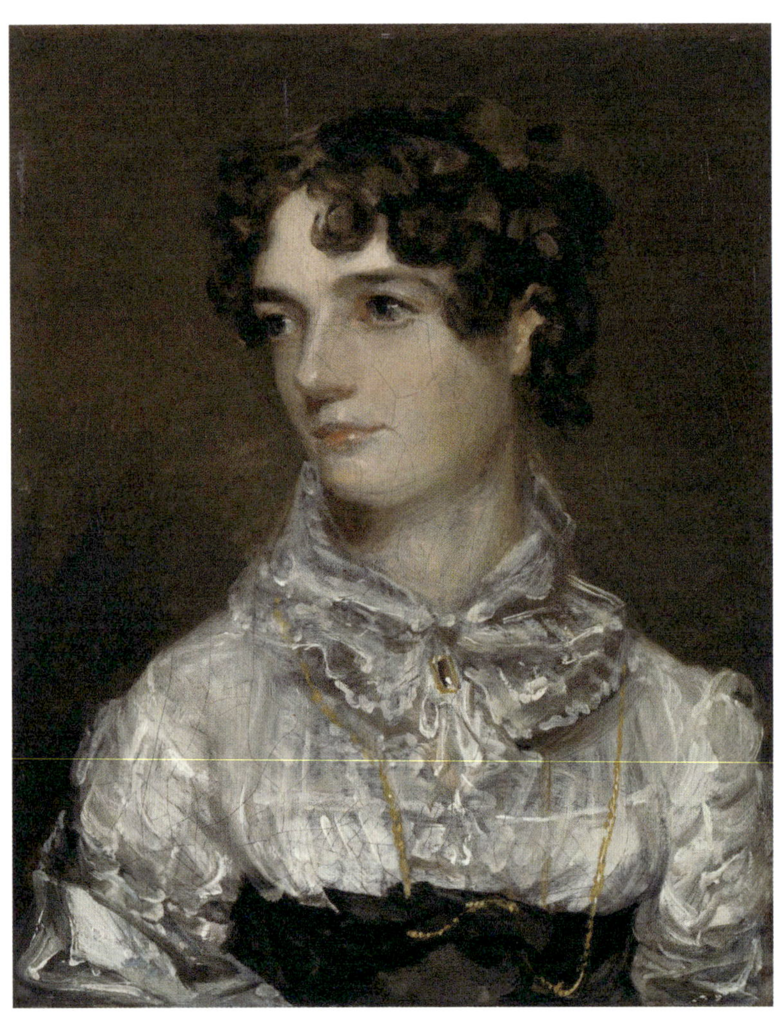

Portrait of Maria Bicknell, 1816. Oil on canvas. Constable was entranced by this portrait of Maria, painted three months before their marriage. He told her that it was 'so extremely like' that he could 'hardly help going up to it'.

as though roughly scratched with a stick in the sandy dirt of the towpath. As a new chapter in his life was beginning, he was scraping his mark into the Suffolk earth, as though making a pledge. His old way of life may have ended, but he would find ways to maintain connections to the places he loved. And as his picture failed to find a buyer either at the Royal Academy in 1817 or the British Institution the following year, it returned to him and remained in his possession for the rest of his life: a permanent reminder of a unique season, the chill of which was quite at odds with his emotions.

Old haunts

During their long years of courtship, John and Maria had become resigned to the fact that they would be apart during the summer months of each year. As she had put it to him one winter's day, 'In the summer it comes as a thing of course, we have been used to it, and know it must be, but in the winter, and spring months I think we have always seen each other.' So the first summer they spent together as a married couple was a particularly precious one. Having shared John's bachelor lodgings since returning from their honeymoon, in June they found a more suitable house on Keppel Street, just north of the British Museum. The following month, within days of moving in, they were on a coach bound for East Bergholt, where they would stay until late October. Maria was pregnant. It may have been their first summer – but it was the last they would be able to devote to each other before children began to arrive. It promised to combine delightful novelty with deep familiarity. For Constable, the season would be one of profound emotion.

He soon embarked on a series of drawings in a sketchbook, larger than those he had used in 1813 and 1814. Over time, these kinds of drawings had been making the transition from 'little scraps' to fully realized compositions, albeit in miniature – but those he made in 1817 had a quality of their own. He seems to have chosen each view with great deliberation: this was no time for the quick or partial sketches he had habitually made before. That summer he set out to make an album of the most significant places. Some of these drawings exude such intense feeling it is like a sound so low you cannot quite hear it, but its reverberations can be felt. On 25 July Constable walked down a lane he knew intimately, the one that led

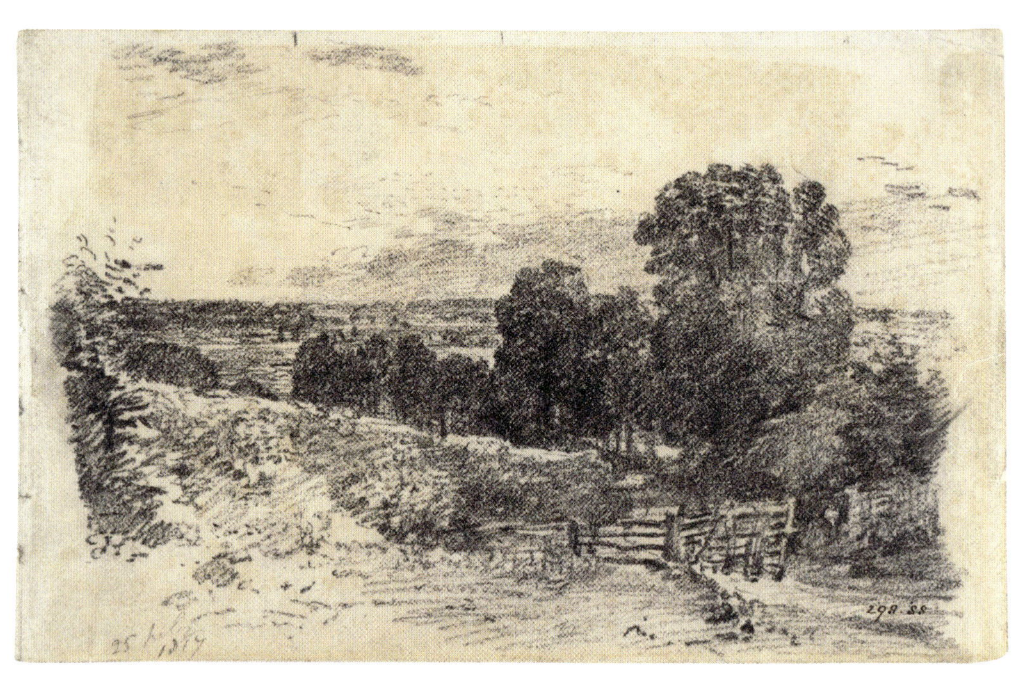

The entrance to the lane from East Bergholt to Fen Bridge, 25 July 1817. Graphite on paper.

from the centre of East Bergholt, opposite the church, down towards his father's mill at Flatford. He chose to stop and draw at a spot where Fen Lane opened to the right, through a gate; if you went that way you would cross a bridge over the Stour and arrive at Dedham. It was the path he had taken to his grammar school, a walk of about half an hour. Standing in the lane, looking towards the gate, you can see the land dip down into the vale, the distant expanse of which can just be made out through the dark masses of summer foliage. But this drawing is not really about a view, or even the foreground, but a feeling. Constable chose to work with a soft, blunt pencil, creating lines so fuzzy and shadows so deep that nearly all detail is obscured. The picture he created is not so much of what was in front of him as what was deeply impressed in his mind. He could probably have drawn it in the dark.

At some point, Constable turned the sheet over and wrote four lines of Latin verse on the back in unusually careful script:

Hic locus aetatis nostrae primordia novit
Annos felices, laetitiaeque dies.
Hic locus ingenuis pueriles imbuit annos
Artibus, et nostae laudis origo fuit.

Three years later, when they were together in Salisbury in August, Fisher wrote his own translation in his friend's sketchbook:

This spot saw the day spring of my life,
Hours of Joy and years of Happiness,
This place first tinged my boyish fancy with a love of the Art,
This place was the origin of my Fame.

The words – with which Constable identified so strongly that he used them again on the frontispiece to *English Landscape* – were written by an English poet of the late twelfth to early thirteenth century, Alexander Neckam, abbot of Cirencester, who was describing his own youth with the monks of St Albans. William Camden quoted them in his classic topographical and historical survey, *Britannia*, and Thomas Warton in his influential *History of English Poetry* (1774–81), two works Constable would surely have known. In linking these lines to his own drawing, he was supercharging his own memories with layers of history, poetry and Christian faith.

Back in the summer of 1817, just over a week later Constable visited another site and made another drawing. This view is simple, even stark: of a lane and a low hedge; a gate, a field and a cottage beyond. A solitary reaper plods away, scythe slung over his shoulder. Ahead of him is a darkening sky and vertical strokes of falling rain. A quiet lane offers an opportunity for courting couples to stroll and talk. Opening a gate makes a change in the rhythm of a walk, a zig-zag, a crossing, the man stepping quickly forwards, unfasten, and back – after you – forwards, fasten, then turning on the spot; a rural dance. A pause, and sudden proximity. A kiss? A declaration of love? Perhaps this drawing commemorates a stage in a shy, protracted courtship. In this and the drawing of the entrance to Fen Lane, the emotion is almost tangible, making it hard to look away.

On 15 August, between six and seven in the evening, while the trees lengthened their shadows, Constable drew a field with reapers still diligently at work, pushing forwards in a neat line as they cut the crop. He had drawn reapers at work before, of course, many times. But this view is subtly different. There is a framed formality about it rather than his usual easy familiarity. It is a drawing by an artist aware that his life is at a turning point; that he will no longer have the freedom to wander and sketch for weeks on end. He drew East Bergholt church with the same solemn intensity, recording every flint and brick. On 20 August he went to Mistley to sketch the port where sacks of flour from Constable mills were transferred from barges to be shipped to London – he drew the shore and the boats twice, from the east and the west. The family's brig, the *Balloon* – which had replaced the *Telegraph* – is probably the tall-masted focus of these two, its portrait captured within the covers of his sketchbook. He was bottling the atmosphere with these drawings so that, in future, he could uncork it, breathe it in and remember.

In late October, when he had nearly completed the rounds of his old haunts, covering his sketchbook pages with an almost ritualistic series of drawings as he came to terms with the transition from old life to new, he attempted a yet more ambitious subject. It was to be a magnificent farewell while the trees

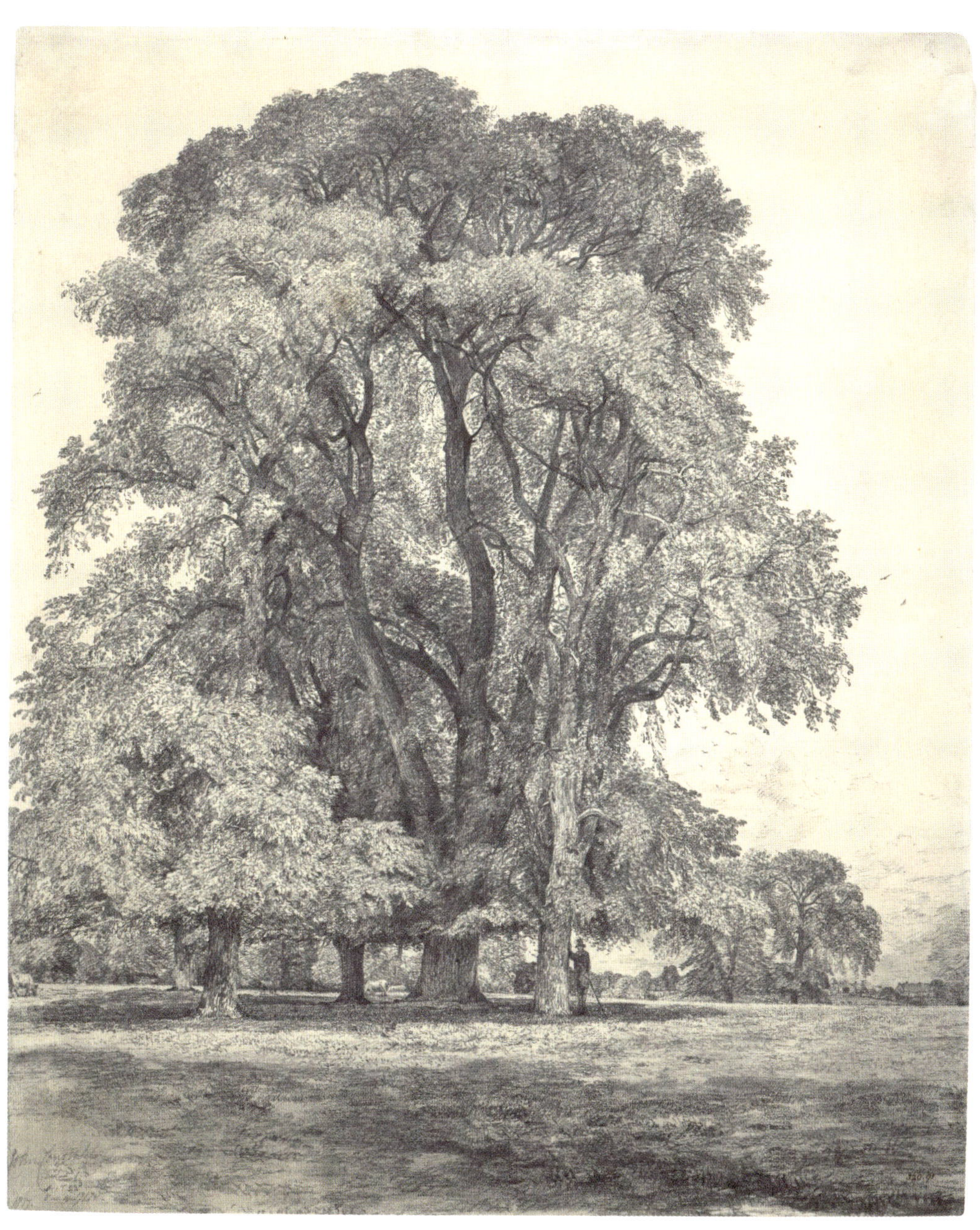

Elm trees in Old Hall Park, East Bergholt,
22 October 1817. Graphite on paper.

were still dressed in their summer foliage – and one for which he needed a much larger sheet of paper. He sought permission from Peter Godfrey to draw in the parkland of Old Hall, where there stood a group of elms (the top-hatted figure leaning against the tree trunk may well be Godfrey himself). This time Constable used at least two grades of graphite pencil, soft for the deepest tones and a harder, silvery one, more capable of fine detail. Having spent weeks drawing places of emotional resonance, this large-scale drawing is a triumphant feat of sustained observation. He honoured the trees by looking at them with a forensic eye – not falling back on conventional squiggles to represent foliage but instead by following the twisting route of each branch and drawing virtually every leaf. The drawing rings with a sense of place. The sketchbook drawings he made that summer and autumn were intensely private; but he exposed this tribute to East Bergholt the following year to full public view, on the walls of the Royal Academy.

I am living here but I dislike the place

Summer in London can be dusty and stifling. That is as true today as it was a little over two hundred years ago. Exhaust fumes may have been many decades away in the 1810s; but imagine the pollution caused by a coal fire burning in every kitchen, smoke billowing from chimneys and the air tasting of soot. On hot days it could stink. London's sewerage system emptied human waste from the fast-growing population into the fetid Fleet River and thence into the Thames. The bodies of the dead were packed, sometimes ten deep, into crowded burial sites. Until his marriage Constable had had limited experience of London at this time of year; but by the August of 1819 he and Maria, with their one and a half-year-old son John Charles and baby daughter Maria Louisa (usually known as Minna), were spending their second summer in Keppel Street. Maria's health had always been delicate, and the smoky atmosphere was bad for this young mother's lungs as well as her children's. Looking around for temporary summer accommodation away from the miasma of the city but not too far from the family's base, Constable thought of the village of Hampstead, to the north of London. It had the twin advantages of being higher up, with fresher air – and of being on the edge of a heath, the closest approximation to the country that the city could offer. Constable was pleased: lodgings in Hampstead, just three miles door to door from their London house, allowed him to 'see nature – & unite a town & country life' – the twin poles that he had never been able to integrate before. So began a pattern of life in which Constable family summers were largely spent away from the centre of London. They took lodgings in Hampstead most summers from 1819 until 1827, when they moved permanently into a house on Well Walk, close to the heath. Over time, however, it became worryingly apparent that Maria was failing to thrive, even in the healthy air of north London. '[T]his warm weather has hurt her a good deal,' Constable reported to Fisher in early May of 1824, 'and we are told we must try the sea'. For the next few years after that, family summers were shaped by the coastal resort of Brighton.

Maria knew Brighton well and had stayed there before her marriage. John, however, took a hearty dislike to this former fishing village, which George IV had made into a fashionable destination when he first began to visit as Prince of Wales. He made a brief visit in May of 1824 to settle Maria and the children into their accommodation (the journey took just a few hours from London by coach) and went down again in June, but he mostly remained in London: this new arrangement meant that the family was separated for long periods. In July he felt able to leave town, and took the coach down to Brighton for a longer stay. The following month he catalogued his feelings about the place in a letter to Fisher. The passage is worth quoting in full.

Brighton is the receptacle of the fashion and offscouring of London. The magnificence of the sea, and its (to use your own beautifull expression) everlasting voice, is drowned in the din & lost in the tumult of stage-coaches – gigs – 'flys' &c. – and the beach is only Piccadilly… by the sea-side. Ladies dressed & *undressed* – gentlemen in morning gowns & slippers on, or without them altogether about *knee deep* in the breakers – footmen – children – nursery maids, dogs, boys, fishermen – *preventive service men* (with hangars & pistols), rotten fish & those hideous amphibious animals the old bathing women, whose language both in oaths & voice resembles men – all are mixed up together in endless & indecent confusion

It did not, in other words, remotely resemble his beloved Suffolk, with its (in his view) traditional, purposeful rhythms of life and work. But he ends his diatribe on a positive note despite himself. 'In short there is nothing here for a painter but the breakers – & sky – which have been lovely indeed and always varying.'

Given a free hand, Constable would not have chosen to spend time there. But there he was, and as usual he drew and painted his immediate surroundings. He did so, however, in a highly selective way. It was as though he were training a telescope on a particular spot, blinkering out the summer's informally dressed visitors, boisterous children, cheerful paddlers and brightly painted bathing machines. He focused his notional viewfinder on working boats, a subject that had always absorbed him. It was, in fact, almost as though he were looking into the past: when he made oil sketches and drawings on the beach, he pictured summer in Brighton as it was before the tourists came. He was even ambivalent, he confessed to Fisher, on the subject of fishing boats, because he felt the subject had become so 'hackneyed', too many appearing each summer on the Royal Academy's walls. What caught his eye instead was the incongruous presence of the coal ships, or colliers, which were brought right up onto the beach at high tide in order to unload. Perhaps they offered Constable a connection to his father's brigs, the *Telegraph* and the *Balloon*, which sometimes carried coal that had been shipped down the coast from the north, alongside their cargo of Suffolk flour, to London. On 19 July, a fine summer's day with a little fair-weather cloud, Constable settled himself on the beach with his paintbox resting on his knee as usual and painted three beached colliers, stark black against an aquamarine sea, sounding a harsh industrial note in the midst of this pleasure town. The beach – as Constable painted it – is nearly empty, save for a handful of small blobs and smudges that stand for holidaymakers. And he evidently got over his reservations about fishing boats, because they appear again and again in his drawings and oil sketches. He repeatedly drew fishermen at work, hauling their nets and furling their sails. He even made a diagram-like drawing of fishing tackle on the beach, observing it with the same level of fascinated attention he normally reserved for varieties of plough.

Even taking his ambivalence into account, it can come as a shock to discover what Constable was thinking when he was sketching. On 3 August, a

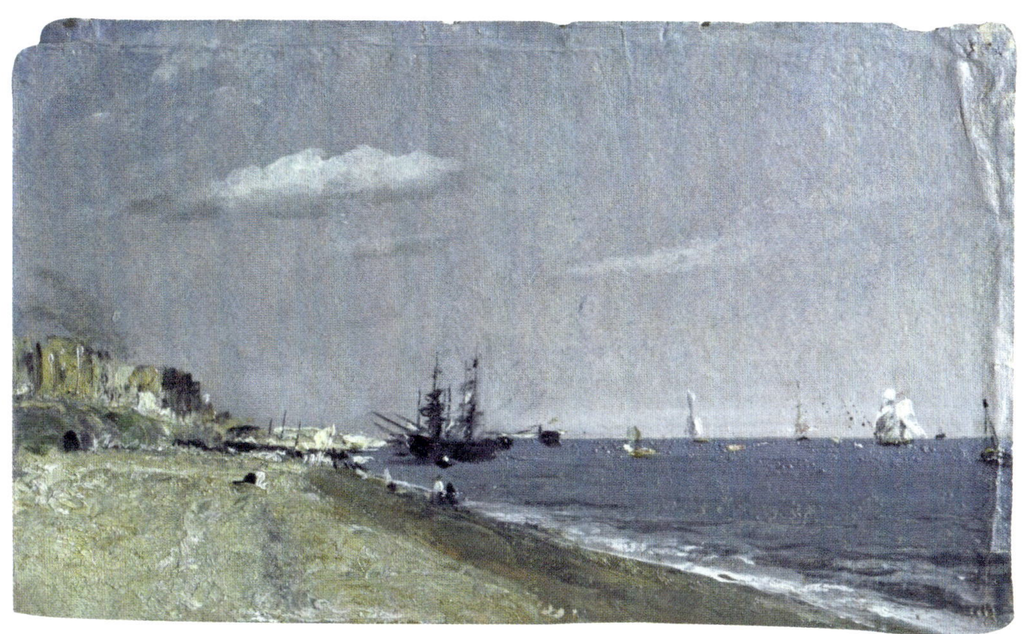

Brighton beach with colliers, 1824. Oil on paper. '3d tide
receeding left the beach wet', Constable noted on
the back of this sketch, '– Head of the Chain Pier
Beach Brighton July 19 Evg., 1824 My dear Maria's
birthday … Very lovely Evening – looking
eastward – cliffs & light off a dark grey effect –
background – very white and golden light'.

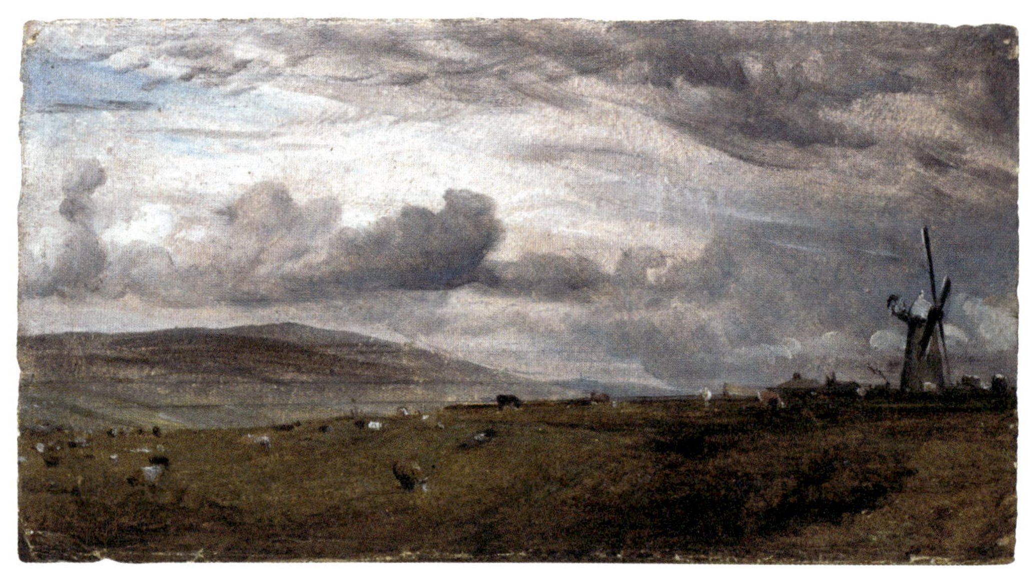

A windmill near Brighton, 3 August 1824. Oil on paper.
Following spread: A rainstorm over the sea, c. 1824–28. Oil on paper.

day of racing clouds in which hints of blue were evenly matched by threats of darkening grey, he made an apparently lyrical oil study of the downs with grazing cattle and a windmill. But if you turn this exercise in earth and sky tones over in your hands and read the words he has written on the back, it reveals a different story. He notes the date and – characteristically – that the windmill is a particular kind called a 'Smock or Tower mill'. Then he writes this: 'west end of Brighton the neighbourhood of Brighton – consists of London cow fields – and Hideous masses of unfledged earth called the country'. To a man who had grown up loving the intensively farmed arable land of Suffolk, this stretch of the down with its close-cropped turf, not far from the lodgings he and Maria had found at the western edge of Brighton, was wild in just the wrong way.

The breakers and the sky, however, put on their daily show regardless of holidaymakers or local farmers, and Constable made his most vivid oil sketches when he turned his back on the town. He must have been one of very few visitors to Brighton during those summers who did not welcome a clear blue sky. His interest was hooked by gathering clouds and foaming waves, by the trout-skin greys and pinks that stained and streaked the sky when a summer storm was on its way. One of the very first sketches he made in Brighton, on an elongated sheet chosen to emphasize the horizontal strips of beach, sea and sky – the latter almost purple with storm clouds – shows two women, bundled in shawls, making their slow way along the shingle, backs bent as they brace themselves against the gale. 'June 12 1824 / taking the air', was the wry comment he wrote on the back. Another, undated, is of a rainstorm over the sea. The relish with which he painted it is almost tangible. The beach and sea are squashed into a narrow strip at the bottom to make room for the spectacular drama of the sky. Racing the storm with his brush and poised to dash for shelter, he splotted in boiling black clouds and bright shafts of light, then dragged his brush violently down the paper, again and again, using the bristle-tracks for the torrents of rain lashing down on the sea, getting closer by the second.

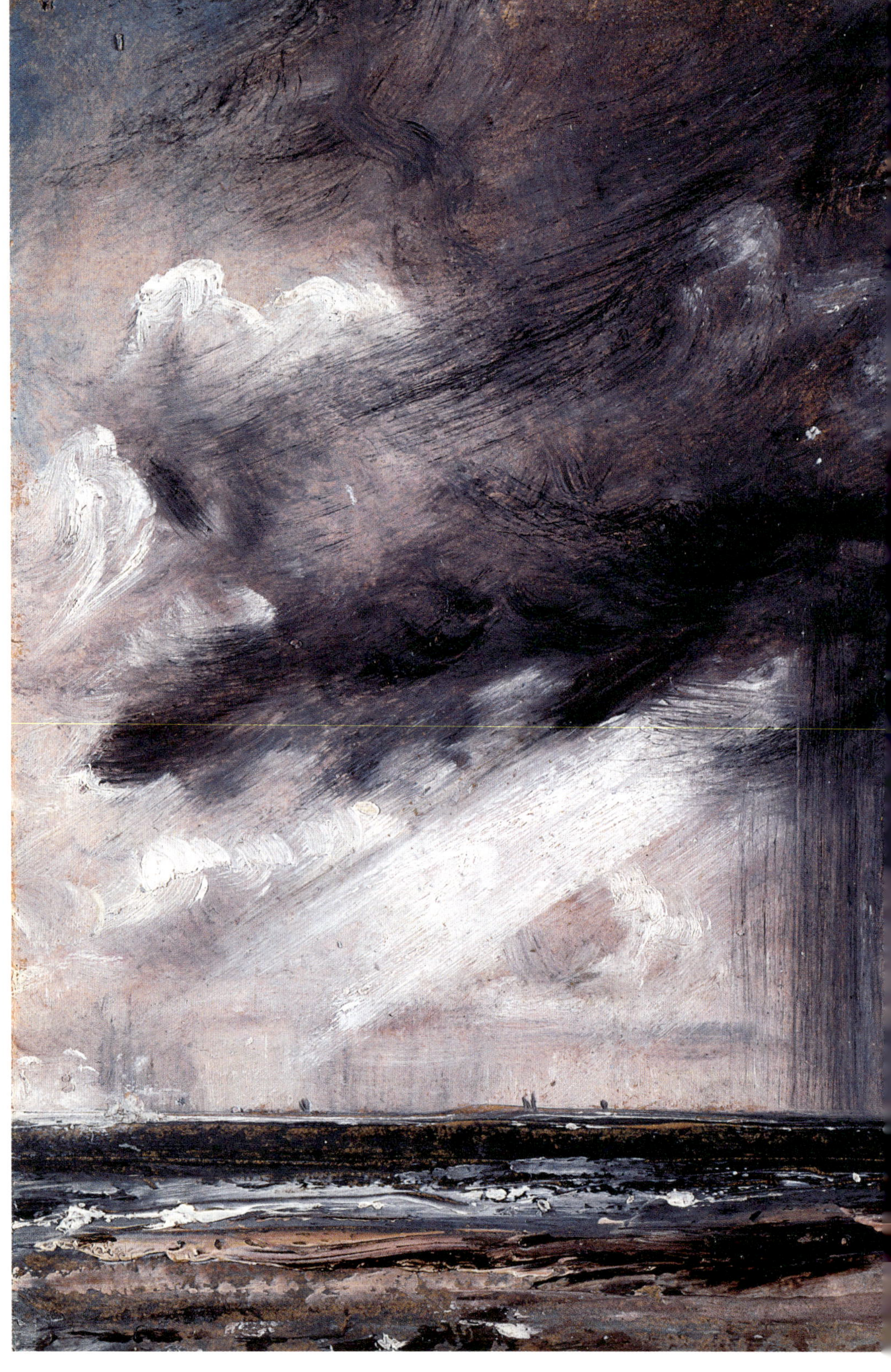

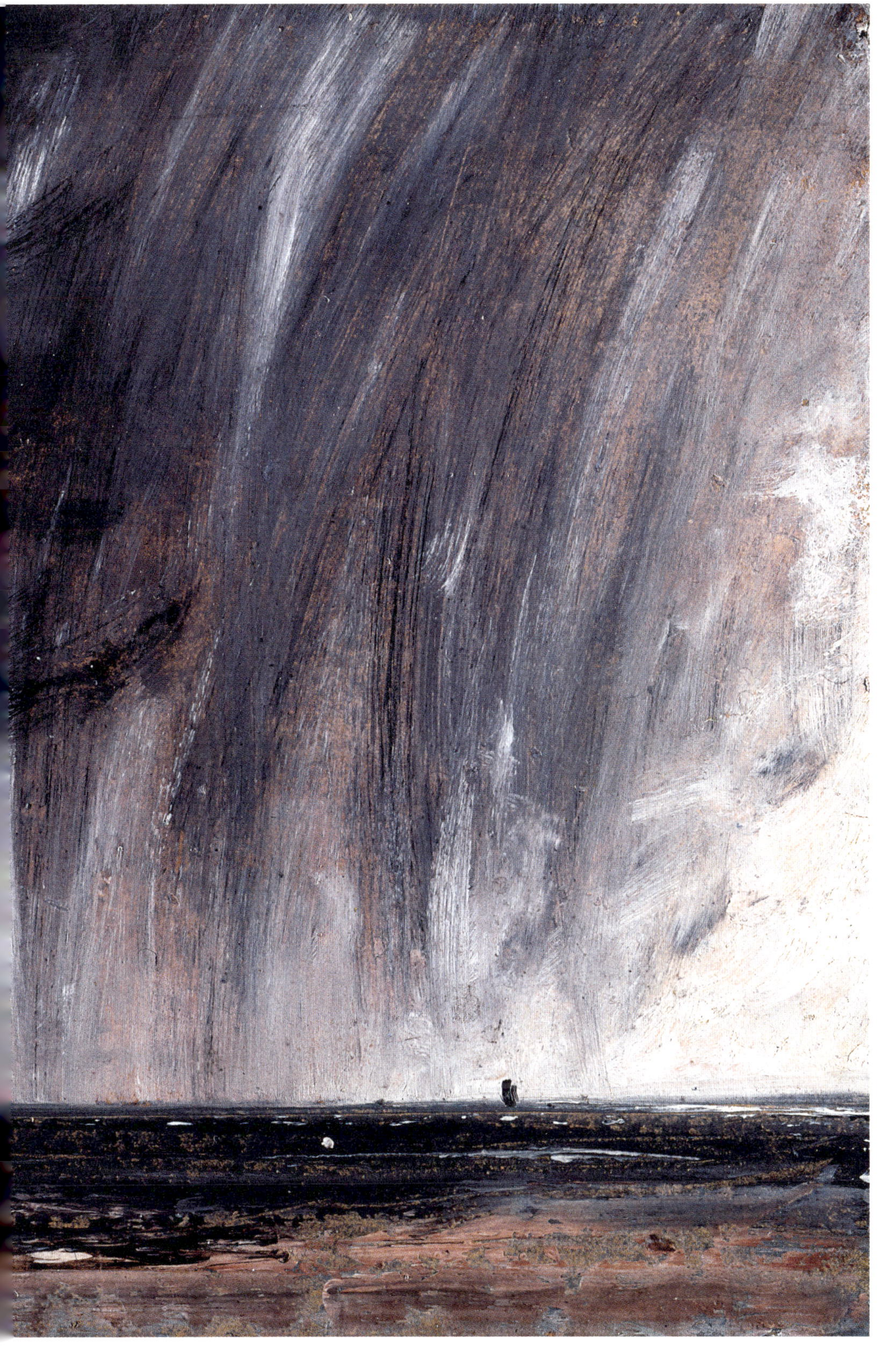

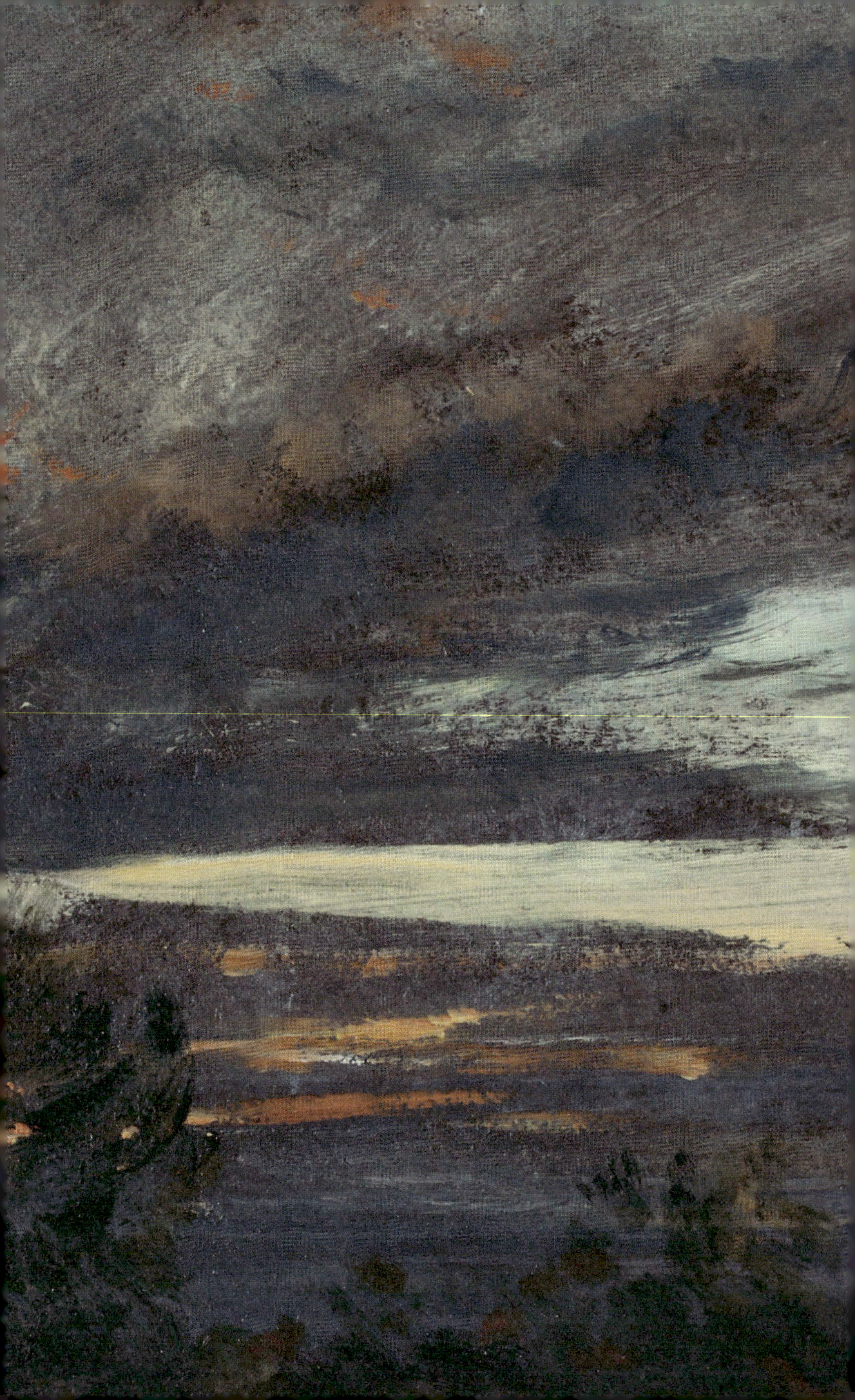

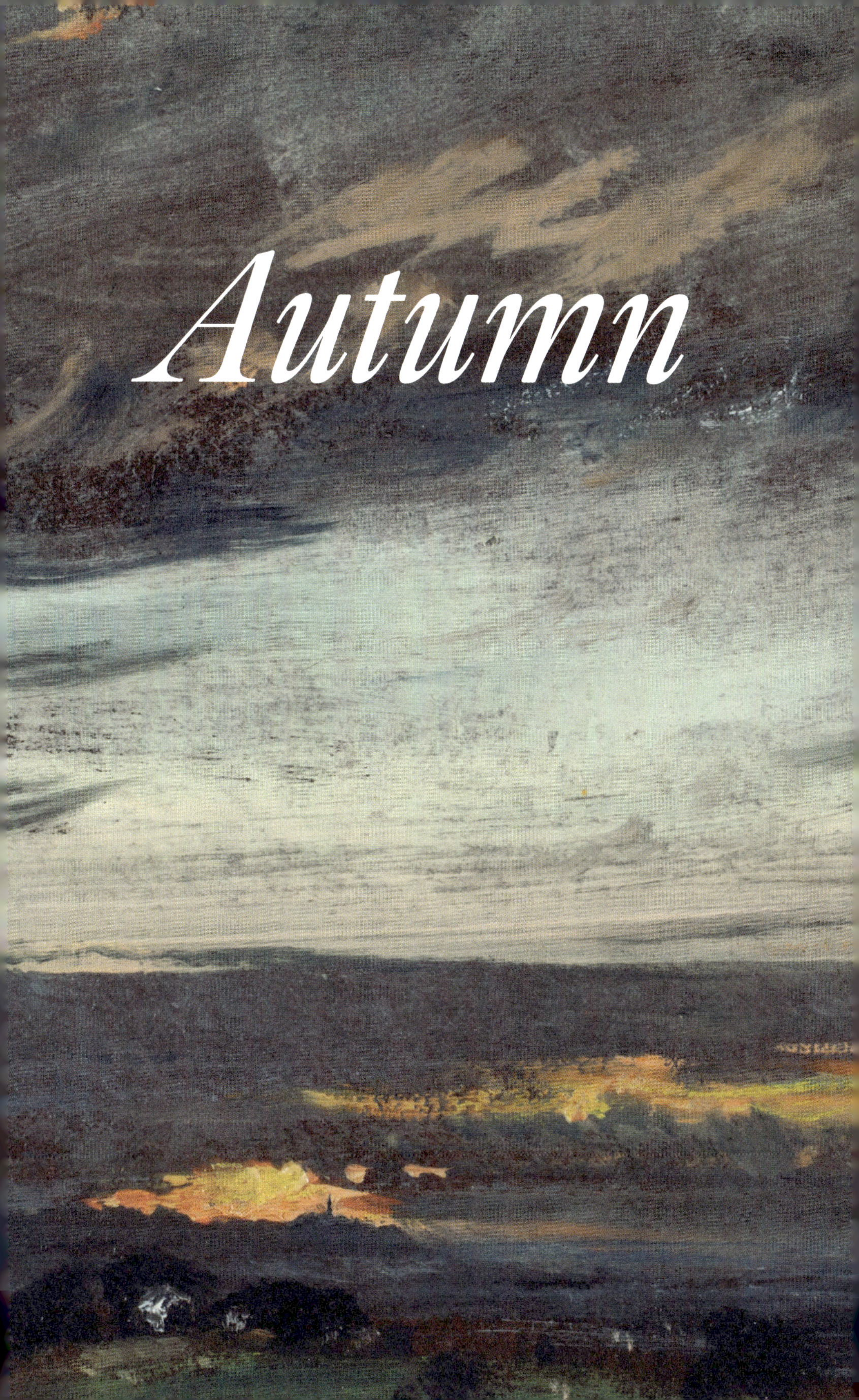
Autumn

'After all this is the painter's season'

The painter's season

Constable had mixed feelings about autumn. Despite his routine of sketching from nature throughout October and into November, it is so rare to find him depicting foliage in autumnal colours that one can only conclude that he deliberately avoided it. One of his favourite hobbyhorses, repeatedly expressed, was his preference for spring over its opposite number. Here he is in April 1833 writing to his friend George Constable with a wish that his health would continue to improve: 'the coming season is in your favor. I have always heard of the autumn being the *painter's season*, but give me the spring, though "with tears and sunshine in her fickle eyes".' And here he is again, just a month later, writing to his friend C. R. Leslie, who was about to set off on a four-month visit to the United States: 'The loss of you is a cloud casting its shade over my life, now in its autumn. I never did admire the autumnal tints in nature, so little of a painter am I in the eye of commonplace connoisseurship – I love the exhilarating freshness of spring.' In both letters he begins with one subject, but the mention of autumn sends him swerving back to his own preoccupation with the rival claims of the seasons.

Constable's reactions to the season tended to depend on his mood, the weather – or a combination of the two. One evening in the autumn of 1812 he made an oil sketch from the westernmost edge of East Bergholt, looking towards Langham and Stoke-by-Nayland over a valley bathed in gold by the light of the setting sun, with a flight of rooks making their way home. In late October of 1818 he could write to Maria from East Bergholt, where

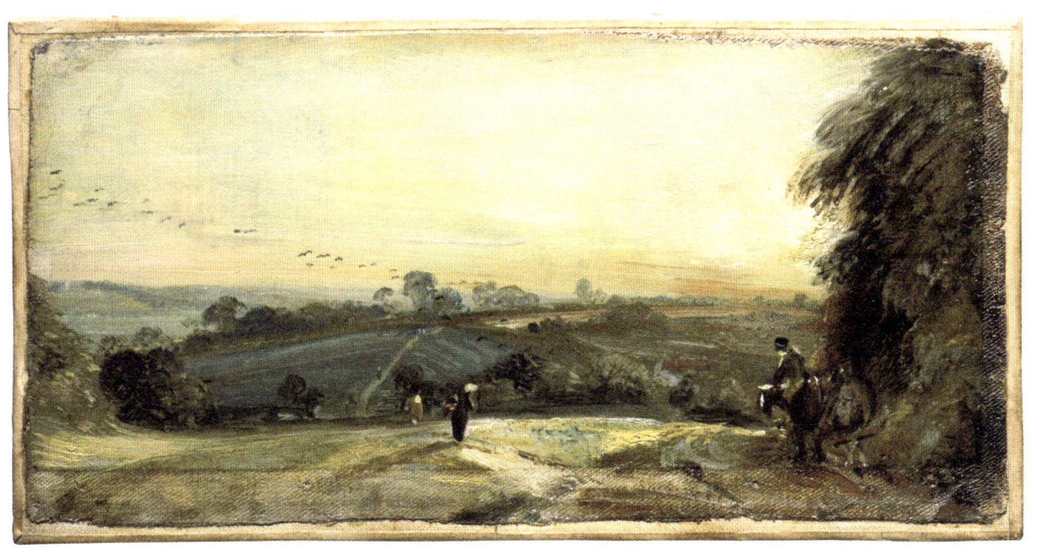

Autumnal sunset, 1812. Oil on paper. Constable
prepared the paper with a ground of grey-blue paint,
introducing subtle evening-sky tones to the golden
glow produced by the setting sun. His vantage point
was the far end of Cemetery Lane in East Bergholt,
the westernmost point of the village.

the sale of the family house was on the point of being agreed: 'This has been a lovely day – early this morning I walked into a wood at Stratford, which was lovely with its rich autumnal tints – after all this is the painter's season.' On a visit to Fisher in Salisbury in November 1821 he made an oil sketch close to his friend's house in the Cathedral Close, with the silvery spire and an old stone gateway all but engulfed in a blaze of golden foliage. On another autumnal day two years later, however, he ended a letter to Fisher from Hampstead: 'I want to get to my easil in Town – & not to witnes [the] rotting melancholy dissolution of the trees &c – which two months ago were so beautifull – & lovely.'

What rubbed him up the wrong way was not so much autumn itself as its revered place in artistic convention. The notion that it was 'the painter's season' had its roots in works by the most highly influential landscape painter of them all in Constable's day, the seventeenth-century French artist Claude Lorrain. Claude spent most of his working life in and around Rome, creating beguiling images in which scenes from classical myth or the Bible take place in enchanted natural settings. Loosely based on the Italian campagna, these extensive landscapes, framed by trees or rocky outcrops, are usually bathed in the golden glow of an early autumn afternoon. Paintings by Claude and his follower, Gaspard Dughet (also known as Gaspard or Gaspar Poussin), were exceptionally popular with British collectors, and as a result their vision of the landscape was widely imitated by artists in the UK. Claude's first and most accomplished disciple was the Welsh artist Richard Wilson, who in the middle of the eighteenth century spent time absorbing the Claudean tradition in Rome and the Italian campagna. When he arrived back in Britain he zhuzhed up the landscape's natural contours in his paintings, making peaks higher, views more extensive and applying a flattering Claudean filter to the rain-soaked hillsides of north Wales. Many artists followed in his footsteps: George Smith of Chichester, for example, had never been to Rome but still managed to make the Sussex landscape look like Italy.

Constable himself was not immune to the habit of seeing the landscape through the filter of the old masters: back in October 1806, while sketching in the Lake District, he wrote admiringly of a 'Dark Autumnal Day at noon … the effect exceeding terrific – and much like the beautiful Gaspar

I saw in Margaret St [the London home of his friend Bishop Fisher].' No, it wasn't Claude himself who was the trouble: Constable remained passionately attached to his paintings. Nor was it Wilson, whom he revered. It was the multitude of ham-fisted, unprincipled imitators that bothered him, the landscape artists who subjected British scenery to a Claudean makeover in an appeal for admiration and commercial success.

Constable could find it difficult to remain calm when these artists were singled out for praise, and his temper crackles uncomfortably around the subject in an exchange of letters with John Fisher in the early spring of 1821. In the course of reporting various bits of news, Fisher recommended a recently published book that had attracted some attention: *The Diary of an Invalid*, an account of the author's travels on the continent. It is clear from Fisher's tone that he was offering his friend something he was confident they could both laugh at. 'You will be much amused with it … when you come to his critiques upon painting & statuary you will find another corroboration of our often repeated opinion, that persons of the highest education in the sciences are mere children in their knowledge of the *art*.' Fisher was no doubt thinking of a passage in which the 'invalid', Henry Matthews, opines upon the paintings in the Galleria Doria Pamphilj in Rome. '*Gaspar Poussin's* green landscapes have no charms for me', he begins.

> The fact seems to be, that the delightful green of nature cannot be represented in a picture. Our own Glover has perhaps made the greatest possible exertions to surmount the difficulty, and give with fidelity the real colours of Nature; but I believe the beauty of his pictures is in an inverse ratio to their fidelity; – and his failure affords an additional proof, that Nature must be stripped of her green livery, and dressed in the *browns* of the painters, or confined to her own autumnal tints, in order to be transferred to the canvass.

Constable replied through gritted teeth: he tried to make light of it, but Matthews had cut too close to the bone. Since 1802 he himself had done nothing but paint 'the real colours of Nature' with the greatest fidelity he could muster, and for his pains had experienced year after year of rejection by the Royal Academy when he had put himself forward for election as an

Associate member, only scraping in, in 1819, when artists happy to follow convention had been ushered in before him. Before even mentioning the book, he tells Fisher of the 'clever pictures' that he has heard will be in the forthcoming annual exhibition, crossly contrasting his own knowledge with others' ignorance.

> They are chiefly in the historical & fancy way – I hear little of Landscape – and why? The Londoners with all their ingenuity as artists know nothing of the feeling of a country life (the essence of Landscape) – any more than a hackney coach horse knows of pasture.

'The Diary is delightfull', he continues.

> [Matthews] mentions the landscapes of Gaspar Poussin (whose works contain the highest feeling of Landscape painting yet seen – such a union of patient study with a poetical mind). The Invalid … imagines defects in the Landscapes that he may afford an opportunity to 'our own Glover' of remedying them – this is too bad and one would throw the book out of the window – but that its grossness is its own cure - and one is led on for the fun of the thing – to be amused with the novelty of shapes which Ignorance appears in –

If he could not entirely conceal his irritation, it was understandable. Paintings by John Glover were everything Constable's were not. Glover aimed at grandiose effects, often used a dark, predominantly brown palette – imitative of the discoloured varnish of Old Master paintings – and could produce embarrassingly slavish imitations of Claude on an eye-catchingly colossal scale. Rather than trying to capture the fresh appearance of nature, he followed convention and strove to impress. And here, in this popular travel book, Glover's most bogus efforts were mortifyingly applauded by a man who thought the best landscape paintings were brown landscape paintings. From that time on, when Constable referred to the artist in letters to Fisher it was as 'our own Glover' – either that or, with bitter sarcasm, 'the English Claude' (that last epithet accompanied by a caricature of the artist at his easel).

Glover perhaps got off relatively lightly. Constable once described a landscape by the Royal Academician William Collins – a man he heartily despised – as looking 'like a large cow-turd'. Presumably it, too, was painted in 'autumnal tints'.

A runover dungle

Constable did approve wholeheartedly of the agricultural work that autumn brought. In September and October 1814, at the same time as he was spending each afternoon painting the boat-building activity in his father's dry dock at Flatford, his mornings, when the light came from the east, were taken up with another painting. Two days before he made the sketchbook drawing that formed the basis for *Boat-Building*, he painted an oil sketch from the edge of the park of Old Hall in East Bergholt. It was the first step in planning a commissioned picture, but one apparently without the constraints that usually made such work so irksome to him. Philadelphia Godfrey, the daughter of Peter Godfrey, who had always taken an interest in the young artist's career, was getting married in November. Her fiancé, Thomas Fitzhugh, had engaged Constable to paint a view from the grounds of Old Hall – the picture was to be a wedding present that would remind his bride of a familiar Suffolk view as she settled into her new home in London.

Was Constable directed by Fitzhugh or the Godfreys themselves to an attractive local view, or was he left to his own devices? We don't know, although a sweeping view over the Stour Valley towards Dedham from the edge of the estate was an obvious enough choice. His vantage point was, in fact, very close to the spot he had occupied the previous year when planning his *Ploughing Scene in Suffolk*. But if Fitzhugh or the Godfreys had actually gone to look at the scene with him, they would have noticed a new feature of the landscape that had appeared in the corner of a field. It might well have persuaded them to rethink.

Constable had learned from his struggles earlier in the year that a landscape without any human activity – especially the gentle farmland of

Suffolk – could look bare and uneventful when scaled up. Well, here, right in front of him, was an abundance of activity. In the summer the local farm labourers had built a gigantic mound of manure at the edge of a field and left it to rot. A hill of this kind, made when the stockyards were cleared in June, was known locally as a 'runover dungle'. When it became too high for loads to be tipped directly on top, ramps were put up to allow a horse to pull a laden cart up the slope, pause for the load to be emptied, then pull the cart down the other side. The weight of the horses and carts gradually compacted the manure into a solid hill, which could be six feet high. Now that autumn had arrived, labourers were busy digging the manure out and loading it onto carts in preparation for spreading on the nearby fields. As a subject, Constable found it irresistible.

Perhaps only Constable could have painted a dunghill as a wedding present. He even modified the composition from his initial oil sketch, making the mound more prominent. It looms enormously, frilled here and there with weeds and catching the rays of the morning sun. It probably never crossed his mind that Philadelphia might have shrunk from contemplating a view of the Stour Valley over the top of a giant hill of manure. This countrywoman would probably have accepted it in reality, if leaning over the fence of her father's estate and surveying the valley – muck-spreading was crucial for a good harvest the following year, and for that you naturally needed a well-sited dungle. But a muck heap in a painting? What she or her husband thought of the picture, and where – or if – they hung it in their smart London house, is not recorded.

To Constable, however, the dungle was an important aspect not only of the landscape but also of the activity of the agricultural year. He chose to paint it because he was fascinated by the processes of farming – the carefully crafted mound of manure was every bit as interesting to him as a ripe crop. It was another aspect of the mentality that led him to paint the construction of a vessel – a working barge at that – when other artists were painting picturesque fishing boats. Constable's attitude to landscape was deeply rooted in the agricultural tasks that needed to be done, which were pegged to the calendar. It is possible to trace time passing as he worked on the painting: in the oil sketch dated 5 September harvesters can be seen in the field on the left, while in the final picture – which Constable

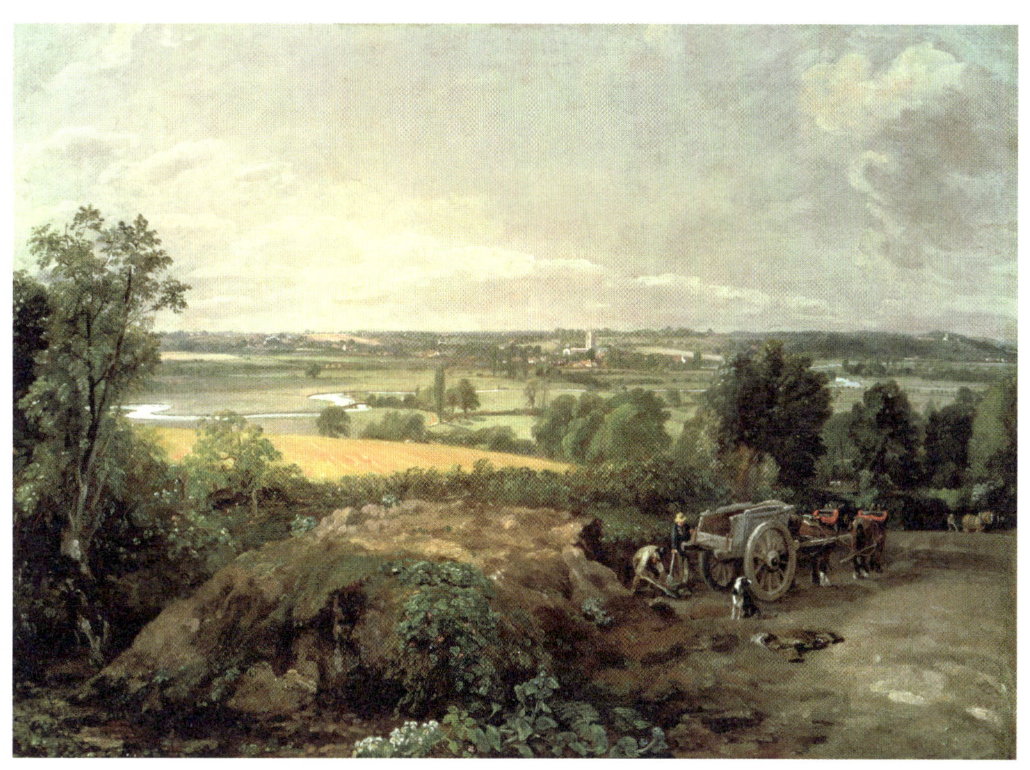

The Stour Valley and Dedham Village, 1815. Oil on canvas. *Detail overleaf.*

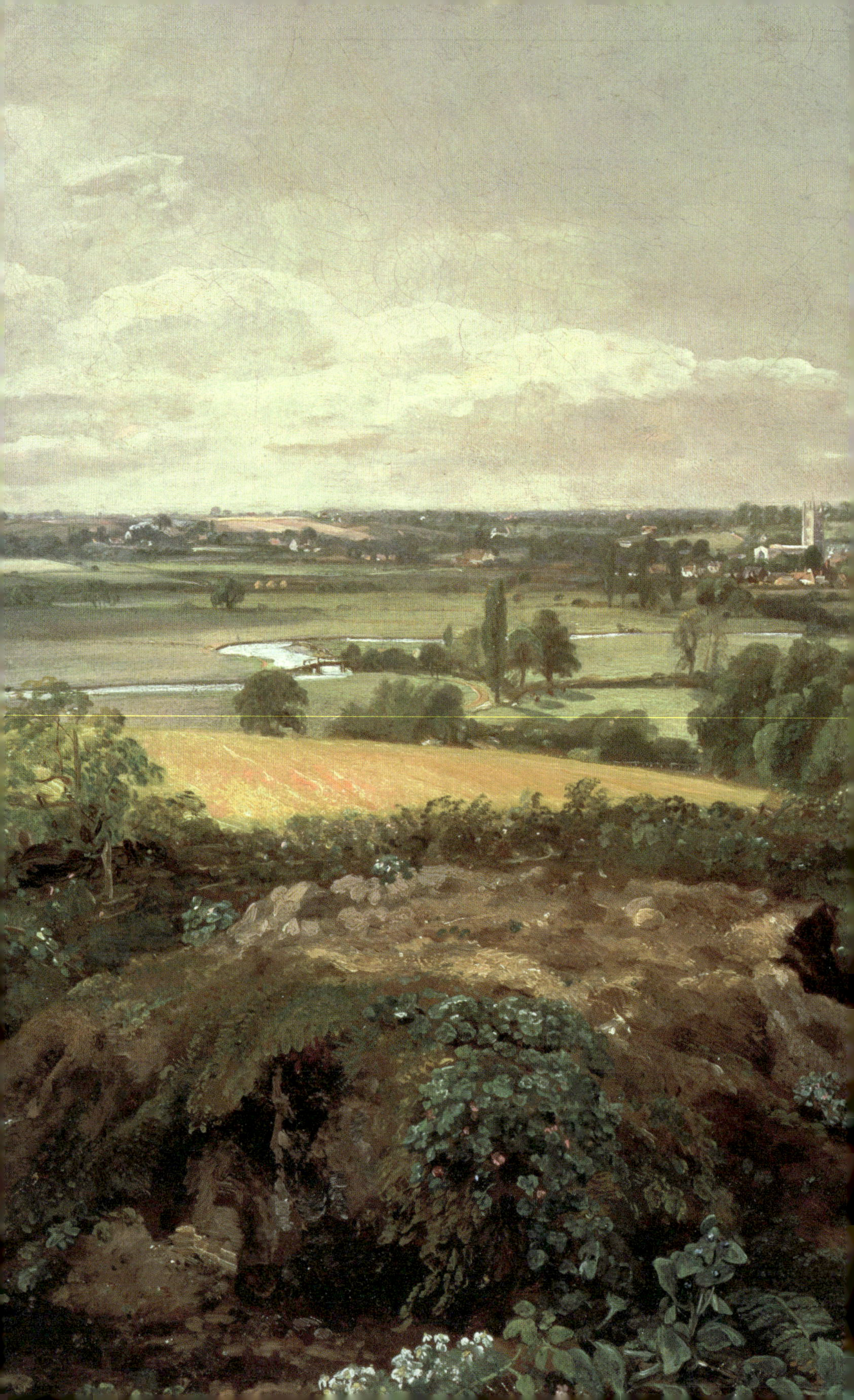

described as being 'almost done' on 25 October – a man is ploughing on the right. Late summer has given way to autumn. Dungles being temporary structures, this one shrinks between 26 September, when he made one sketchbook drawing of the scene, and 9 October, when he made another.

Constable felt an unusually strong sense of purpose during those weeks spent sitting in front of his portable easel in the autumn sunshine, on the edge of the village he loved. 'We have had a most charming season, and I hope I have endeavoured to avail myself of it', he wrote to Maria on 2 October. 'It is many years since I have pursued my studies so uninterruptedly and so calmly – or worked with so much steadiness & confidence.' There is a new ease and expansiveness to the contents of that season's sketchbook, a sense that all was right with the world: fewer fractured bits of views and more whole ones. A boat was being built. Fields were being manured. The autumn's tasks were balanced against the following year's yield. That evening he went out and made a drawing at the top of the very last page of his sketchbook, showing the family house silhouetted by a nearly full moon, noting the date underneath; the next day he sketched the house bathed in sunlight on the lower half of the sheet. Just a few days after the autumn equinox, he himself was experiencing a contented equilibrium.

Constable was busy during those weeks, spending most days outside. He was even able to enjoy the autumnal spectacle of red and yellow leaves without reservation. Towards the end of October he told Maria he had put off writing to her on the Sunday – when he usually caught up with his correspondence – because 'the beauty of the day (which perhaps might be the last this autumn) tempted me to take a walk to Neyland … My way was cheifly through woods and nothing could exceed the beauty of the foliage.' On other days he was out painting. 'I am considered rather unsociable here', he reported; '– my cousins could never get me to walk with them once as I was never at home 'till night – I was wishing to make the most of the fine weather by working out of doors.'

It could not last. The days shortened, the final weeks of autumn arrived, and on 4 November Constable had to get on the coach and return to the city. It was, as ever, a shock to his system. A few days later he admitted to Maria: 'I am hardly yet got reconciled to brick walls and dirty streets, after leaving the endearing scenes of Suffolk.' By dirty streets he probably meant horse droppings: what was wholesome and useful in Suffolk was, in London, distasteful waste. And a painting by a rival that had the misfortune to look like a cow's turd was very different from one that actually celebrated animal dung.

An autumn honeymoon

John Fisher relished the prospect of showing his friend the landscape around Osmington, where he had been vicar since 1813. 'The country here', he wrote, inviting John and Maria to stay with him after their wedding in October 1816, 'is wonderfully wild & sublime & well worth a painters visit. My house commands a singularly beautiful view: & you may study from my very windows.' Wild and sublime were not words that could be used to describe the landscape around East Bergholt; in his working life Constable had generally avoided both. Left to his own devices, he would probably never have travelled to Dorset in search of such scenery: his reluctance to be parted from his familiar towpath by the Stour at Flatford had surprised even Maria, who knew his attachment to his local places better than anyone. But, as ever, he threw himself into drawing and painting the places in which he found himself.

Constable's drawings make a visual itinerary of the couple's progress towards Osmington that October. After the wedding he and Maria went to Salisbury, where they stayed for a few days at the Palace as guests of his old friend and mentor the Bishop, the younger Fisher's uncle, whom Constable had met in East Bergholt many years before. The Bishop had provided steadfast support to the young artist in his early, hesitant London years. 'For long [I] floundered in the path – and tottered on the threshold – and there never was any young man nearer being lost than myself', he later recalled, paying tribute to his friend's kindness and the part he had played in galvanizing him. He now provided spectacular surroundings for John and Maria to begin their honeymoon. East Bergholt church had long had a hold on Constable's imagination and he had drawn and painted it countless times and from numerous angles; here, on his doorstep in Salisbury, was a far grander and more challenging ecclesiastical subject, and one that

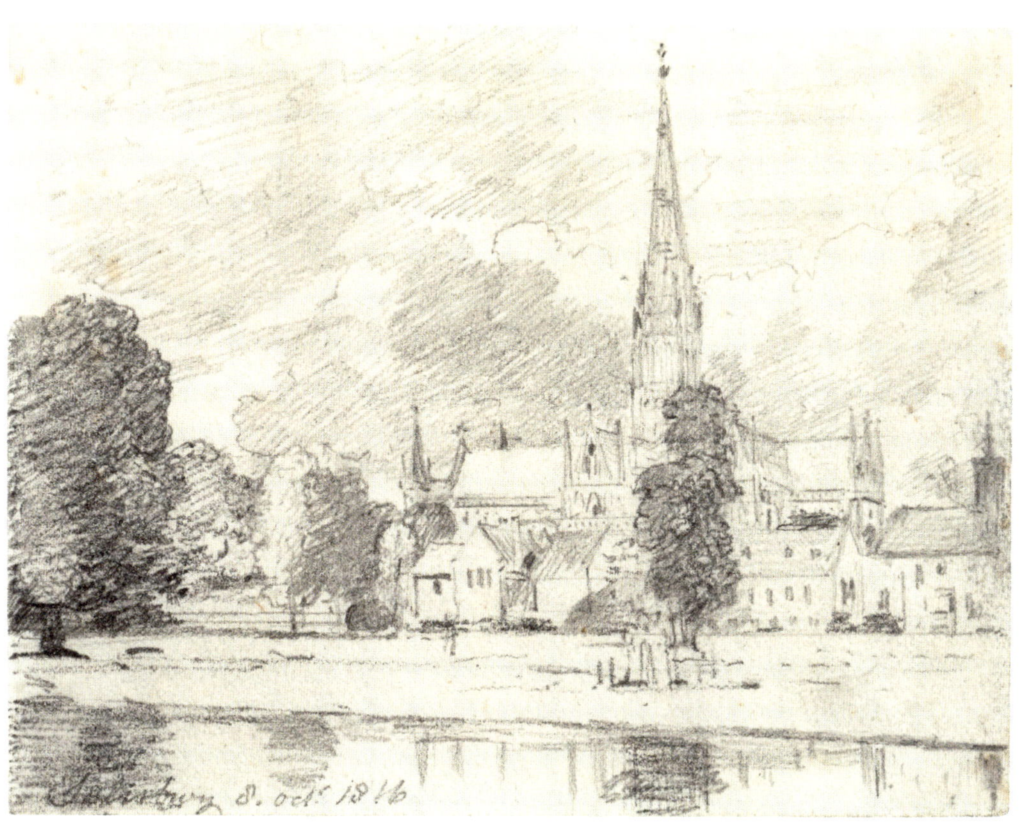

Salisbury Cathedral and the Bishop's Palace, 1816. Graphite on paper.

demanded to be tackled straight away. During the week the couple spent at Salisbury he made several drawings, including one from a vantage point to the south-east, on the far side of a small lake, from which he could frame both the cathedral and the Bishop's Palace which stood in front of it. At first glance there might not be much to distinguish this little sketchbook drawing from others of its kind. In reality, it was an emotional milestone so big you could trip over it: a meticulous record commemorating the setting of his first days of married life in the context of both the friendship and the Christian faith that had sustained him over the years.

After Salisbury, the couple travelled down to Southampton to visit an aunt of Constable's. While there he drew the ruins of Netley Abbey, a picturesque spot popular with artists; it offered a dramatic and shadowy counterpart to the pale stone of Salisbury Cathedral. Practicality, however, accompanied romance: on the back of a sketch of a ruined arch flanked by tall trees he traced a map of the roads that led from Ringwood to Osmington. The first drawing he made after the couple arrived there is dated 17 October; you might expect it to be a landscape, but Constable chose to draw the interior of the church at the nearby village of Preston in which Fisher preached. Friendship and faith took precedence, even over expansive new scenery. But Constable soon set about exploring the hilly coastal country around the Fishers' house, taking advantage of the high vantage points to draw Weymouth Bay and Osmington Church and village. In one view of the bay from the downs a figure sits dead centre with her back to us – perhaps Maria, absorbed in making her own sketch. On another there is an inscription noting the date of John and Mary Fisher's wedding: 'Weymouth Bay. Osmington 22nd. Octr. 1816. noon J. F. married July 2 1816'. Place, date and time were commemorated along with the people he loved: with his pencil and his sketchbook Constable was mapping the emotional contours of these precious weeks, consciously infusing places with associations. On a bright, calm day he made a small painting of Osmington Bay under a big sky, which he gave to his hosts as a gift. A figure stands on the beach, quite close, leaning on his stick and watching the artist as he works: this is surely Fisher himself. After seeing this man crop up a few times in drawings and paintings you start to recognize the shape of his hat and his characteristic slouch. I think I could point him out in a crowd.

One stormy day that autumn the group visited Bowleaze Cove, a beach within walking distance of Osmington where the River Jordan flows across the sands and into the sea. Constable found a spot on high ground looking west, put a piece of paper in his paintbox lid and prepared to sketch. The weather outdid the scenery in wildness and sublimity that particularly autumnal day; the sky was the colour of whale skin and a shaft of sunlight dramatically illuminated the sodden beach and a patch of feverish sea. Constable focused with a new, sensuous intensity on details, textures and colours: the foam deposited on the sand by the waves; a pulpy line of yellowish seaweed left at high tide; a startling flash of angled gulls' wings against grey cloud. A lady and gentleman – the Fishers, I think – walk on the beach, bent sideways by the wind's force, the woman's dress billowing absurdly. They are small and prosaic against the backdrop of this elemental weather: for once in Constable's work, men are not in control of the natural world. Heavy drops of rain began to fall before he had time to shut the lid of his box. They came down so hard that they dented the surface of the wet paint.

Storms must be expected in autumn, but the weather was particularly volatile in the strange global climate of 1816. In London, the meteorologist Luke Howard recorded an unusual degree of thunder, lightning, strong winds, frosts and snowfalls in his weather journal during October and November. Constable normally chose to ignore dramatic weather, to stay indoors and wait for it to pass; his touchstone had always been the calm of a summer's noon. Look at his sketch of Bowleaze Cove, however, and it is plain that something fundamental had changed. His handling of paint has a new fluency and sensuality, teetering on the edge of control. The longed-for intimacy with his beloved Maria after so many years of thwarted desire – successive seasons in which the crops had been sown, grown and harvested while their own field lay fallow – had sent his restraint tumbling. There is a new relish for wildness in his sketch of Bowleaze Cove, as though he were looking up at the sky and willing the rain to fall in torrents, to soak him to the skin. To the passing observer he was sketching a cove on a stormy day; inwardly he was painting the newly released energy that had transformed his world.

Overleaf: Bowleaze Cove, Weymouth Bay, 1816. Oil on millboard.

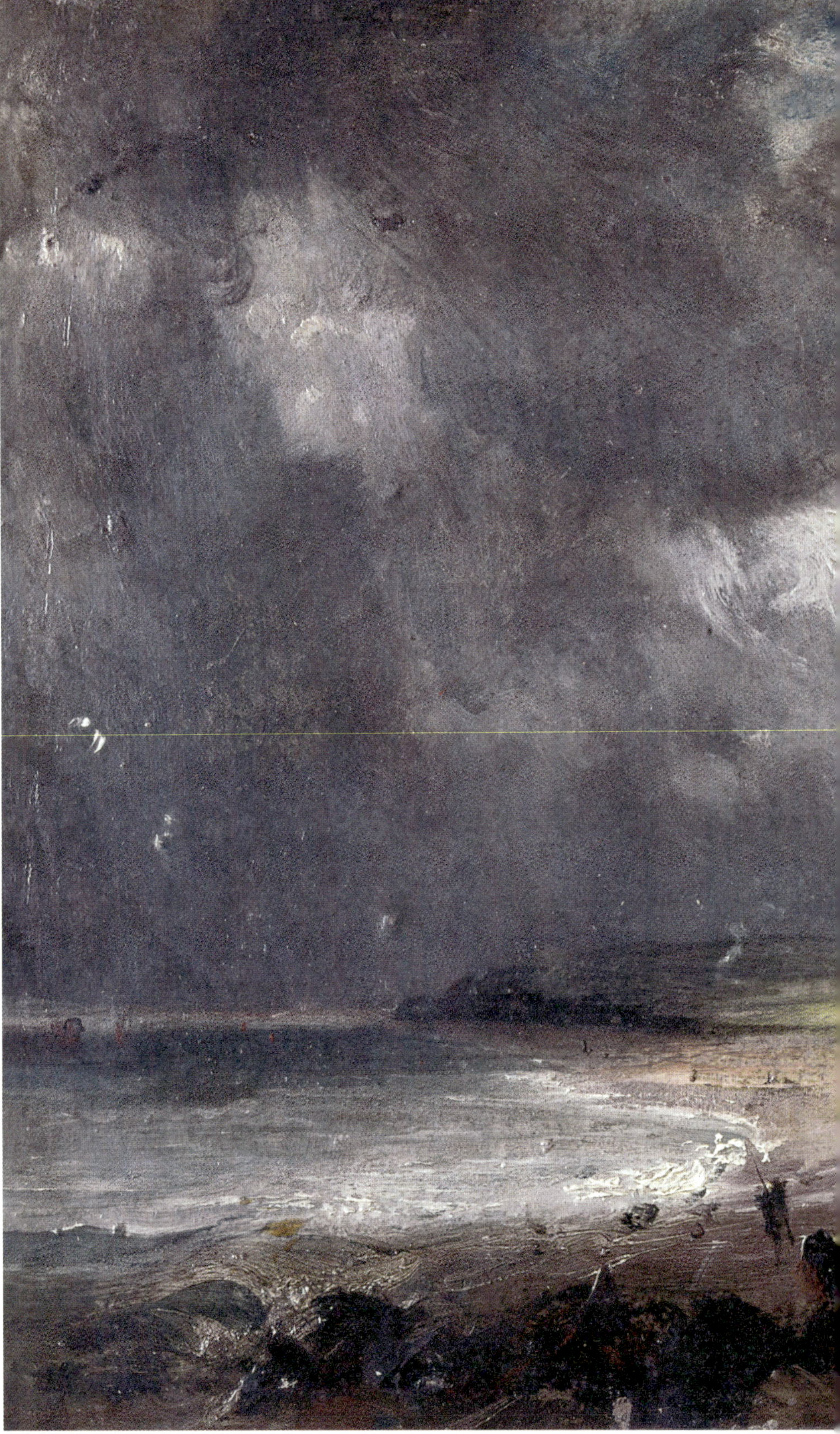

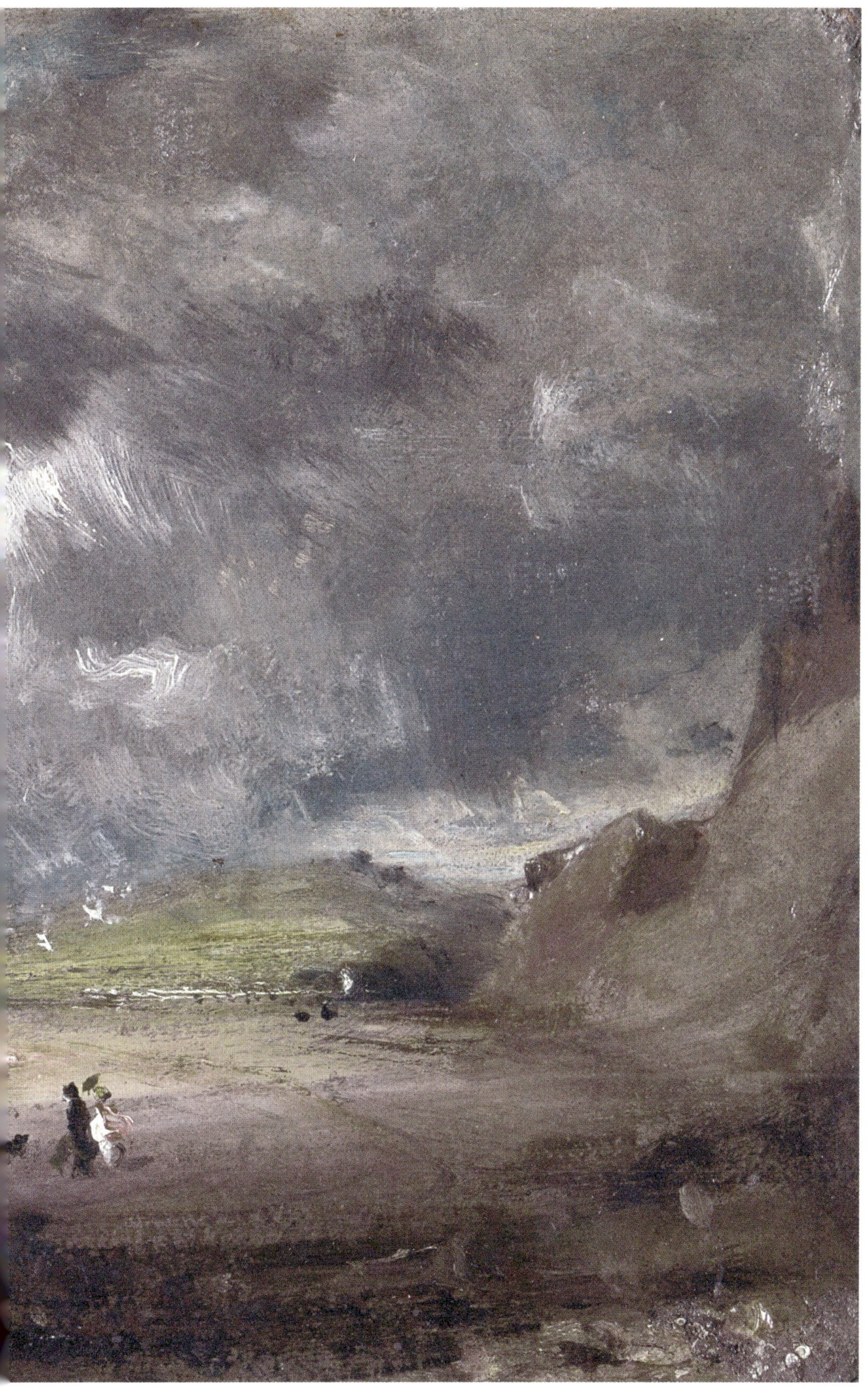

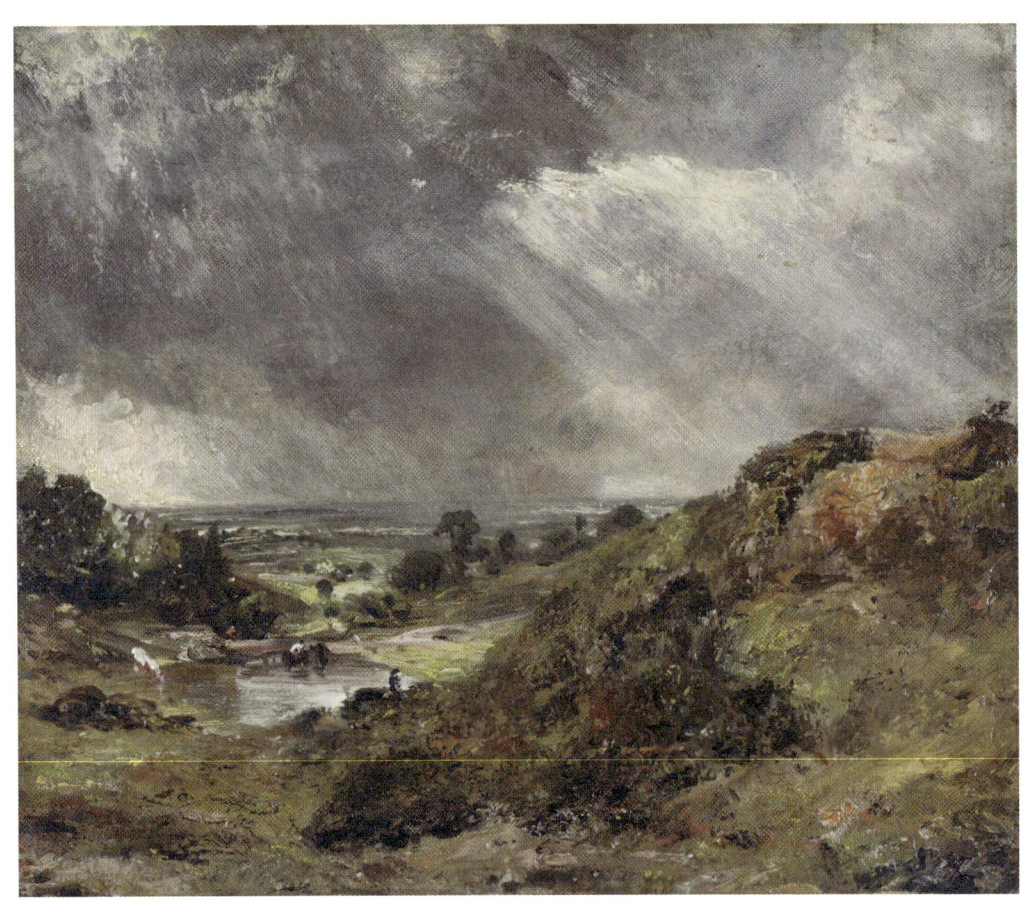

Branch Hill Pond, Hampstead, October 1819.
Oil on canvas. This is the first oil sketch
Constable is known to have painted
on Hampstead Heath. He would often
return to the same high vantage point
for compositions.

The man of clouds

Hampstead Heath, where the Constable family first stayed in the summer and autumn of 1819, was the closest approximation of Suffolk within easy reach of central London. Like the country around East Bergholt, it had beautiful tall trees and high vantage points offering sweeping views over valleys and bodies of water. What it lacked, however, was an agricultural dimension. The Suffolk landscape was always in flux: each season brought work that needed to be done to prepare for the next. Fields were ploughed and crops were sown and harvested. Even a field lying fallow was part of a careful pattern of land management. Cattle and sheep may have been grazed on the heath, but all that really changed at Hampstead was the weather.

Constable was in the habit of regarding autumn as an extension of summer and, therefore, as a time for wandering and drawing. That first Hampstead autumn he explored this new territory with a sketchbook and, as ever, was drawn to purposeful activity. As he roamed over the heath during October and November 1819 his attention was caught by the sandpits dug out by builders for the new houses that were reshaping the edges of London. He drew labourers shovelling sand, men with wheelbarrows and horses and carts taking it away to the builders' yards. But something else caught his eye too: an oil sketch he made at the end of October shows him focusing on the quality of light he found up there. From the highest vantage point that the heath – and indeed London itself – had to offer, 134 metres (440 ft), he painted the reflective surface of Branch Hill Pond under a sky heavy with dark clouds, sunlight breaking through in dramatic shafts and fitfully illuminating the tussocky foreground. Constable cast his farmer's eye over this sandy ground and carefully painted the rich, burnt sienna earth where it was exposed like signs of buried treasure through the thin, yellowing autumn grass. Another moment, and the lights and shadows would change and the whole composition alter. In this sketch of rough heathland, Constable was worrying at a landscape problem that had interested him for some time: the relationship between the source of light and its effect on foliage and water. Both in the foreground and the distant view, Constable has thought about the sky and the ground not as separate entities, as many landscape painters would, but as inextricably combined. This sketch, alongside a group of chalk drawings he made of clouds that autumn, were the beginnings of a sustained and astonishingly productive study of light and sky that he would conduct from Hampstead. He made the heath his cloud-viewing platform, a laboratory for studying these great aerial structures that utterly transformed the landscapes they drifted over.

The Constables spent the following summer, 1820, in Salisbury, staying with the Fishers in the spacious house on the Cathedral Close that had come with John Fisher's new job as Canon. It was the beginning of September when Maria and the children moved to Hampstead. Constable was busy during those autumn days in his Keppel Street painting room, where he was working towards a large picture of the recent opening of Waterloo Bridge. He usually only returned home in the evenings, and it was not until the middle of October that he was able to reach the heath, carrying his paintbox, while it was still light. The leaves were turning khaki, and as he sketched Constable noticed how they became translucent against the flesh-coloured, yellow-flecked blaze of the setting sun. 'Hampd. 17th Octr 1820 Stormy Sunset. Wind. W.', he wrote. The next day he was back, looking north towards Harrow between four o'clock and half-past five, the wind in the north-west. He returned on 25th – 'fine evening', he noted, 'wind N W' – then again three days later. Standing on the same spot as he had at first, this time he painted the spectacle of peach and apricot clouds cutting across sober grey-blue ones, the sun a creamy splatter in the centre. '28 Octr.', he noted in pencil on the back, 'fine Evening Wind Gentle at S. W.' By the end of the month, however, the temperature had dropped, making it too cold to sketch outdoors in the afternoons, especially when the wind was northerly. It was time for the family to return to Keppel Street. In any case, Constable had a new project in mind that would occupy his time, absorb his thoughts and keep him in his studio over the winter months: the picture that would become known as *The Hay Wain*.

The following July the Constable family was back in Hampstead, this time in Lower Terrace, near the western part of the heath. Constable cleared the mops and brooms out of a garden shed so that he could use it as a makeshift studio and what he called a 'place of refuge'. The months stretched ahead, with all the opportunities they offered for sketching. For the previous two autumns he had gone up to the heath to paint the light and the weather, and by studying the behaviour of clouds and blown-about

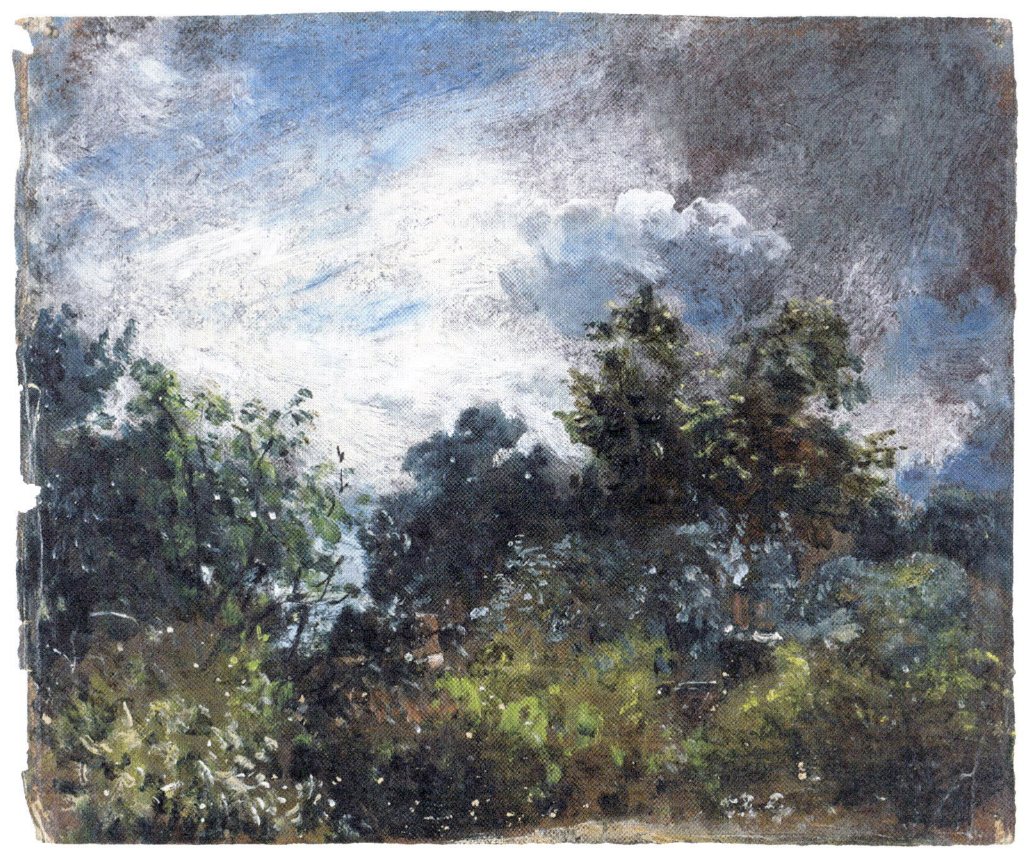

Study of sky and trees, 3 September *c.* 1821.
Oil on paper. This sketch is inscribed
on the back: 'September 3d. Noon. very
sultry. with large drops of Rain falling
on my palate light air from S. W.'

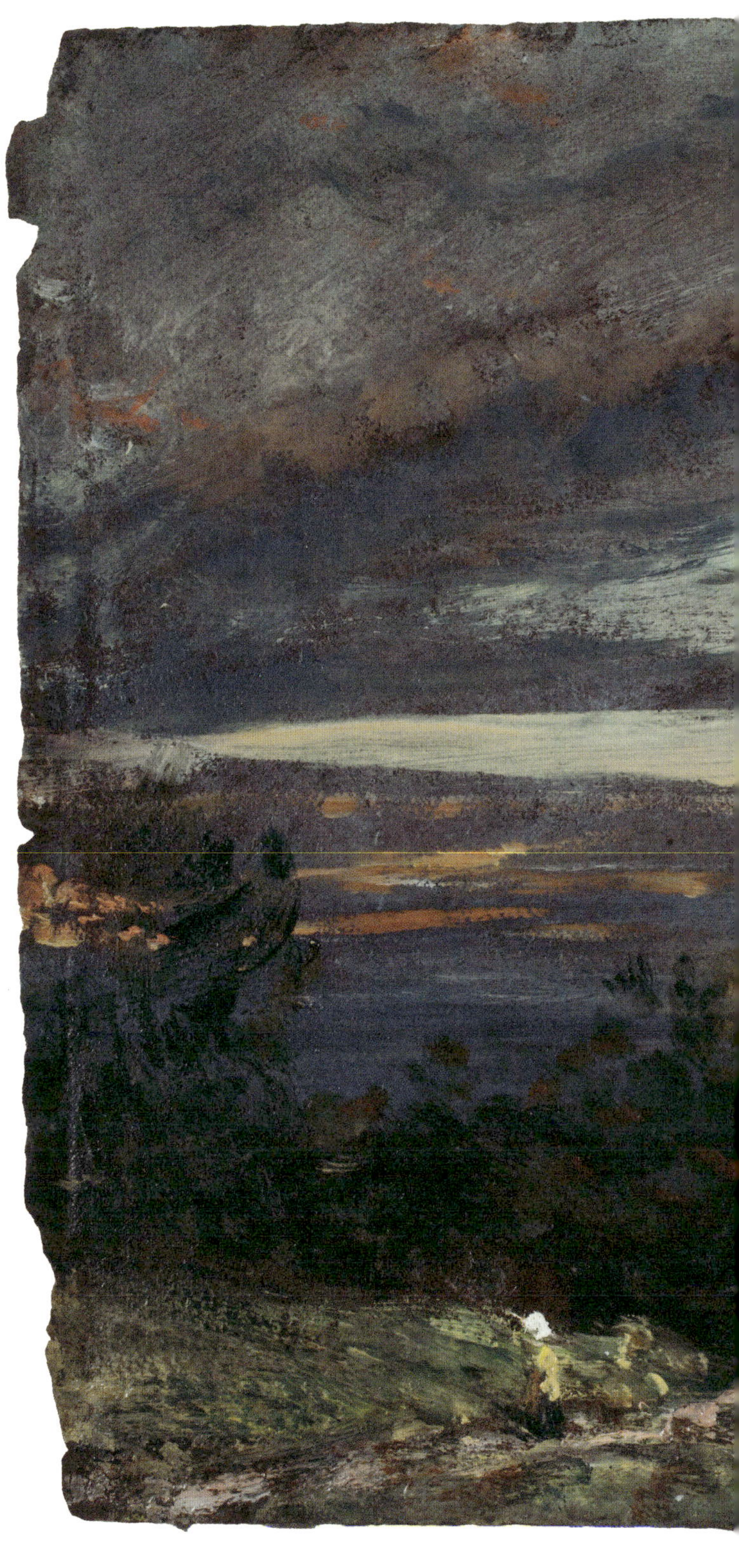

Hampstead Heath, looking towards Harrow, at sunset, 12 September 1821. Oil on paper.

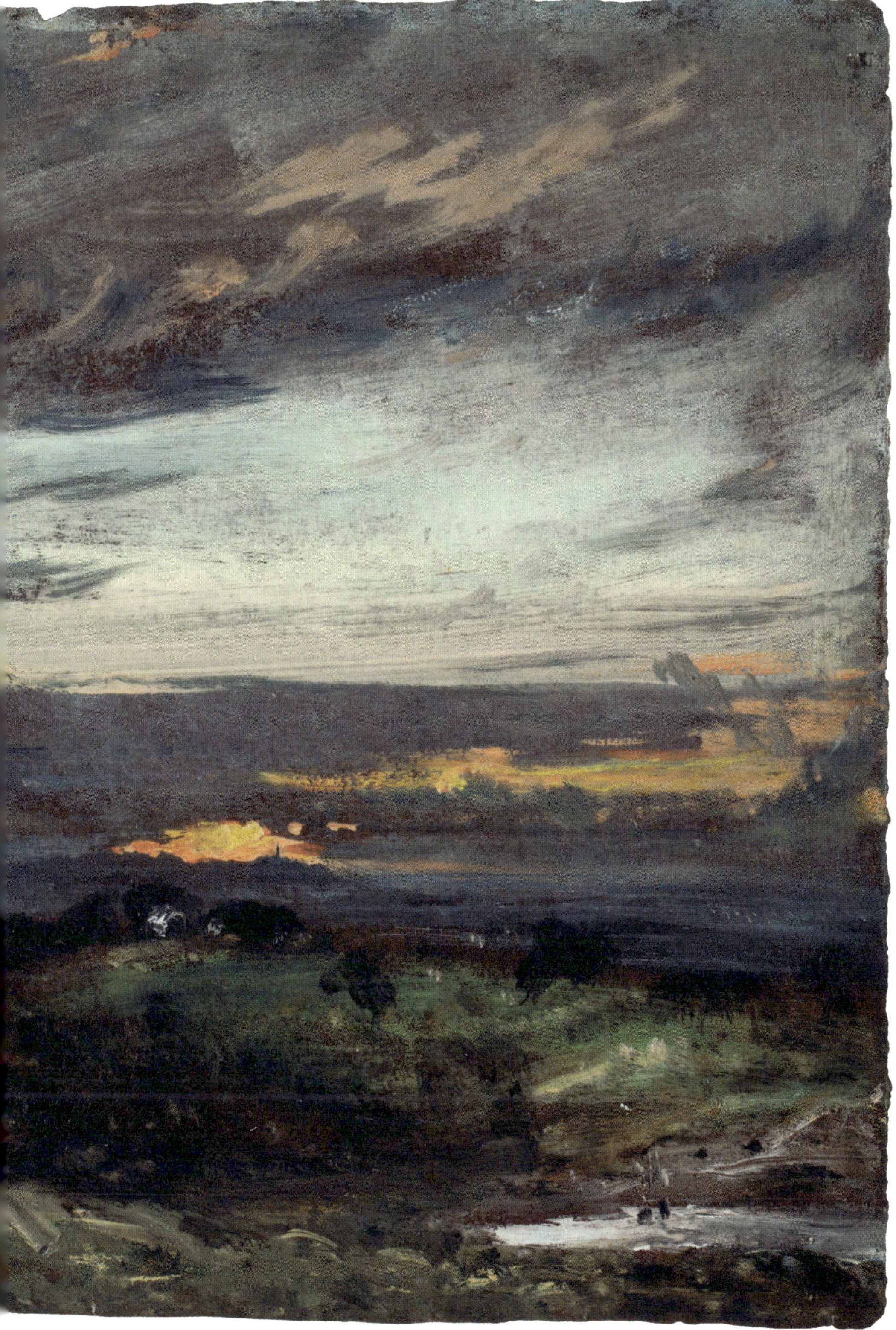

foliage had come as close as he could to painting the wind itself. But the prevalence of sunsets reveals that he had been obliged to fit these forays around more pressing studio work. Now he had time to dig deeper. During the spring he had been thinking about Gilbert White, the clergyman-naturalist renowned for his *Natural History of Selborne* (first published in 1789), telling Fisher he had just acquired a copy that included a memoir of the writer. White's patient, highly focused study of the plants and creatures living in his village, his garden and right outside his back door, had struck a chord deep within him:

> The mind & feeling which produced the 'Selborne' is such an one as
> I have always envied. The single page alone of the life of Mr White
> leaves a more lasting impression on my mind than that of Charles
> the fifth or any other renowned hero – it only shows what a real love
> for nature will do – surely the serene & blameless life of Mr White,
> so different from the folly & quackery of the world, must have fitted
> him for such a clear & intimate view of nature.

The chord continued to reverberate. Not long after moving to Lower Terrace, Constable produced the first sketch in a concerted campaign of what he called 'skying'.

Because Constable added inscriptions, dates and often times of day to so many of his sky sketches, from this moment on they can be read like the pages of a diary. He was up on the heath in July and August, noting afternoons that were windy, that felt as though a storm was on its way, or were fine and bright after a shower. But in September the pace quickened. He had been waiting for the autumn because he felt it brought a 'peculiar tone and beauty' to the skies. This was when he began his most intensive period of study, focusing on the clouds themselves with a new, scientific rigour. With the oil sketches he had done in Hampstead up to that time, it was as though he had climbed into the basket of a hot air balloon but had hesitated and continued to scan the sky with the ground safely in view. Now he was ready to untie the ropes. From the beginning of that autumn on he would look decisively upwards, reduce the landscape element to strips of sky-reflecting foliage or do without it

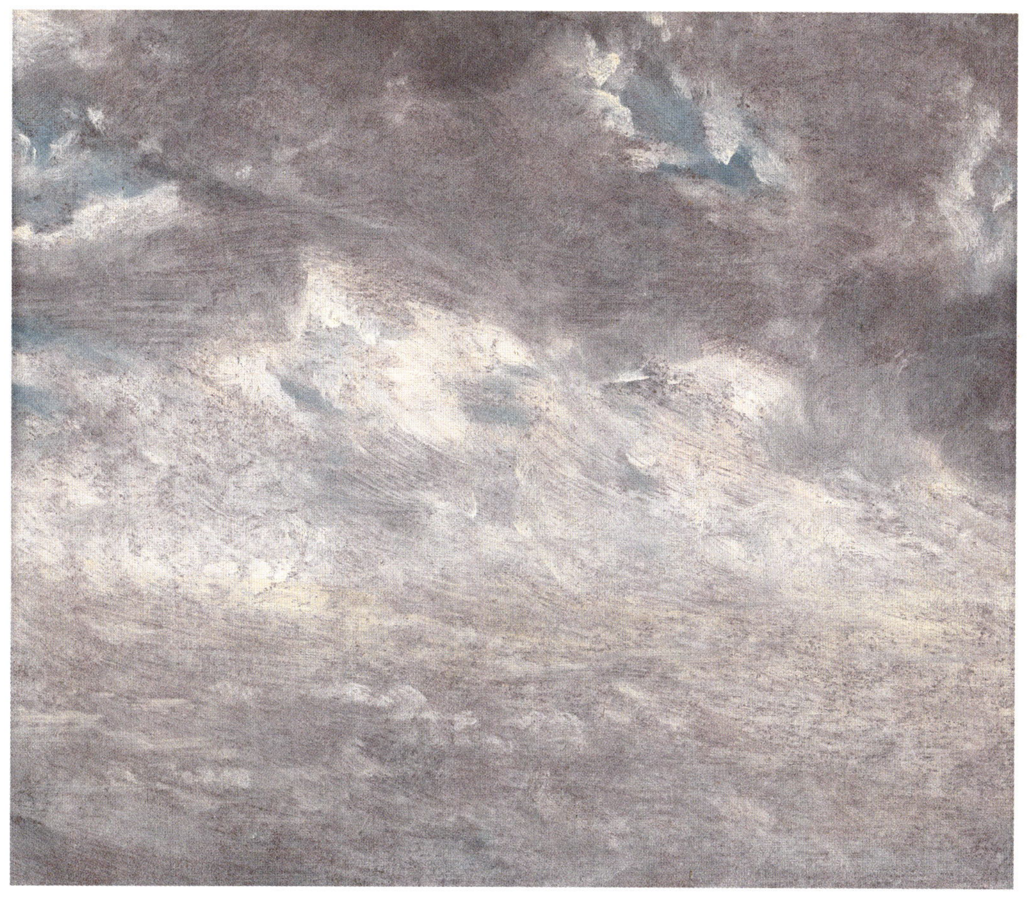

Study of altocumulus clouds, 13 September
1821. Oil on paper. Constable's weather
notes on the back of this sketch read:
'Septr 13th. one o'clock. Slight wind at
North West, which became tempestuous
in the afternoon, With Rain all the
night following.'
Overleaf: Cloud study, 25 September 1821.
Oil on paper.

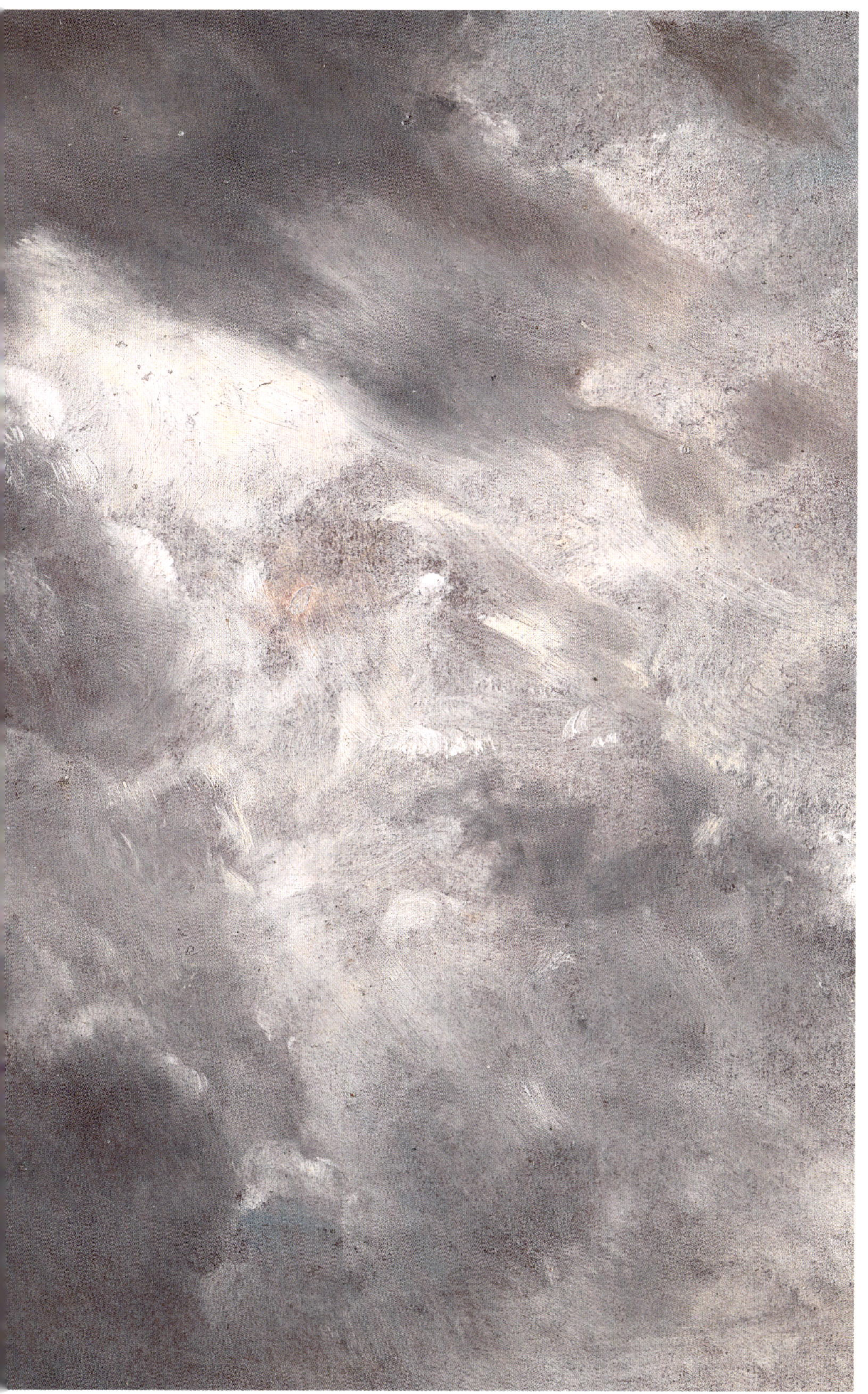

entirely. His art would be changed by this immersion in a new element, and so would he. 'I am the man of clouds,' he announced to Fisher two autumns later.

Constable worked rapidly, taking around an hour to make each sketch, some days painting two or even three. He had to be quick if he was going to capture the forms and colours of the skies with his brush as they were changing before his eyes – or before a shower. 'Noon. very sultry. with large drops of Rain falling on my palate light air from S. W.,' he wrote on the back of a sketch he made on 3 September, in which he had examined the ways leaves reflected the light from the sky. On another, made just over a week later, he noted: 'Hampstead, Sepr 11, 1821. 10. to 11. Morning under the sun – Clouds silvery grey, on warm ground Sultry. Light wind to the S. W. fine all day – but rain in the night following.' Making his weather notes later, sometimes the next day, gave him the chance to put his rapid studies in a wider context, to look back at the cloud formations he had captured and ask: what came in their wake? The next day, 12 September, he made two sketches. One was painted at noon: 'Sun very Hot. looking southward exceedingly bright vivid & Glowing, very heavy showers in the Afternoon but a fine evening. High wind in the night.' The other was done later in the day as the sun was setting over Harrow, 'after a very heavy rain … while making this sketch observed the Moon rising very beautifully … due East over the heavy clouds from which the late showers had fallen'. At one o'clock the following day, he tilted his head right back and – for the first time, as far as we know – painted a study purely of clouds, without a single leaf to anchor them to the ground. A few days later, on a particularly stormy afternoon with dramatically dark skies, he did it again, noting the 'bright light coming through the Clouds which were lying one on another'.

Throughout September and October Constable watched the skies, dodging showers and noting the shapes and speed of the clouds. He must have kept his painting box by the door, so it was ready for him to tuck under his arm as he hurried out towards the heath. He relished the autumnal weather and the dramatic contrasts it brought. As he wrote to Fisher on 20 September: 'We have had noble clouds & effects of light & dark & colour – as is always the case in such seasons as the present.' All

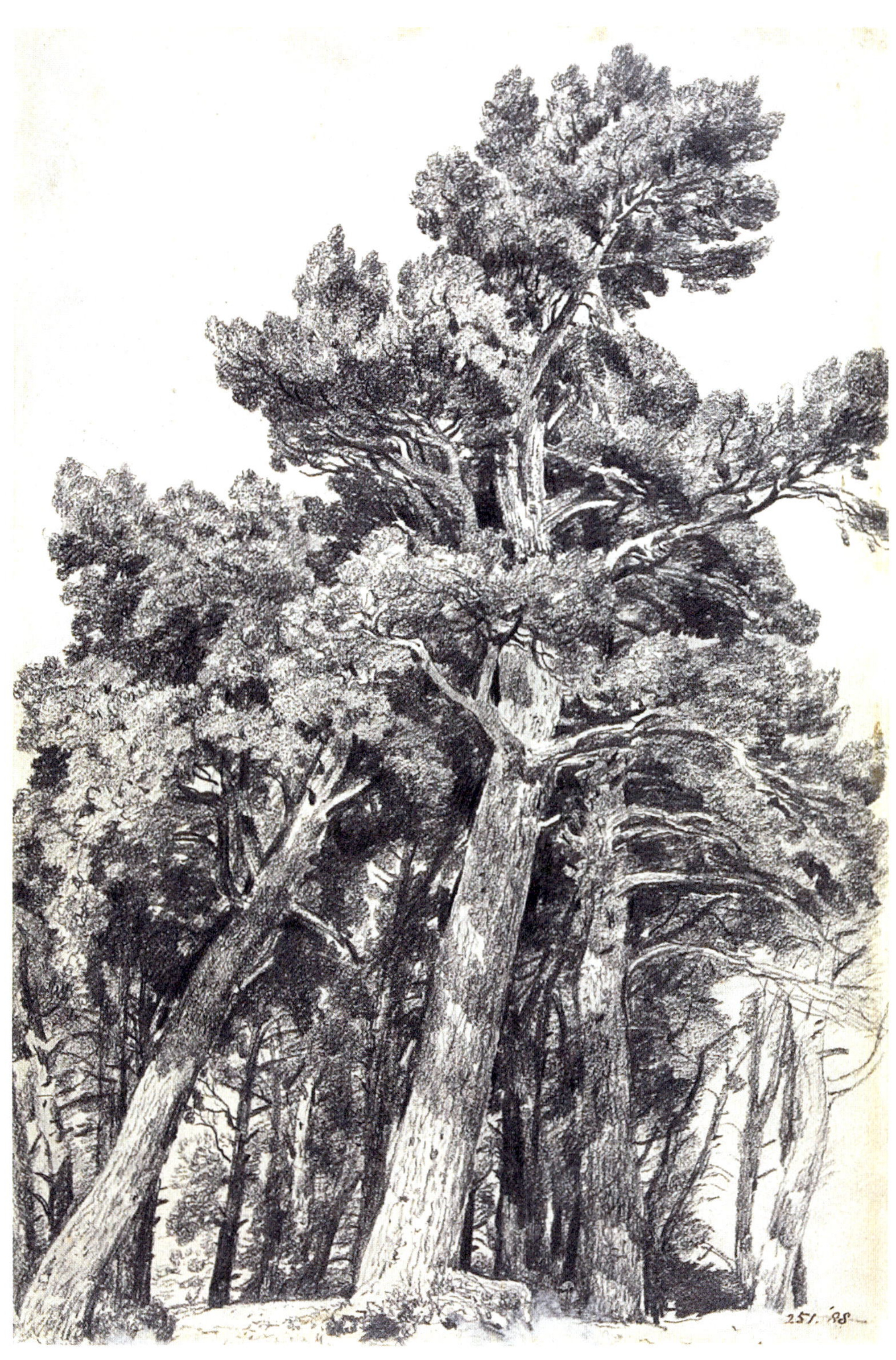

Fir trees at Hampstead, 2 October 1820. Graphite on paper. C. R. Leslie describes how William Blake was once looking through Constable's sketches and, coming to a drawing of fir trees on Hampstead Heath – perhaps this one – exclaimed 'Why, this is not drawing, but inspiration!'

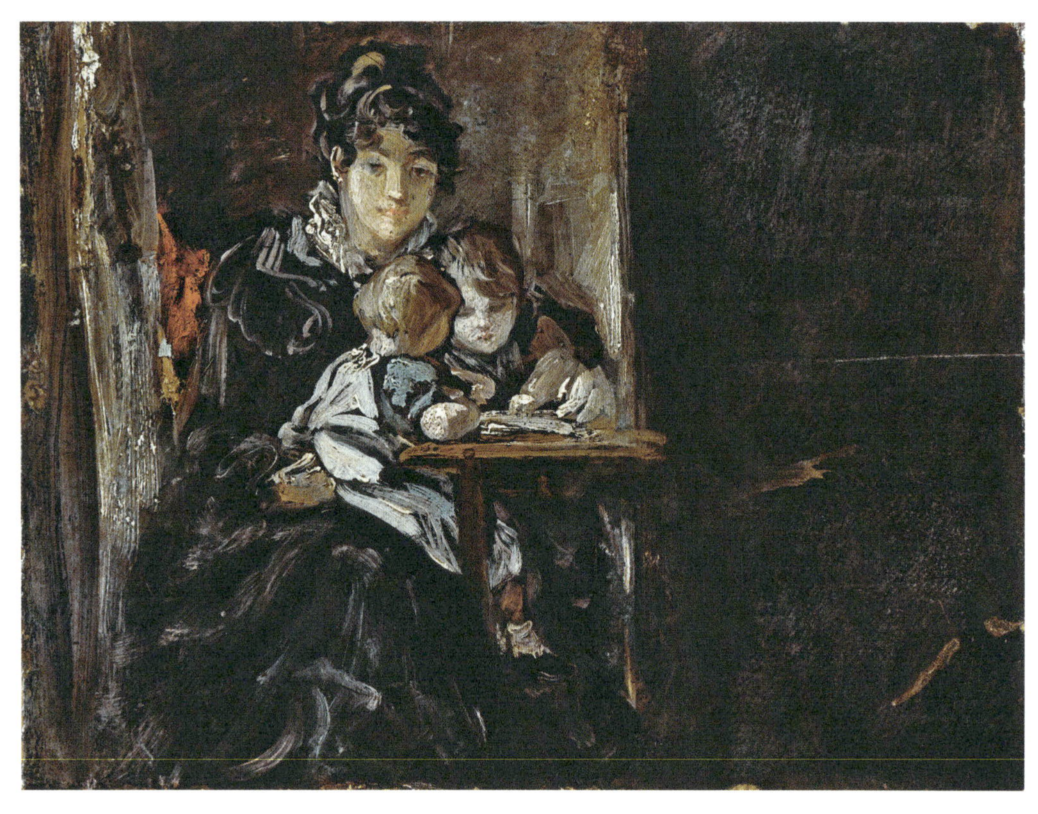

Maria Constable with two of her children, 1820. Oil on panel.

this time he was thinking about skies, how Old Masters like Rembrandt had painted them and how he could get better at representing them in his own exhibition pictures. As he explained to his friend on 23 October, 'I have not been Idle and have made more particular and general study than I have ever done in one summer … I have done a good deal of skying – I am determined to conquer all difficulties and that most arduous one among the rest.' 'I have often been advised,' he continued,

> to consider my *Sky* – as a 'White Sheet drawn behind the Objects'. Certainly if the Sky is *obtrusive* – (as mine are) it is bad, but if they are *evaded* (as mine are not) it is worse, they must and always shall with me make an effectual part of the composition … The sky is the 'source of light' in nature – and governs every thing. Even our common observations on the weather of every day, are suggested by them but it does not occur to us.

Arguments of this kind must have revolved around his mind as he was outdoors cloud-watching, brush in hand. Fisher, the amateur artist and astute critic, was the ideal sounding board.

Constable may have pursued his research that autumn with intense drive, but this did not dull the joy that – if you caught him in the right mood – he could find in the beauty of the season. 'The last day of Octr was indeed lovely so much that I could not paint for looking,' he told Fisher; '– my wife was walking with me all the middle of the day on the beautifull heath. I made two evening effects' (see p. 2). And for all that he had made Hampstead his laboratory for the study of clouds and the fall of light, the place itself became important to him over the months he spent there. He came to associate it with his family, and inscribed his emotional history into the heath just as he had done at East Bergholt. In the autumn of 1820, on the fourth anniversary of his marriage to Maria, he made a large and magnificent drawing of a group of trees – a match for his 1817 farewell-to-East-Bergholt study of elms – and wrote in the top corner: 'Wedding day. Hampstead Octr. 2. 1820.' The trees he chose to draw were firs. Evergreen, like their love.

Sitting at the breakfast table one morning in the second week of October 1823, Constable opened a letter that contained an irresistible invitation. It came from Lady Beaumont, the wife of a wealthy patron, collector and amateur artist whom Constable had first got to know in 1795. Sir George Beaumont had come into contact with the Constable family through his mother, who lived in Dedham with her second husband, a mill-owner, and had taken Golding Constable's talented young son under his wing because of their shared love of art and of drawing from nature. The two would surely have teamed up for sketching expeditions in and around Dedham Vale. Beaumont also offered Constable his first sight of serious Old Master paintings. He was a collector with such a passionate admiration for Claude Lorrain that he took his prized landscape painting *Hagar and the Angel* with him when he travelled, in a specially constructed box that fitted on the roof of his carriage. Despite their different positions on the social scale, the two men had kept in friendly touch over the years. Beaumont had been kind to Constable in his bachelor years in London, at one point issuing an avuncular invitation when the latter was unwell to walk to his London house on Grosvenor Square, look at any painting of his for as long as he pleased, then go home and paint it again from memory, returning as often as he liked. It was an unconventional prescription, but one Beaumont knew his friend would appreciate. Paintings by Claude, Rubens, Rembrandt and Wilson hung in his specially constructed top-lit gallery. Given Constable's profound love of these artists, it probably worked.

Lady Beaumont's invitation of 1823 was an urgent one: autumn was slipping away. 'Sir George would wish to shew you this place before the trees are stript of their leaves on which account there is no time to lose,' she wrote. Presumably, Constable suppressed remarks about 'rotting melancholy dissolution' in his reply. Despite having recently returned home to his wife and children after a lengthy stay with Fisher, he accepted. Here was an opportunity not to be missed. As he wrote triumphantly to Fisher on 19 October:

At the time you receive this letter I shall be at breakfast with Sir George Beaumont at Colorton [*sic*] Hall, Leicestershire, near Ashby de la Zouch … I look to this visit with pleasure and improvement. All his beautiful pictures are there, and if I can find time to copy the little Grove, by Claude Lorraine (evidently a study from nature), it will much help me.

Travelling north on the coach from Charing Cross the next day, he must have watched the Midlands countryside that unfolded outside the window – much of it new to him – with keen interest; but his thoughts were full of Old Masters.

Constable seems to have regarded his visit to Coleorton as a kind of artists' retreat, offering respite from the demands of family life and a precious opportunity to devote his days entirely to art. He did not have to go far to experience aesthetic delight. 'Every step from this door is a picture,' he wrote to Maria, entranced; 'the garden is beyond all description, rock, ruins, the Church, the house, the mountain &c &c.' The house itself ran like clockwork, with a bell ringing for breakfast on the dot of nine o'clock, dinner at four and tea at seven, after which Constable would be given a portfolio of prints and drawings to inspect while Beaumont read aloud from a sermon, a poem or a play. The bell rang again at ten for prayers, after which it was time for bed. Constable was so impressed by the order that governed the Beaumonts' days that he renewed the vow he had made to Dunthorne twenty-one years before to be more discerning about how he spent his time, and with whom. This time he assured Maria that he would no longer 'let low people get an influence over me but keep to myself much more'.

During the first part of his stay, horses were brought to the door at two o'clock and, guided by Sir George, Constable explored the decidedly picturesque countryside around Coleorton Hall. 'I had the opportunity of seeing the ruins at Ashby, the mountain streams and rocks,' he told Maria. One day, riding with Beaumont along a shady lane at Staunton Harold, a couple of miles from Coleorton, Constable was apparently struck by the beauty of a particular tree. He asked his friend to hold his reins while they stopped for long enough for him to make a pencil sketch from the saddle, his horse shifting beneath him. 'I think it was the finest ash I ever saw', he noted later on the back of his drawing.

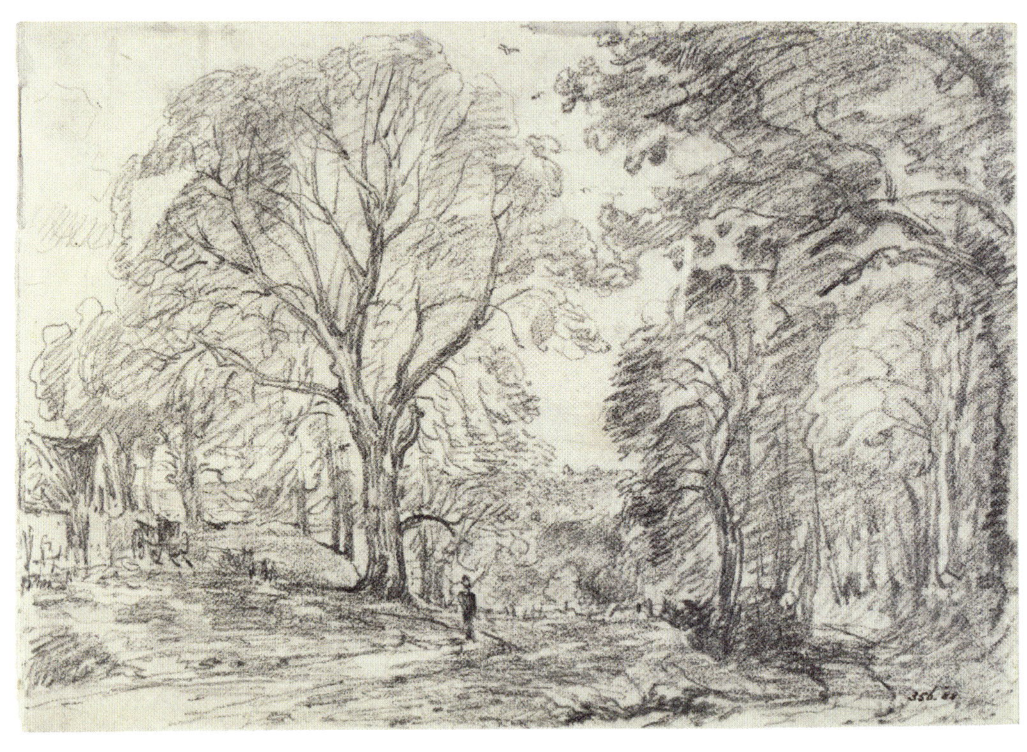

Trees in a lane at Staunton Harold, Leicestershire, 1823. Graphite on paper.

If, however, you were to take the catalogue of Constable's works and turn to October 1823 expecting to find a wealth of drawings recording the lanes, fields, rocks and ruins in and around Coleorton, and oil sketches of trees in glorious autumnal foliage, you would be disappointed. One almost wonders whether the drawing of Leicestershire's finest ash, executed in suspiciously stagey circumstances, was made to satisfy Lady Beaumont's insistence that he must enjoy the trees in their autumn colours. For the most part, rather than drawing out of doors as he usually did, Constable stayed in the house and made copies: some of drawings by Beaumont himself, but mostly of paintings by Claude. To copy was to learn an artist's secrets: brushstroke by brushstroke he could feel his way into the methods of another and take something for himself. The trees in the park and beyond could turn every shade of scarlet, ochre and gold without him. It was Claude he had come for.

'Only think', Constable wrote in a letter to Maria the morning after he arrived, 'that I am now writing in a room full of Claudes (not Glovers) – real Claudes, and Wilsons & Poussins &c.' Today we take it for granted that we can walk into public galleries and see paintings, but Constable was writing the year before the National Gallery was founded – a venture in which Beaumont himself was instrumental – and long before most regional museums were established. This prolonged exposure to Old Master paintings was a rare privilege, especially to someone with no desire to travel abroad. It was to be savoured, moment by moment. Constable set himself the task of copying in oils not just one but two paintings by Claude: a landscape of a grove of trees under which a goatherd and his goats shelter from the noonday sun, and a sunset scene, *The Death of Procris*. Two oil paintings was an ambitious task. As luck would have it, the weather in Leicestershire took a turn for the worse.

'This is a dreary morning,' he announced cheerfully to Maria after nearly a week,

> but I do not mind, I have so much that I want within … Sir G. has kindly allowed me to make a study of a little Claude, a Grove – probably done on the spot … It rains gently – so that probably I shall get a good day's work.

A few more days passed, and Constable explained that 'the weather has been bad,' adding 'I do not at all regret being confined to this house.' A week later and it was, he claimed, still so poor that he could 'scarcely look out of the window'. By 18 November he was freely admitting to being kept indoors by copying Claudes. He had, he said, 'worked so hard in the house that [he] never once went out of the door last week' and as a result was 'getting quite nervous'. The following week he resolved to 'get a few more walks and rides as I have not been out hardly at all – and only made you one little sketch of the house, which is all I have done from nature'.

Writing exuberantly to Fisher, he felt no need to mention the weather. Instead, he relished telling his friend about the sensuous artistic medium into which he had plunged. 'I am left entirely to do as I like with full range of the whole house,' he announced, 'in which I may saturate myself with art'. 'O, when I think of the "Ancient Masters",' he continued, 'I am almost choaked in this breakfast room. Here hang 4 Claudes, a Cousins & a Swanevelt. The low sun in the morning sets them off to great advantage.' He drank this atmosphere by night as well as day, teasing Maria with his quasi-erotic passion for Claude. 'You would laugh to see my bed room,' he told her. 'I have dragged so many things into it, books, portfolios, paints, canvases, pictures &c, and I have slept with one of the Claudes every night.' Claude's paintings seduced him into turning aside from the natural world that normally entranced him, beguiled him with delicious southern sun-light filtered through green foliage. November's winds may have been blowing around the walls of Coleorton Hall, but inside Constable was basking in a gentle Claudean glow.

He would probably have stretched out his visit to the Beaumonts even longer than the six weeks he did stay, happily immersed in a warm pool of art and unwilling to haul himself out to face the chill autumnal air. To Maria's exasperation, he was even invited to stay over Christmas. 'It was complimentary in Sir George to ask you to remain the Xmas, but he forgot at the time that you had a wife', she wrote with understandable asperity. His two-and-a-half-year-old son Charley began to say that papa would 'never come home', and Maria herself came close to losing patience. She informed him that she was 'heartily sick' of his 'long absence' and suggested he not show her his 'Claude', as she would throw it out of the window. But

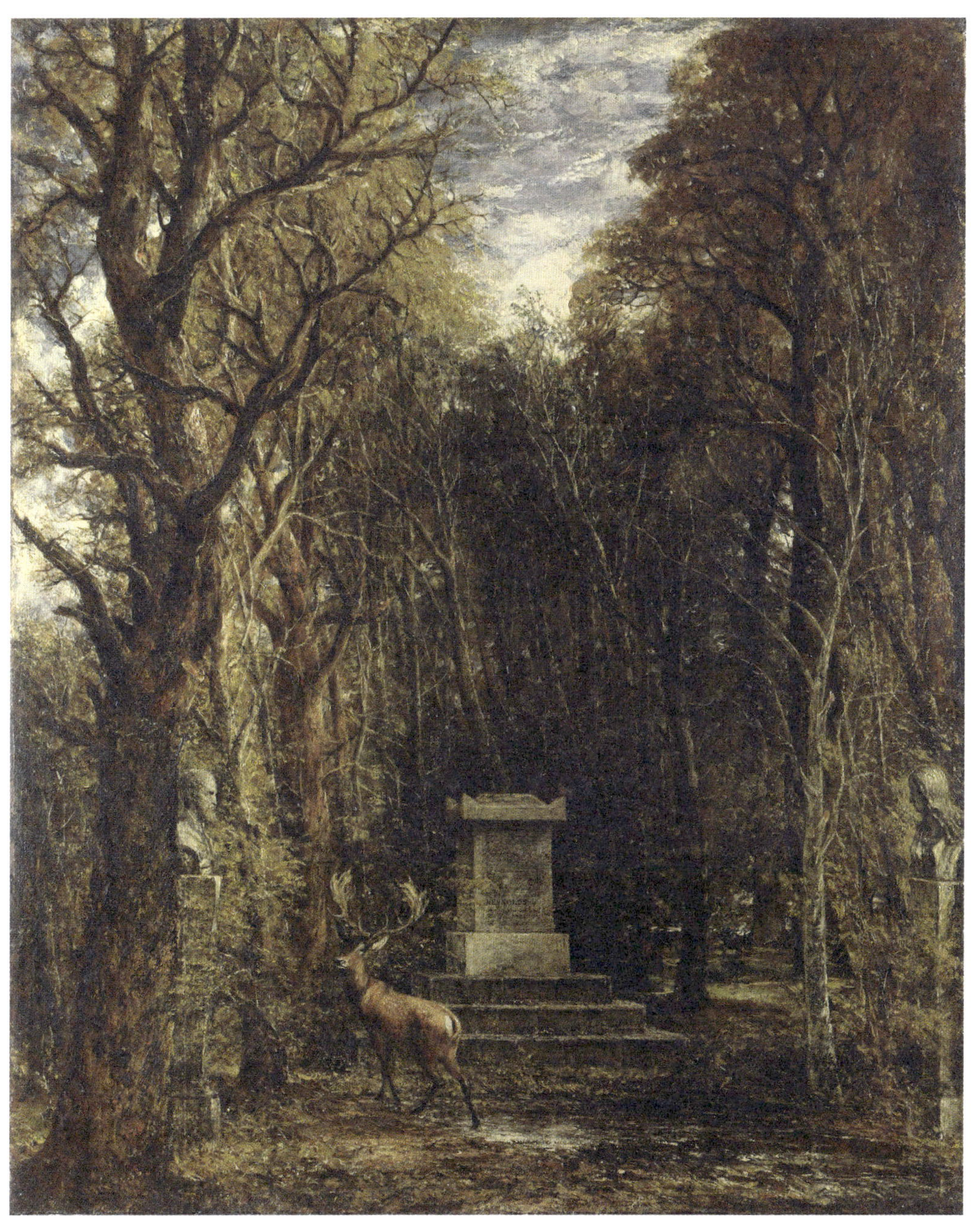

Cenotaph to the Memory of Sir Joshua Reynolds, 1833–36. Oil on canvas.

Constable still delayed his return, determined to finish his copy of Claude's noonday landscape with goatherds and internalize what he described as its 'life & breezy freshness'. Finally, on his last day, 28 November, he found an hour or two to walk in the garden, where he made a clutch of drawings. Even then, they were as much about art as nature. One shows a monument to Sir Joshua Reynolds that Beaumont had constructed at the end of an avenue of lime trees, with an inscription composed by William Wordsworth; another, a boulder dedicated to the memory of Richard Wilson.

Ten years later, by then a widower, Constable returned to a drawing he had made at Coleorton that late November day. He used it as the basis for a grand oil painting of the Reynolds monument, surrounded by towering trees in the brown foliage of late autumn, fallen leaves thick on the ground. More than any other picture he painted, it acknowledges the reverence for the Old Masters in which he indulged that autumn in 1823: on the left of his composition is a bust of Michelangelo, on the right one of Raphael. It also commemorates a friendship: *Cenotaph to the Memory of Sir Joshua Reynolds*, the most autumnally melancholy painting Constable ever produced, was a tribute to Beaumont himself. The picture was finally completed in time for the Royal Academy exhibition of 1836 – the year before his own death. It did not find a buyer, but when in 1888 it was bequeathed to the National Gallery by the artist's daughter Isabel, it found its most appropriate setting among paintings by Michelangelo, Raphael, Claude and Reynolds, in the institution that Sir George had done so much to support.

Places of the heart

One late September day in 1827, Abram Constable, now quietly living at Flatford Mill with his unmarried sister Mary and her beloved collection of old china, received a letter from John that left him aghast. He took pen and paper and scribbled a hurried response in an attempt to avert the coming catastrophe. The next day he nervously wrote another, this time directing it to Hampstead rather than his brother's London house, just to make sure it was received. John had proposed a visit – and was intending to bring his children. Presumably he had not meant to bring the baby, Alfred Abram, who had yet to reach his first birthday and would naturally stay behind with

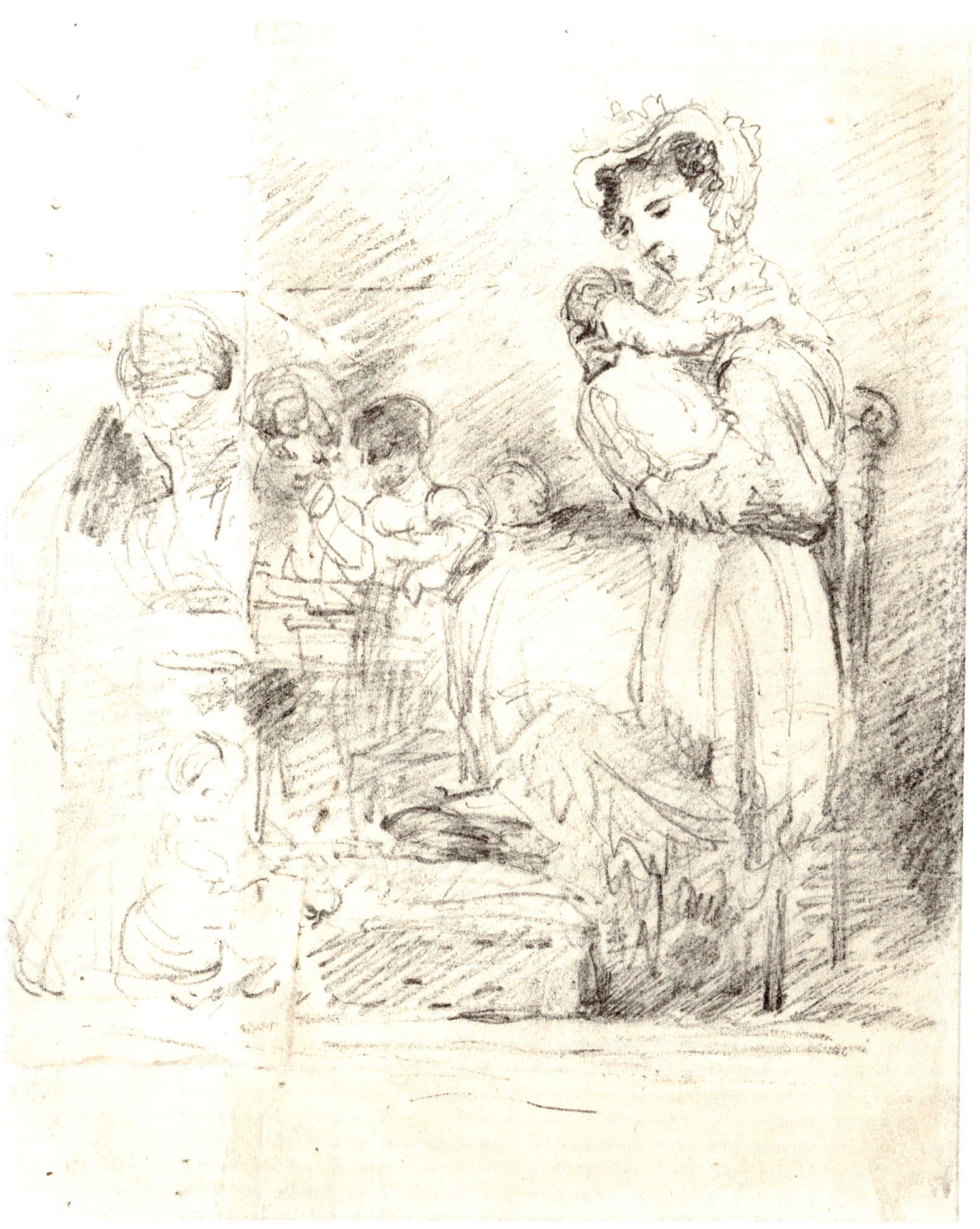

The nursery, 1826. Graphite on paper. This drawing
shows Maria holding her sixth child, Alfred, who was
born in November 1826. The older two children are
John Charles, who was nearly nine, and Minna, who
was seven; the younger ones are Charles Golding,
aged five, Isabel, aged four, and, on the floor, Emily,
born in March the previous year.

Maria, who was then pregnant with their seventh child. But that still left nine-year-old John Charles, eight-year-old Minna, six-year-old Charley, five-year-old Isabel – perhaps even two-year-old Emily. It was 'impossible', he wrote. It was not just the advanced season – think of those long, cold nights! consider the dangers of the journey! – or even the impossibility of accommodating them all. It was Flatford itself. 'I think a more dangerous place for children could not be found upon earth,' exclaimed Abram, forgetting in his panic that his oldest siblings had spent their earliest years there without mishap. He entreated John to consult 'reason & prudence' and postpone the visit – 'let us see what time may do', he wrote soothingly.

It didn't work. John was extravagantly fond of children and remarkably indulgent of noise and boisterous play. When one of his young sons accidentally put a broom handle through a painting he was working on, making a large tear in the canvas, he gently asked the boy if he was responsible, then said: '"Oh! My dear pet! See what we have done! Dear, dear! What shall we do to mend it? I can't think – can *you?*"' He probably had no idea of how alarming the prospect of a lengthy visit from several children under the age of ten might be to a pair of middle-aged, childless siblings. And to him, Flatford was a place of ancient enchantment. How could he possibly see it as a death-trap? As a compromise, though, he only took his two eldest children. They had never been to Suffolk – his own trips back to East Bergholt had, since his long holiday with Maria in 1817, been solitary, fairly brief and on family business. John Charles and Minna's childhoods, shaped by their mother's illness, had been very different to his own. They had known little stability, but had been shuttled between central London, Brighton and lodgings in Hampstead; it was only in August that year that the Constable family had settled into a permanent home in north London, at no. 6, Well Walk. Constable wanted them to know and love the dear familiar scenes that were so deeply rooted in his own soul.

At first, Minna was unimpressed. 'O no, this is only feilds', she said when her father told her they were in Suffolk. But it was not long before they were 'overcome with delight at all they see – Mini thinks Suffolk very like Hampstead', he reported. Constable took a large sketchbook with him and spent the unusually fine days of early October drawing while keeping an eye on his children. There is a relaxed lyricism to these drawings, a holiday

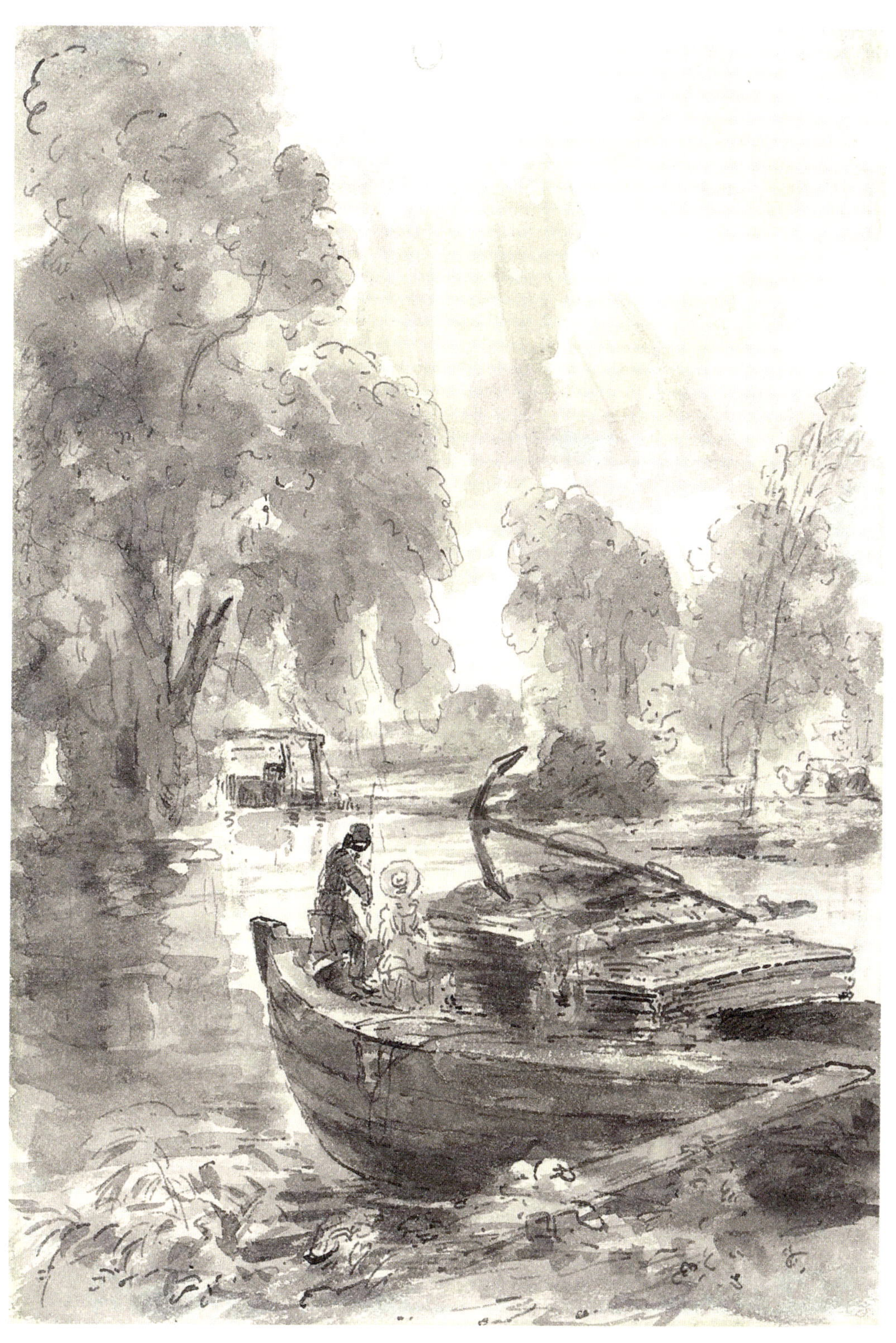

*John Charles and Maria Louisa Constable
fishing from a barge at Flatford*, October
1827. Pen and wash on paper.

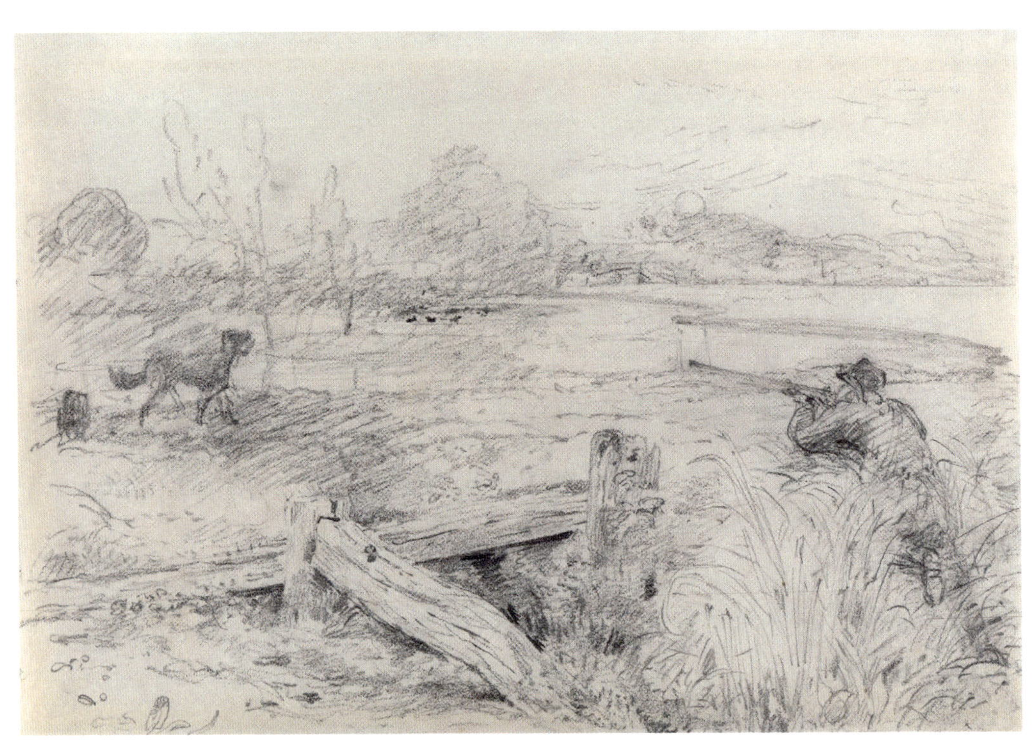

A sportsman shooting duck on the River Stour,
October 1827. Graphite on paper.
Constable's older brother, Golding,
was a skilled shot. He was employed
as a gamekeeper in woods at Bentley,
near East Bergholt, by Constable's
patrons the Dysart family.

spirit quite unlike the intense precision of his earlier Suffolk sketchbooks. He sketched barges on the Stour, willows, a cart, a bridge and – taking out his watercolours – a rainbow. A sportsman with a dog and a gun shooting duck from the towpath is surely his brother Golding; he lived at the nearby Wheeler's Cottage with their sister Nancy, and was at that time repairing Pie's Nest, a tumbledown old farmhouse opposite the windmill. From the bank, Constable drew John Charles and Minna fishing from a moored barge at Flatford. The sun's rays pour down on the scene with the splendour of a religious painting, while liquid washes make the trees' shade wobble on the water. Constable was harvesting these sunlit minutes to store up, merging his own childhood with that of his eldest boy and girl. Half-observing and half-remembering, he was creating a Suffolk idyll in pen and ink.

By 10 October, however, it was 'pouring with rain at so steady and great a rate that I doubt not but the beauty of the weather & season is over.' It was time to return to London and to work. Now that his family was permanently settled in Hampstead, he had let out most of their house in Charlotte Street, where they had moved from Keppel Street in 1822, keeping only his studio and a few rooms for his own use. But the painting he started to plan for the next year's exhibition would allow him to return to the Suffolk countryside in his imagination. It was of a subject he knew intimately and had recently had time to show his children: what Abram called 'that well known (& to me & you) beautiful view' of Dedham Vale from Gun Hill, looking along the course of the River Stour towards the sea.

The face of the World is totally changed to me

A fourth son, Lionel Bicknell, arrived on 2 January 1828. The strain of yet another labour, and of nursing the baby as well as looking after the other children, took its toll, and in the spring Maria's health went into a steep decline. In May, in desperation, the couple travelled down to Brighton, still hoping that the sea air would help her and her sickly baby to gain strength. John returned to London and rejoined her in July, his picture *Dedham Vale* on the wall of the Royal Academy (from where it failed to sell; his vivid evocation of breeze and sparkling sunlight remained baffling to many exhibition visitors). He made some sketches at Brighton, but not many;

anxiety rises from those that survive like a vapour. One Sunday evening he went out to paint the sea under boiling storm clouds, rain thrashing down over the waves. The picture's agitated, choppy appearance – the result of using a palette knife rather than a brush to apply the paint – chimed with the raw edges of his emotional state. Mostly he stayed indoors where he could be near his wife, and occupied his time by painting dock and burdock leaves and trollius flower heads – cramped little sketches that must be among the most joyless botanical studies ever made.

John and Maria returned to Hampstead at the end of the month. She was sinking fast and might as well be at home in Well Walk, high above London, where her spirits could be lifted by views over the heath. C. R. Leslie called in the middle of November. He recalled that his friend had seemed cheerful when they were in the parlour with Maria, but that before he left Constable took him into another room for a moment. He said nothing, but squeezed Leslie's hand and wept. Maria died, aged forty, on a short, dreary day in late November.

Nothing Constable thought, saw or felt would ever be the same again. As he wrote to his brother Golding, 'the face of the World is totally changed to me'. His brothers and sisters urged him to visit. He would like to see them, he explained, but Suffolk? No. Even that nurturing place that had such a hold on his heart had no comfort to offer him. '[P]oor dear Bergholt will fill me full of – sad – sad – associations', he admitted, ' – especially the sight of the Rectory – & its dark trees'. He had always poured his feelings into the fields, hedgerows, lanes and gardens of home; now, saturated, they would only mire him in profounder grief.

Constable usually spent the latter part of November planning the major painting he would send to the Royal Academy the following spring. Wise, forthright Fisher, knowing that his friend would need his work to give shape and purpose to days grown formless with grief, urged him on: 'you should apply yourself rigidly to your profession', he advised. 'Some of the finest works of art, and most vigorous exertions of intellect, have been the result of periods of distress.' Constable followed his advice. His thoughts turned to a subject he remembered in a 'little book of hasty memorandums of the place which I saw' that he had made back in the summer of 1814 when he had visited southern Essex with a friend. One day, as he had told Maria,

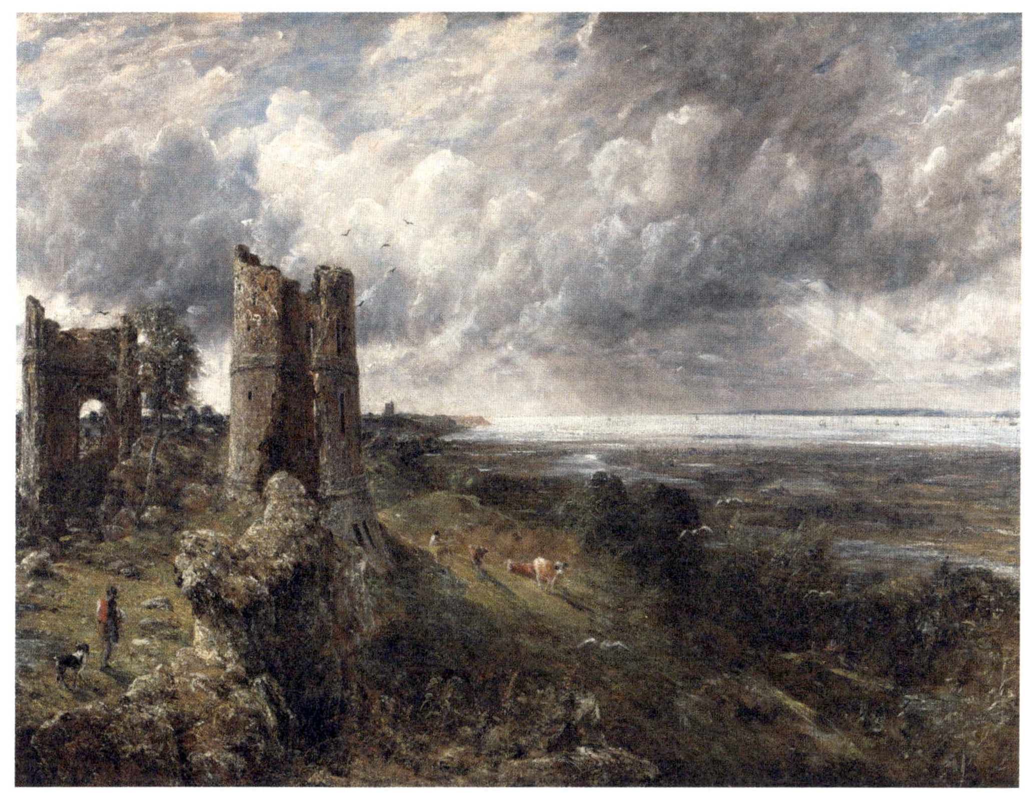

Hadleigh Castle, 1829. Oil on canvas. *Detail overleaf.*

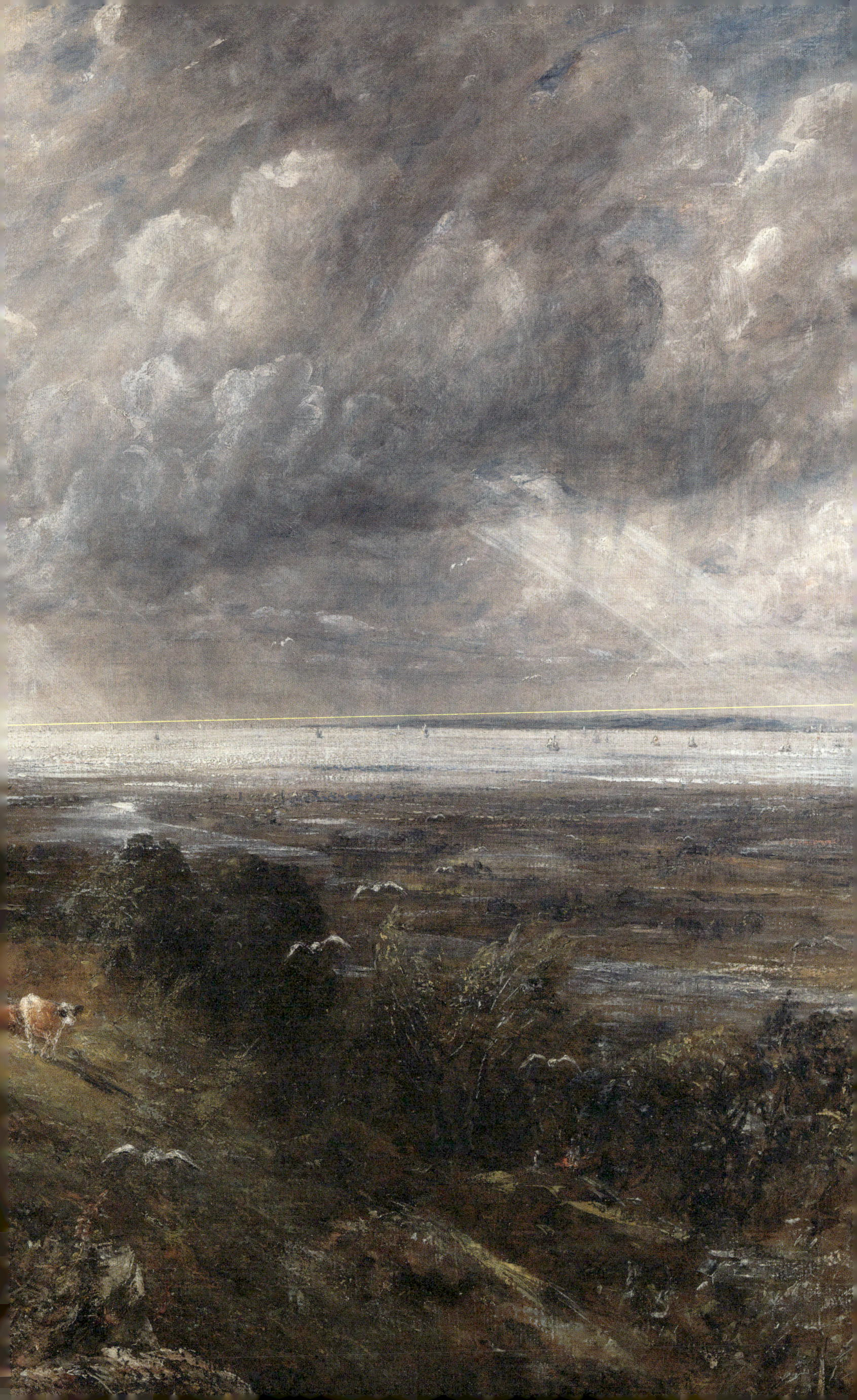

I walked upon the beach at South End. I was always delighted
with the melancholy grandeur of a sea shore. At Hadleigh there is
a ruin of a castle which from its situation is a really fine place – it
commands a view of the Kent hills, the Nore and North Foreland &
looking many miles to sea.

He fetched the sketchbook and flipped through its pages until he found
a drawing he had made of the thirteenth-century castle. From this little
pencilled seed would grow two great canvases, each six feet wide – one a
full-scale oil sketch, the other a finished composition that he would send to
the Academy. He called this picture *Hadleigh Castle, the Mouth of the Thames
– Morning after a Stormy Night*. In the catalogue he quoted a few bleak lines
from Thomson's 'Summer': 'Rude ruins glitter; and the briny deep, / Seen
from some pointed promontory's top, / Restless reflects a floating gleam.'
For a description of summer, it has a great deal of winter to it. The same
could be said of Constable's picture, with its dull olive greens and silvery
greys. The day may have broken and the storm clouds begun to dispel, but
it is hard to imagine a more comfortless light. The coruscating reflections
that play on the stones and the marshes threaten to hurt the eye, make one
wince and look away. Compared to this, night would be preferable.

The ruined walls of the castle and the view over the bleak Essex marshes
towards the Hadleigh Ray, which meets the Thames estuary under billowing storm clouds, can be seen as an expression of grief and desolation: a
ruin offers no shelter and a marsh no safe place to stand. But there is more
to the finished picture than that. The anguish of sorrow and loss can sometimes be assuaged by conventional forms and simple poems; most hearts
can be comforted by platitudes, even while their owners acknowledge the
triteness. Constable's contemporaries had been painting ruins for decades,
but he had rarely bothered with them. By the late 1820s they were something of a cliché. Now, as that terrible autumn darkened into winter, he
reached for ruins and marshes under stormy skies as a way of coping; perhaps they represented a conventional mould into which to pour his grief.
One suspects that the true face of his anguish was represented by the neatly
tended garden of a village rectory, with its too-sorrowful trees.

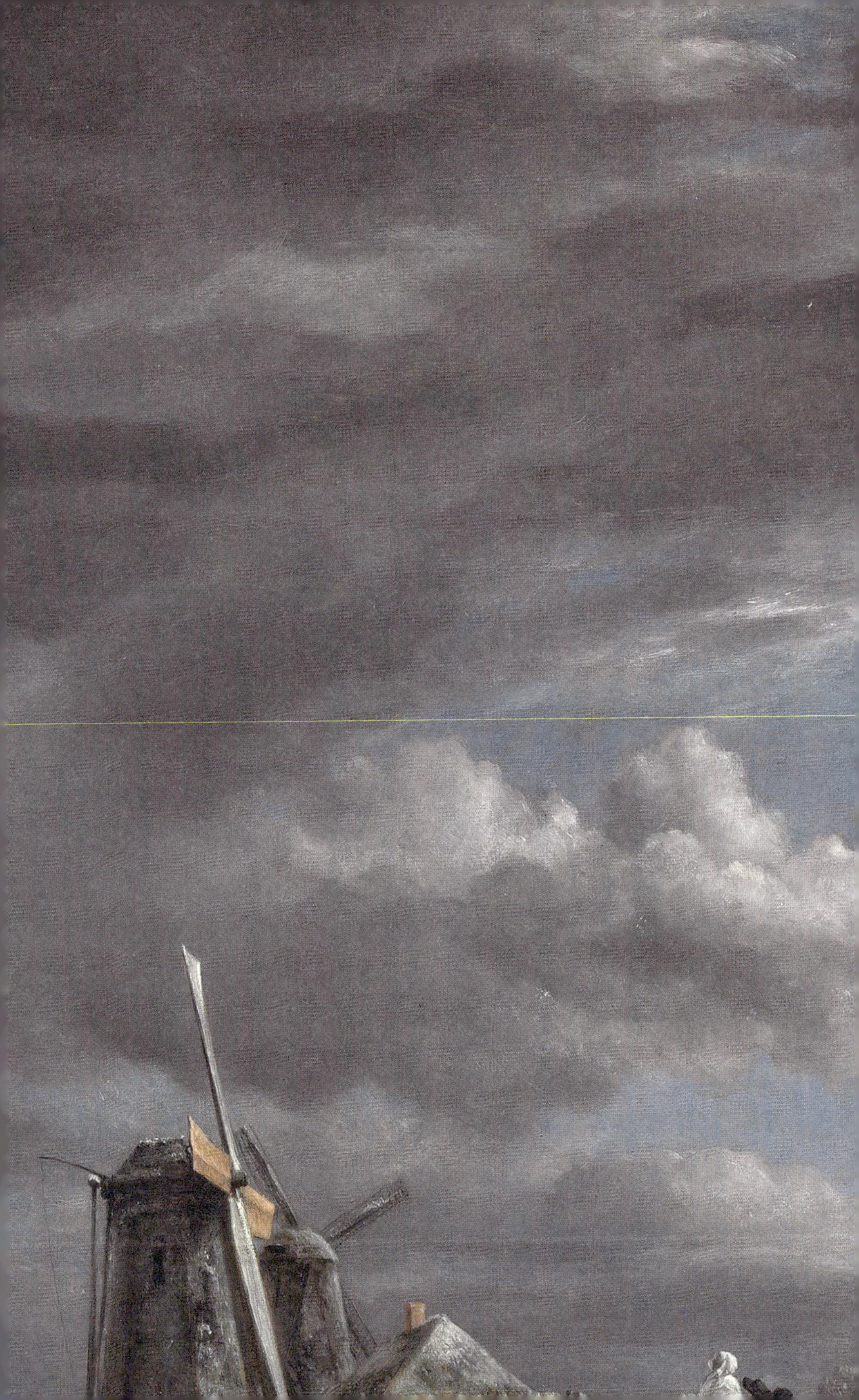

Winter

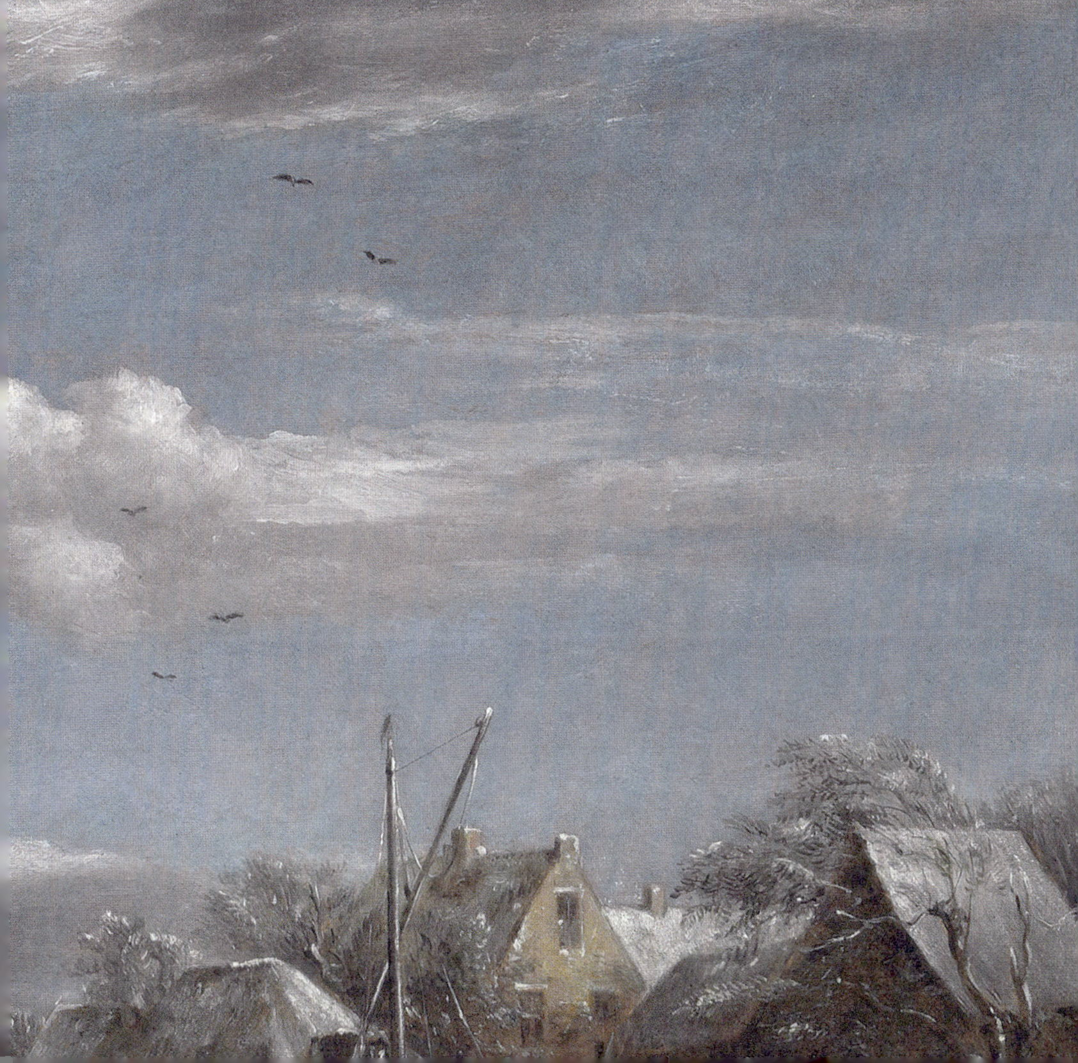

'Can it therefore be wondered at that I paint continual storms?'

Constable's snow

Bare branches silhouetted against a cobalt sky; streets and fields made pristine by snow: winter remakes the world for us to marvel at. But it hasn't always been this way. Constable had been dead for two decades before artists began to paint snow scenes for a British public newly alive to the season's beauties. In Dutch and Flemish art there was a long tradition of snow scenes that stretched back to Pieter Bruegel the Elder, but in Britain, few wanted to be reminded of harsh winter weather. In British versions of the medieval Labours of the Months, daily chores like trudging through frozen mud and slush with armfuls of brushwood were omitted from the sequence in favour of cheerful fireside scenes. Constable's favourite poet, William Cowper, was highly unusual in writing about the awe he felt when stopping to admire a snowy landscape during a winter's walk: 'The vault is blue / Without a cloud, and white without a speck / The dazzling splendour of the scene below'. But then, Cowper did not have to worry about food or fuel – others reliably supplied that – or travelling, which he seldom did. We often have to distance ourselves from a subject before we can see it with enough objectivity to find it beautiful. It was only in the mid-Victorian period, when for the first time more people lived in towns and cities than in the country, that the necessary focal length for admiring rural snow scenes was achieved. Thus framed, winter weather acquired a new aesthetic dimension – and a touch of pleasurable nostalgia – that it had never had before.

Constable never painted a snow scene from nature, and he set the majority of his exhibition pictures in high summer. Ever since he had begun to sketch in oils outdoors, his aim had been to catch the natural world on the move, to represent the sparkling surface of a river or the flicker of sunlight on the pale undersides of foliage as it was stirred by the summer breeze. 'I have seen him lying at the foot of a tree watching the motion of the leaves', recalled Henry Trimmer, the son of a friend. The intense stillness of a frost-bound landscape never held the same appeal. And yet from the early 1820s critics affected to misunderstand the dabs and flecks of white oil paint he applied with a palette knife to represent what he called the *freshness – sparkle – brightness* of nature: 'there is a flittering mannerism in his foliage and handling which gives to all his trees and herbage the appearance of sleet or snow having fallen', wrote a reviewer in 1823 of Constable's *Salisbury Cathedral from the Bishop's Grounds* when it was exhibited at the Royal Academy. After that, Constable's 'snow' became a popular jibe by critics who objected to his increasingly loose and expressive handling of paint. On one occasion the misunderstanding was genuine: Constable himself told the story of an old attendant at the Royal Academy who congratulated him on one summer scene, saying: 'That's a good picture, sir; so natural, all the frost on the trees.'

But Constable did find inspiration in winter scenes. 'I have been out with him after all colour of the landscape had disappeared,' recalled the artists' colourman George Field, 'and objects were seen only as skeletons and masses, yet his eye was still active for his art … Constable found undecorated beauties in the nakedness of winter when he lavished admiration on the anatomy of trees.' And although winter was a time for studio work rather than outdoor studies, there were occasions when his sketchbooks could not supply the data he needed and only the raw material of nature would do. 'When at work, he was life and soul in his subject,' remembered Trimmer, 'and the last time I saw him he told me he once put on his great coat, and sallied forth in a snowstorm to Hampstead Heath, to sketch an ash for some picture he was about.'

Constable may have appreciated the beauty of winter, but rooted in his mind was anxiety about the havoc bad weather could bring. In the country it was not only perilous and isolating but also dangerously disruptive for a business like Golding Constable's that relied on the movement of goods. Ann wrote anxiously to her son in early January 1811, reporting 'severe frosty air … snow & frost, almost constant rains, and great floods, which has greatly impeded navigation & dispatch of business'. She paused, remembering to tell him that she was about to send him a box of Christmas provisions and to exhort him to take care in the cold. Then her thoughts flew back to problems at home: two days ago, she continued, she had heard that the barges were frozen fast in the river at Cattawade, a village on the Stour just east of Bergholt, and the family's brig, the *Telegraph*, was stuck in the port at Mistley: 'so you may know it is severe', she concluded. Four days later she wrote again. The weather was still 'intensely cold', with snow drifts deeper than she could remember. As her pen moved busily across the paper, she imagined her son walking along London streets made slippery and treacherous. The bottled cherries she had sent him would, she hoped, bestow a 'cordial warmth … either before or after the Academy these very sharp evenings'. He must be sure not to sit around in damp socks, because it could lead to 'sore throats, inflammation of the lungs and tooth ache'. And he should keep a good fire.

Winter in London may have been damp, dark and often bitterly cold, but for Constable in the years before 1816, it had one wonderful advantage: Maria lived there. Her family home was at Spring Garden Terrace, a short stroll from St James's Park. He could meet her in the open air and walk by her side, although the park was a far cry from East Bergholt and stricter social rules applied. She was always chaperoned, usually by her sister Catherine. A much greater obstacle was her father's continuing opposition to John as a suitor, which meant that these encounters on the park's avenues had to be made to seem as though they happened by chance. It was far from easy. A day or two before Christmas, 1813, Maria received a plaintive letter from John.

> I have been all this morning looking for you – and at last had the mortification of seeing [you] come up New Street and enter your door without my being able to make you or dear Catherine see me – though I was close under the iron rails directly opposite. I wasted some time hoping you might join your Mother but when I saw your Sisters without you I gave up hope of seeing you and I began to get very cold as I had been out hours without a great coat.

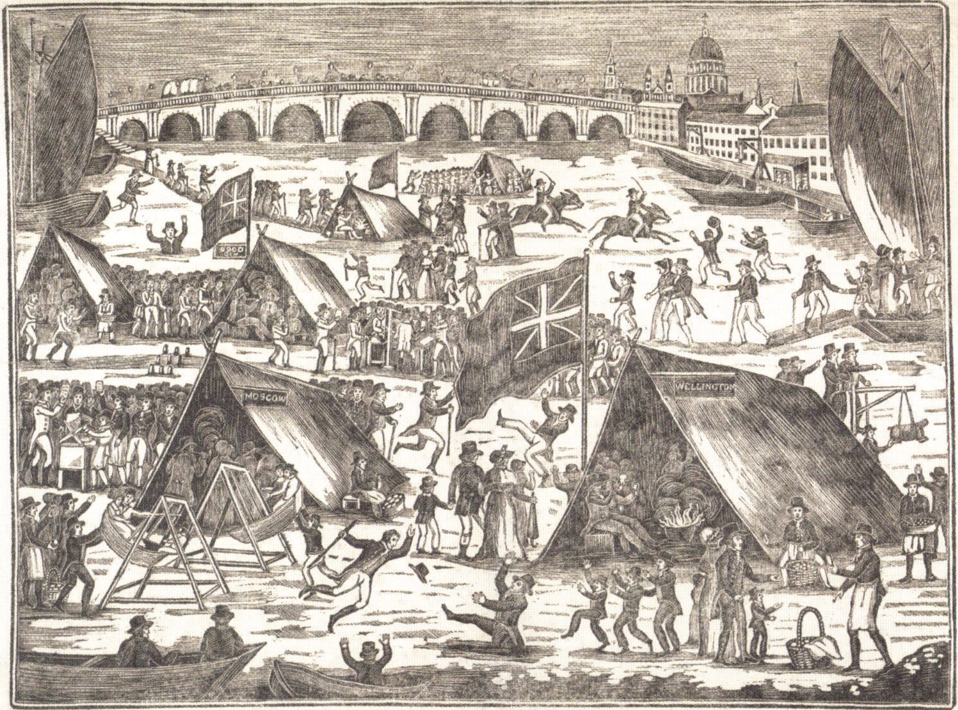

The Year 1814 will be long remembered for the severe frosts and heavy falls of snow with which it commenced, and by which the rivers were rendered innavigable, and the public roads for several days impassable. At the beginning of February the river was completely blocked up with ice, between London and Blackfriars Bridges, where a fair was kept, 3 or 4 days, with booths, swings, skittles, presses printing tickets in commemoration, &c. &c.

Published by T. Batchelar, 115, Long Alley, Moorfields.

Anonymous, *A view of the frost fair on the Thames*, 1814. Woodcut. Two factors led to the regular freezing over of the Thames between 1600 and 1814. One was the period of regional cooling known as the 'Little Ice Age'; the other was the narrowness of the gaps between the medieval piers of London Bridge, which allowed ice to form.

It was intensely poignant, and also a little ridiculous. Constable was thirty-seven and being forced by circumstances to lurk around behind railings like a teenager, when he knew he should have been getting on with his work and furthering his career. He was so upset by the time he got back to his rooms that he hated the sight of his own pictures. He would try his best to bear up, he told Maria, but it was 'almost enough to turn a *painter's* mind.'

The weather was not kind to the couple that winter. December had been unusually cold. 'You must have found the weather lately very unfavourable to painting,' remarked Maria to John in the middle of the month, 'so dark, and now so cold, that I should think you could hardly feel the brush.' It was a taste of what was to come. Two days after Christmas, a thick, freezing fog rolled into London. In early January, which turned out to be the third coldest on record, it began to snow heavily. Streets became entirely blocked and yard-long icicles hung from buildings. The temperature dropped so low that the Thames froze over – the very last time it did so. An impromptu Frost Fair was held on the frozen river, before a thaw in late February cracked the ice into great chunks that went crashing down the river towards the estuary. For week after bitter week, walks in St James's Park were out of the question. Now it was Maria's turn to express how upset and thwarted she felt; 'for my defence,' she wrote unhappily to John towards the end of January, 'I can say I did not expect such a continuation of bad weather to prevent our seeing each other.'

Above all, however, for Constable as well as most artists of this period, winter meant work at the easel. It was a demanding time, both physically and mentally. 'I am so well that I seem quite equal to a winter's campaign', John announced to Maria one December, having just returned to London from a visit to Suffolk. Whether he felt up to it or daunted by the prospect, he had little choice but to marshal his brushes, drawings and oil sketches and advance. It might have been the end of the year, but Constable's thoughts – when not on meeting Maria – were fixed on the following spring's exhibition.

Landscape: Noon

In the late autumn of 1820, when dusk darkened their Hampstead rooms a little earlier each afternoon and the trees dropped yellowing leaves on the heath, the Constable family packed up their belongings and moved back to the house on Keppel Street. John had spent the autumn months tinkering with what, for him, was an unusual subject. It was not a landscape at all, but an urban scene: the ceremonial opening of Waterloo Bridge by the Prince Regent in June 1817. He had been there on the day, sketching the colourful, bustling crowds just as he used to do at East Bergholt fair. Now was the time to decide on the direction of that winter's campaign. When he showed the picture to his friend and mentor Joseph Farington, however, the older man advised him to stay closer to the riverine subjects upon which he was slowly building his reputation. That year and the year before, Constable had exhibited Suffolk scenes at the Royal Academy exhibition. Both were tranquil Stour views that breathed the warmth of summer days. *The White Horse* (1819) is just the kind of working scene Constable loved: it shows a horse standing in a barge, being ferried across the Stour near Flatford Lock where the towpath switched banks. *Stratford Mill* (1820) has a more leisurely atmosphere: boys fish in the foreground, while men pull up a barge on the opposite bank. But there was a difference between these and his previous pictures. Both were 'six footers' – impressive, ambitious canvases, designed to catch the eye. Although in the end both were bought by Fisher, their scale and confidence revealed a new appetite in the artist for wider recognition. For fame.

Now, in his Keppel Street workroom, Constable turned the pages of his sketchbooks and opened the portfolios of drawings and oil sketches that teemed with details and views of the lanes, towpaths and fields around his Suffolk haunts, those 'dear scenes which I must always prefer and love to any other'. Scanning this visual anthology, he decided to take Farington's advice to heart. The subject he chose was as close to home as any he painted.

Anyone able to make a window into Constable's heart would have seen Flatford lodged at the centre. Though he had been living full time in London for four years by the end of 1820, his father's watermill – now managed by Abram – remained for him a place of intense emotional significance. It was where his parents had lived until his father built East

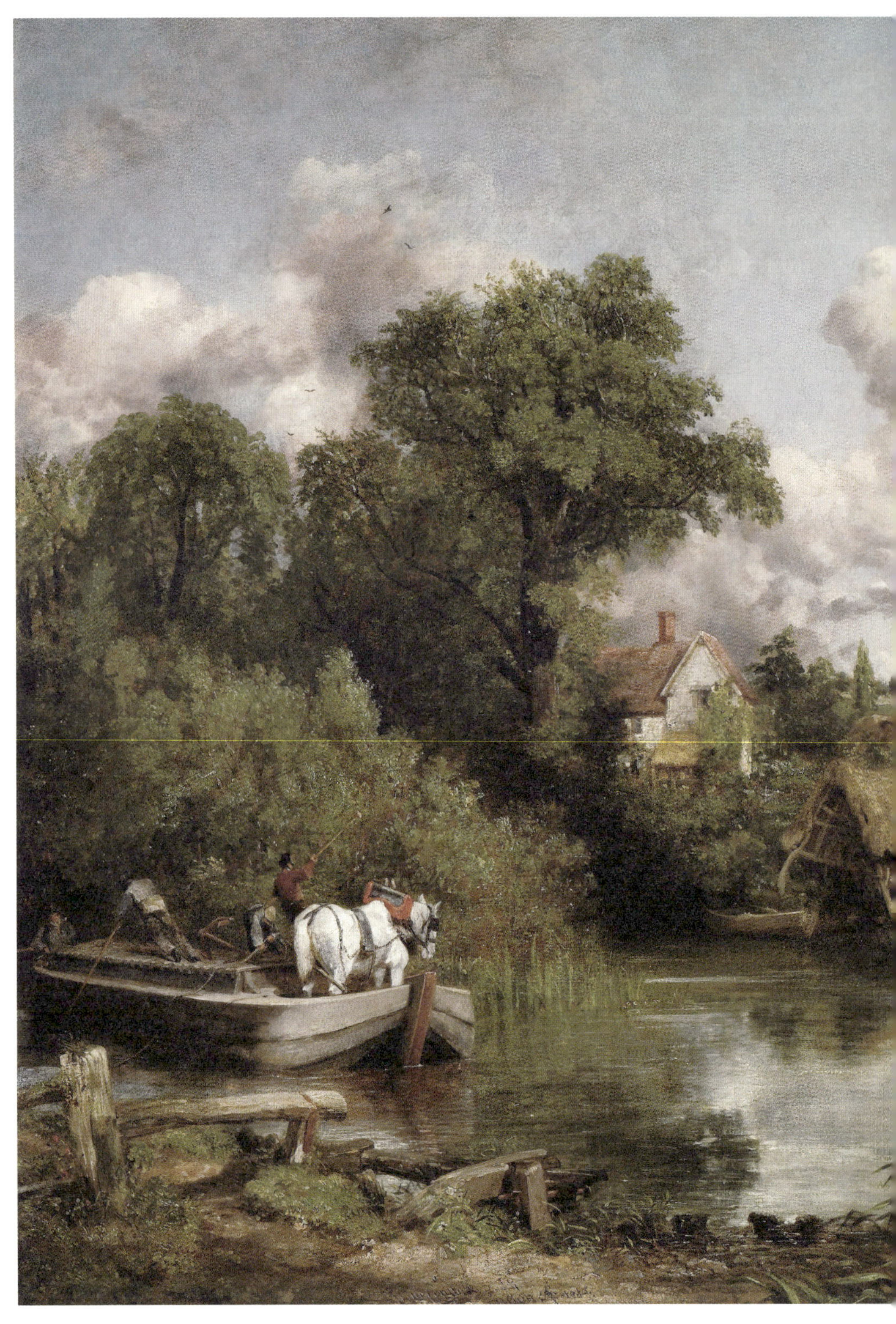

The White Horse, 1819. Oil on canvas. The white gabled house is Willy Lott's; it would also feature in *The Hay Wain*. Constable's vantage point was the right bank of the Stour, just below Flatford Lock.

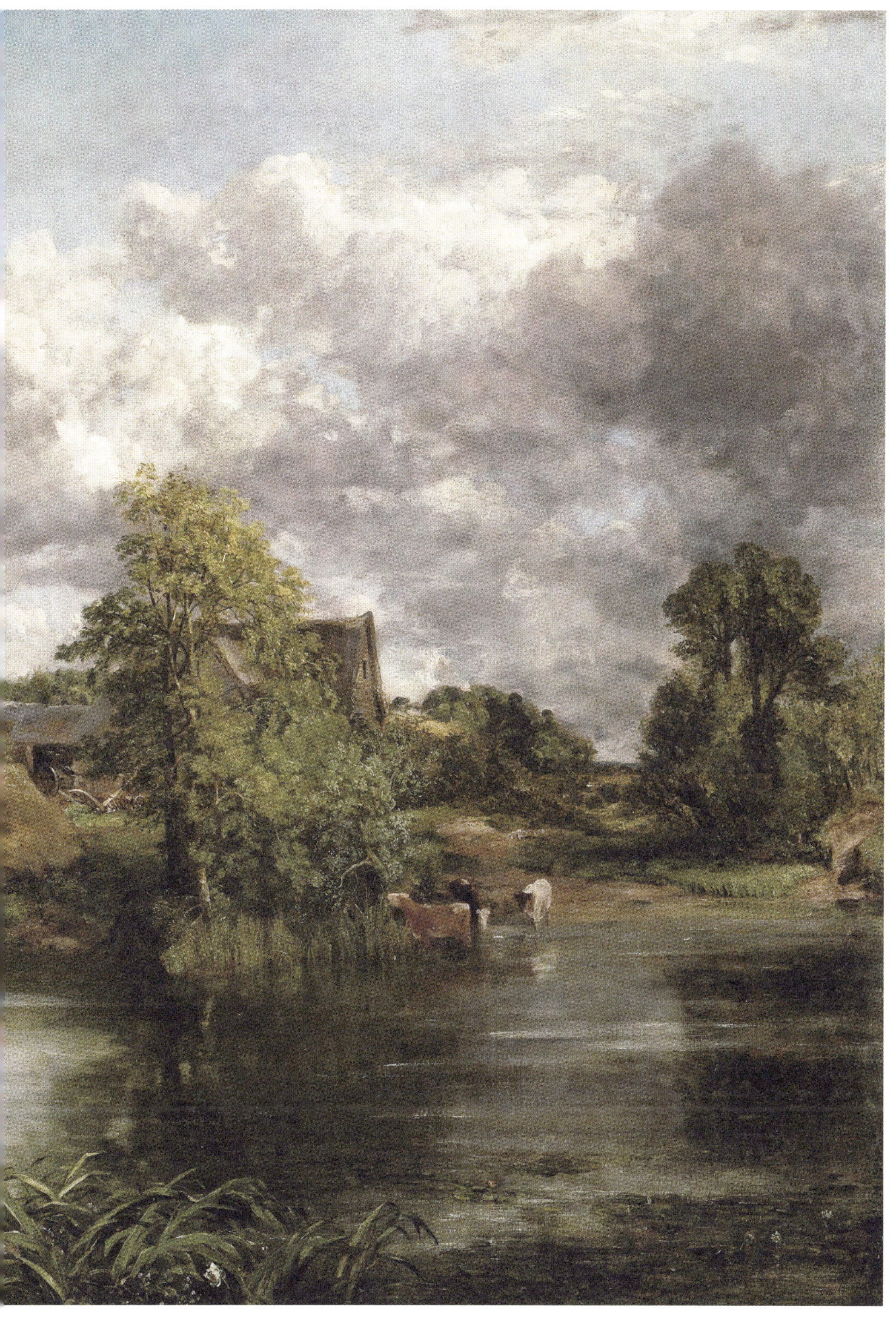

Bergholt House in 1774: the year their third child, Golding, was born, and just two years before his own birth. So Flatford had a sentimental resonance for him of the kind that early scenes of our parents' lives together often evoke. The place was certainly the pivot around which his pictorial imagination had revolved for the past two decades, the site of pictures like *Boat-Building* and *Flatford Mill*, painted on the spot. Anyone who has visited and tried to match up the pictures with the actual views will know how few steps he took in his search for compositions. But there was one scene that he had not tackled so far, though he had sketched it again and again. When he stood on the path with the mill building on his right and looked across the millstream, to his left, close to the water, was a substantial house occupied by a tenant farmer called Willy Lott, shaded from behind by tall trees. In front of him a view opened out over meadows.

From at least as far back as 1802 Constable had been making studies of Willy Lott's house, the millstream and the fields beyond from different angles. Now, in his studio, he got them out and propped them up; he had painted one sheet – rather inconveniently, now it came to it – on both sides. It was not so much that these images told him the facts of the view: he had known those all his life and had them by heart. It was more that they exuded a mood and a feeling: bright sunlight flaring on a white-washed wall, trees in their summer foliage reflecting in the still water. A slight breeze. The hum of insects and the rank, tangy smell of the water. Surrounded by precious sketches in his London painting room during those lamp-lit winter days, Constable was able to call to mind the warm air and sunlight of a long summer's day and let it feed his imagination. He had once described himself to Maria as a conjurer; one of his greatest feats was to express on canvas the feeling of a summer noon in the depths of winter.

Constable needed to animate his scene with incident, so, as usual, he chose agricultural labour. His theme was the process of haymaking, which, depending on the weather, takes place between late June and early September, when meadow grass has been allowed to grow tall and the sun promises to shine for several days. The grass is cut and spread out to dry; turned over and left to dry further; then baled and stored to make fodder for livestock over the winter. In Constable's picture, however, this process

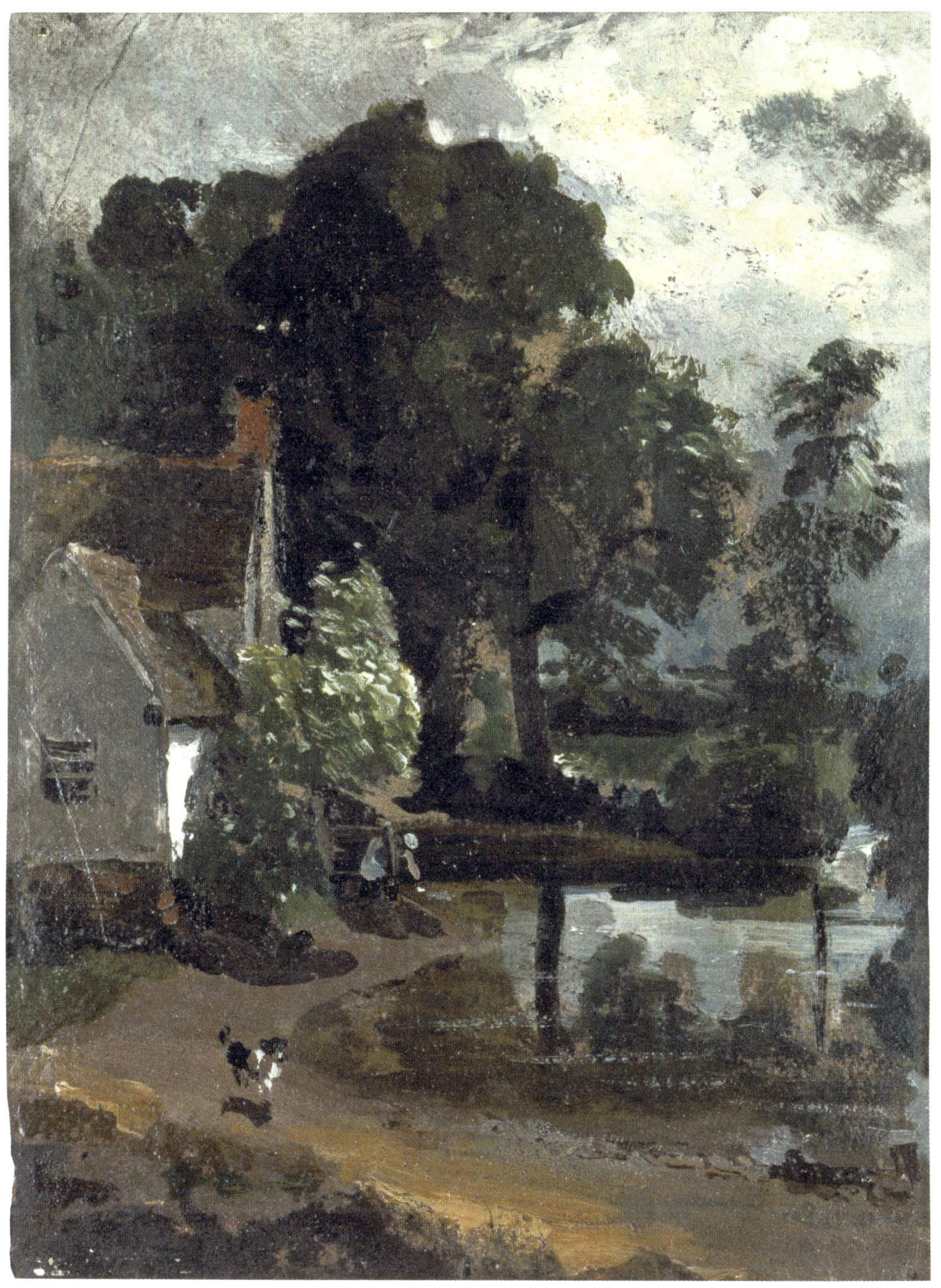

Willy Lott's house, c. 1811. Oil on paper.

happens in the distance and is easy to miss. In the far sunlit meadow a few tiny figures – would we even spot them if their white shirts did not catch the light? – bend forward to cut the tall grass. A man stands to sharpen his scythe. To the left, others pitchfork dried hay onto an already laden wagon or wain, one balancing on top of the bouncing load to distribute it evenly so it doesn't spill or topple over when in motion, though to the untrained eye it looks precarious enough. In this context, the purpose of the empty wagon in the foreground becomes clear. It is no more or less than a delivery vehicle that, having emptied its load, is now on its way back to the meadow. It is being driven through the millstream towards the flat ford across the River Stour that gave the place its name, silvery water running from its wheels as it begins its turn to the right.

Constable was, as ever, particular about detail. He could not find a suitable wagon among his own copious sketches of such vehicles, so he sent a message via Abram to his old friend John Dunthorne to ask if his artistic son, Johnny, who sometimes worked as his studio assistant, would draw the 'outlines of a scrave or harvest waggon' for him. It was hardly the weather for outdoor sketching, and Abram wrote to his brother towards the end of February reporting that poor Johnny had 'had a very cold job but the old Gentleman [Dunthorne senior] urged him forward saying he was sure you must want it as the time drew near fast'. Not only was the appearance of the wagon itself carefully based upon that of an actual Suffolk vehicle, but a technical detail is written into its progress: as the wheels pass slowly through the water, the wood, shrunk by the dry heat, would swell to fit the metal tyre more snugly – which made for a smoother journey. The man in the waistcoat who looks over the side of the wagon gestures to the driver; he may be telling him to slow down to make sure the wheels get a thorough soaking, and to allow time for the horses' legs to be refreshed by the cool water.

Specific features of each season mattered, and in Constable's paintings it is often possible to pinpoint the month and even the week of the year represented. This was easy for him when he was working on the spot. Five years earlier he was painting *A Cottage in a Cornfield* outdoors in Suffolk, carefully noting where the crop was still green because it was in the shadow of the building. From this keenly observed detail, we know that he painted it in July rather than August. Working in his studio was more of a challenge:

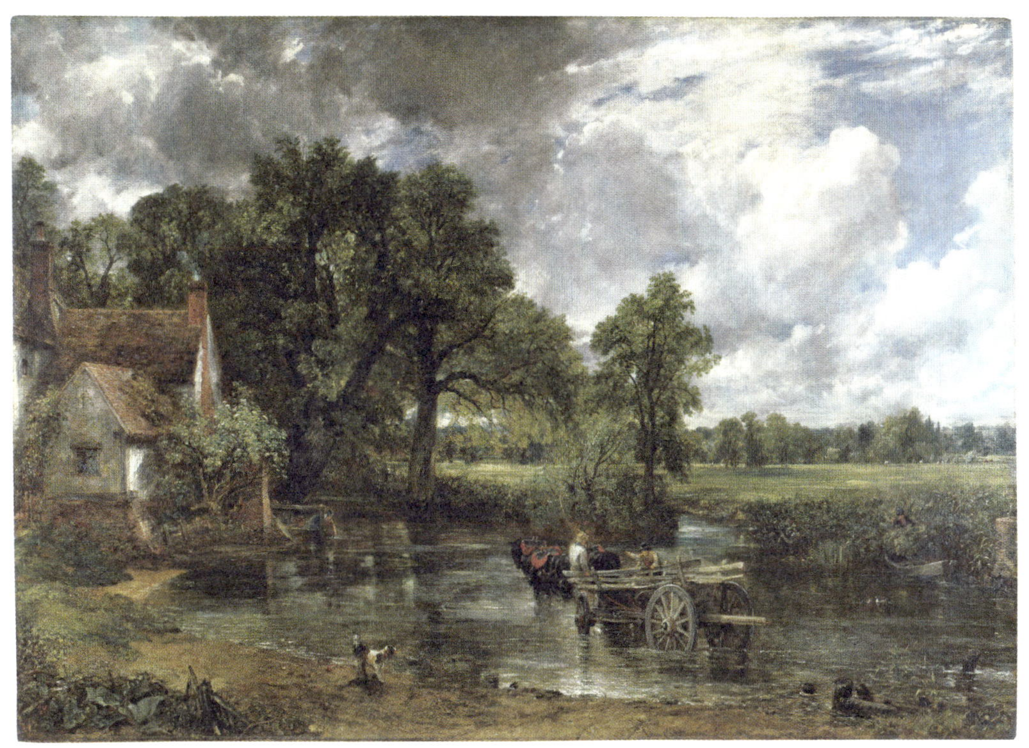

The Hay Wain, 1821. Oil on canvas. *Detail overleaf.*

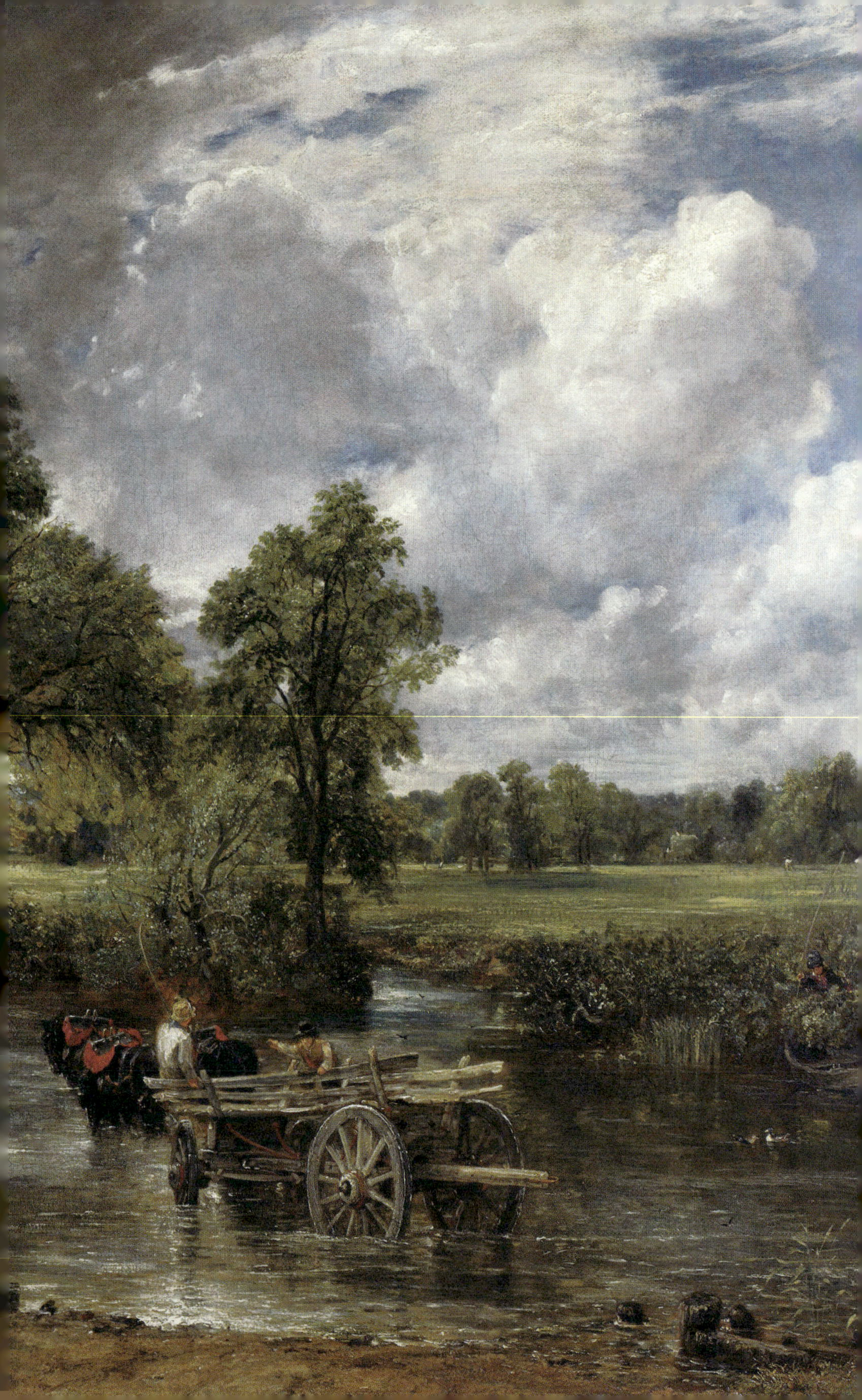

when painting *The Cornfield* in the early spring of 1826, he resorted to a botanist friend to advise him on the wild flowers it would be appropriate for him to include in his picture. 'I think it is July in your green lane', wrote Henry Philips.

> At this season all the tall grasses are in flower, bogrush, teasel. The white bindweed now hangs its flowers over the branches of the hedge; the wild carrot and hemlock flower in banks of hedges, cow parsley, water plantain, &c; the heath hills are purple at this season; the rose-coloured persicaria in wet ditches is now very pretty; the catchfly graces the hedge-row, as also the ragged robin; bramble is now in flower, poppy, mallow, thistle, hop, &c.

But in spite of his insistence on getting the details just right, Constable was constrained to work differently to how he had in the past, when he would set up his easel by the waterside. Or perhaps it wasn't a constraint. His marriage had altered the pattern of his year and disrupted the easy familiarity he had once had with his old Suffolk haunts. He was no longer at the scene to create the bright, outdoorsy realism of pictures like *Boat-Building* and *Flatford Mill*, nor did he benefit more generally from a lengthy annual top-up of East Bergholt and Flatford. Now, he had to negotiate a distance, to look through his mind's eye at scenes he must have witnessed virtually every one of the forty summers he had spent at his parents' home. Constable's vision of Suffolk was complicated by his separation from it. From the vantage point of his London workroom, he now saw the places he knew and loved through veils of memory and imagination. The act of putting brush to canvas was no longer about representation, but about recreation – and as such, it demanded a greater investment of emotion. As he would remark to Fisher the following year, 'Painting is but another word for feeling.' Who else would compare the two and conclude they were the same?

As a result of Constable's new vision, the painting of a cart making its way through a millstream, exhibited in 1821 as *Landscape: Noon* (later known, thanks to Fisher's casual name for it, as *The Hay Wain*), has some elements that are prosaic and others that are almost dreamlike. While the sunlight shining on the meadow and the breeze disturbing the smoke of Willy Lott's chimney come to us as immediate, visceral sensations, the summer atmosphere is more potent for being the product of memory. Constable was diving down through layers of cherished recollections to create a picture of agricultural work that was both seasonal and timeless. 'Whoa', says the man driving the cart. Pause here and now, at this pivot of the year, as the summer's growth is gathered in for the winter's feed. The sunlit labourers in the picture's background are a hazy mirage, ghosts of haymakers who, by 1821, had long since lain in the Suffolk clay, stretching back for generation upon generation, time out of mind.

A dismal day and a new beginning

When Maria was breathing the sea air at Brighton and John was in London at work at his easel, he missed the intimacy and inconsequential chat of their married life. For one reason and another, a significant proportion of their relationship had been conducted on paper, so writing to each other was nothing new. But now that they were separated for weeks at a time, Constable began to find ordinary letters to be ill-shaped vessels for the things they would normally have debated and laughed about: amusing gossip about neighbours; the antics of the cats, Mrs Hook and Billy; or the behaviour of a pair of quarrelsome pigeons that came into the house through a window left open on warm summer evenings. Each of these things may have been trivial in itself, but over time their shared subjects, jokes and bits of news thickened into a medium in which their marriage thrived. So to maintain the sense of continuous conversation, in order to feel close to his wife when they were apart – and she to him – Constable devised a new kind of letter that he would write like a journal. He would stop at the end of the day with no particular ceremony – 'Sat at home all the evening & there was a nice rain', for example – or break off with comic timing. 'Mr Fitzgerald has sent me a cock and two hens', he wrote on the evening of Friday 2 September 1825. 'They came late last night, and this morning – ' he concludes, finishing his sentence the following day: ' – we have commenced with such prodigious crowing, in answer to Mr Blatch's cock, that it is quite ridiculous – they seem quite at home already'. When he had written for several days, he parcelled up the sheets and sent them down to Brighton on the mail-coach.

Constable's journal-letters provide an intimate insight into his daily life, from what he ate for dinner – macaroni, beefsteak pudding, beans and bacon, toad in the hole, boiled mutton, gooseberry pie – to his pleasure at receiving a gold medal for *The Hay Wain* from Charles X of France, after it was exhibited in Paris to great acclaim. The journals (not, of course, intended to be read by anyone but Maria) allow their readers to feel the texture of his life, to hear the thoughts and impressions that are normally left unwritten. They hum with information and slip easily, almost disconcertingly, from reports of grand events at the Royal Academy to intimate domestic details and back again. At times it feels like eavesdropping to read a husband telling his wife about the flannel waistcoat he wore when he had a cold and how very much he wanted her next to him in bed at night.

In early December 1825, Constable went down to Brighton to see his family for a few days. When he returned to London, he took up his journal again. Among a wealth of other information, it tells us how he coped with the short winter days. He needed to get up early on Sunday 11 December to take a parcel of two hares and a pheasant for Maria to the office in charge of the Brighton coach. 'I sat up in bed & struck a light,' he wrote, 'having taken the tinder box up stairs, the night before. It is dismally dark & fogging & wet to day – & so it was yesterday. I had a lonely day.' He had a new pair of slippers that were warm and fitted 'delightfull'. He would bring some money 'to make all merry' when he joined them for Christmas. He had eaten an apple pudding for dinner. Earlier he had gone out without his great coat, and 'was, in consequence, much exposed to a nasty damp, cold air'. The weather was terrible, 'the sun did show itself like a ball of blood – & I dare say was very fine with you, but this is a dreary month here – & dark.' The next day was no better. 'So dark that we had a candle on the table at 10. In the morning could not paint.'

Later in the month, Constable left the painting of Waterloo Bridge that had occupied him on and off for years and joined his family in Brighton for Christmas. Between twelve and two o'clock on the afternoon of New Year's Day 1826, he went out onto the beach with his paintbox and, settling himself close to the water's edge, began to sketch the sea and the

Overleaf: *The sea at Brighton*, 1 January 1826. Oil on paper. Constable noted the place, date, time and weather conditions on the back of this sketch: 'Brighton. Sunday. Jany. 1st. 1826. From 12 till 2 PM. Fresh breeze from S. S. W.'

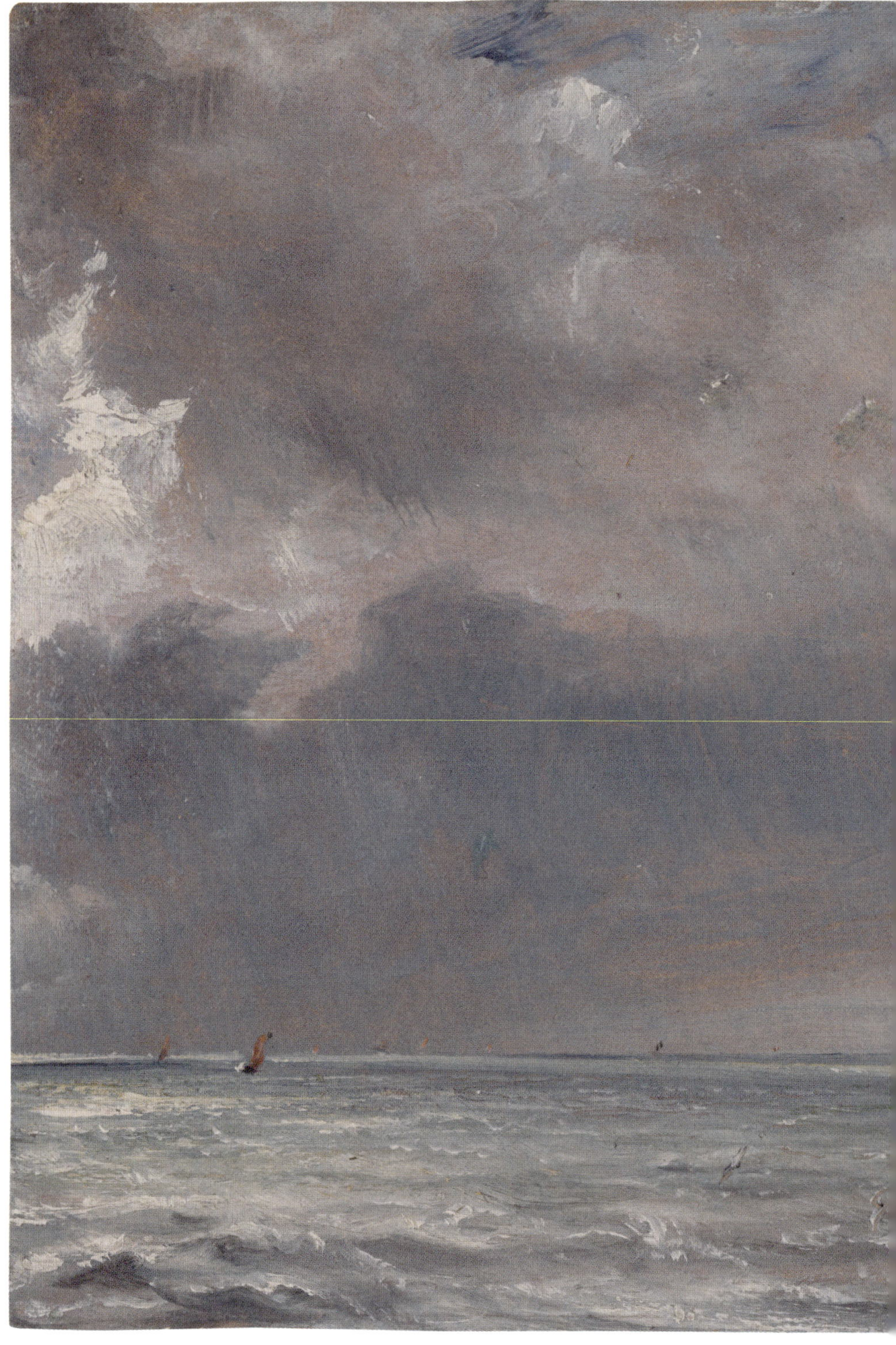

sky. It was a blustery day of fast-moving clouds, and the wind was whipping white foam onto the waves. Gulls were wheeling about, adding to the sense of wildness and melancholy he said he always felt at the shore. The low sun was tinting the clouds a fleshy pink. Just an hour after he finished it would be growing dusk. What drove him onto the beach with his paint-box that day, when he so seldom sketched outdoors in winter? As much as Constable adored children, the desire for an hour or so's respite from their noisy, crowded lodgings cannot entirely be discounted. And yet perhaps there was a deeper reason. He had a lot on his mind. Worry about Maria was nagging at his heart: she was far from strong. His eldest son John Charles was still recovering from a serious illness. But there they all were together. It was worth putting up with the cold on that first day of 1826 to record the sea and the sky, as those ancient elements endlessly renewed themselves in front of his eyes. It was the hinge of the year; but the shortest day was behind them. The cycle of the seasons was already at work on its familiar round.

The source of light

In the years following Maria's death, the emotional support of his close friends was more precious to Constable than ever. The sudden death of John Fisher in August 1832 therefore came as a profound shock. Fisher had been suffering from poor health for some time, and he and his wife had sailed to Boulogne hoping that he would benefit from a change of climate. Contracting cholera, however, he 'was seized with violent spasms' and died within hours. Constable mourned him deeply. 'I cannot say but this very sudden and awfull event has strongly affected me', he wrote to C. R. Leslie. 'The closest intimacy had subsisted for many years between us – we loved each other and confided in each other entirely – and this makes a sad gap in my life & worldly prospects.' He tended to negotiate his emotions with pencil or paintbrush in hand, whether his subject was his parents' tomb in the churchyard at East Bergholt, fir trees at Hampstead on his wedding anniversary or ruins on a windswept estuary, and it was no different now. As it happened, he had arranged to borrow a winter scene by the seventeenth-century Dutch artist Jacob van Ruisdael from its owner, Sir Robert

Peel, in order to copy it for use in a lecture on landscape painting he was planning. Now he saw the picture's terrible aptness. 'I shall pass this week at Hampstead, to copy the winter peice,' he told Leslie ' – for which indeed my mind seems in a fit state.' The composition's windmills, cottages, footbridge, boat and river could all have found homes in one of Constable's own paintings. But the snow and muted colours under a leaden sky? Those had never appeared and never would. So day after day, Constable mourned Fisher by mentally inhabiting a landscape made strange by ice. He mixed steel grey for clouds that would normally be bright, and a dirty white for the ground which in summer would be a variety of fresh greens. The composition he copied with such painstaking attention mirrored the experience of grief – familiar scenes stripped of the warmth and life that give them meaning.

Then came another death, close on the heels of Fisher's. The talented Johnny Dunthorne, son of his old friend and painting companion from East Bergholt, had helped Constable on and off in his painting room since 1814 by grinding pigments, preparing canvases, finishing paintings, copying portraits, admitting visitors and generally keeping things in good order. He had become a necessary member of the household; 'he cheers & helps me so much that I could wish him always to be with me', Constable had told Fisher. Constable recorded this beloved young man's death with a sad inscription on the back of his copy of the Ruisdael: 'Showed this Picture to Dear John Dunthrone [*sic*] Oct 30 1832 … Poor J Dunthorne died on Friday (all Saints) the 2d of November. 1832-at 4 o clock in the afternoon Aged 34 years.' The winter painting, so unlike Constable's lively summer views, became a memorial for both friends.

And yet Constable, with his experienced miller's eye, also saw signs of hope in the scene. Ruisdael's picture, he explained in his lecture on Dutch and Flemish landscapes,

> represents an approaching thaw. The ground is covered with snow, and the trees are still white; but there are two windmills near the centre; the one has the sails furled, and is turned in the position from which the wind blew when the mill left off work; the other has the canvas on the poles, and is turned another way, which indicates

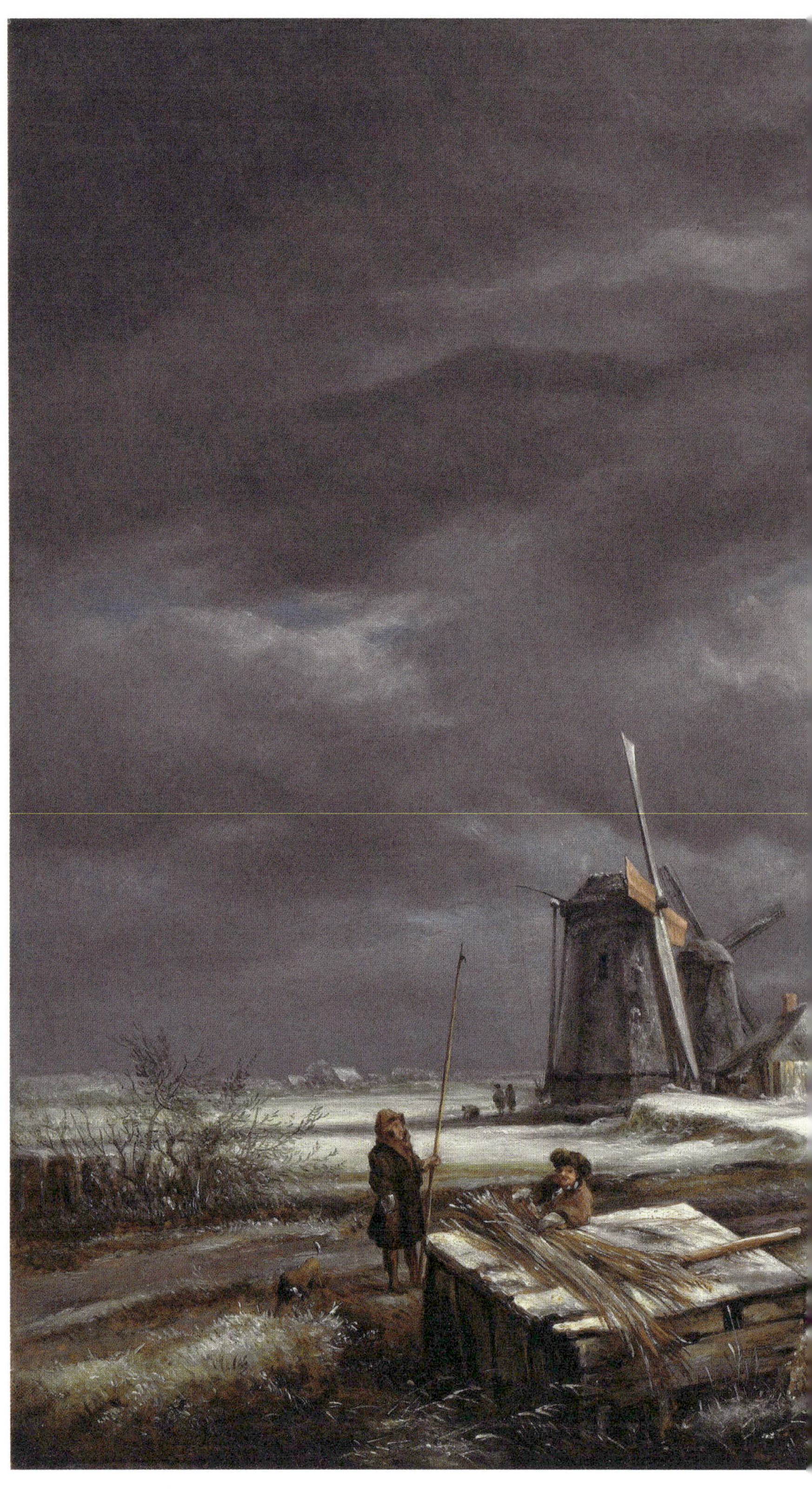

Winter, after Jacob van Ruisdael, 1832. Oil on canvas.

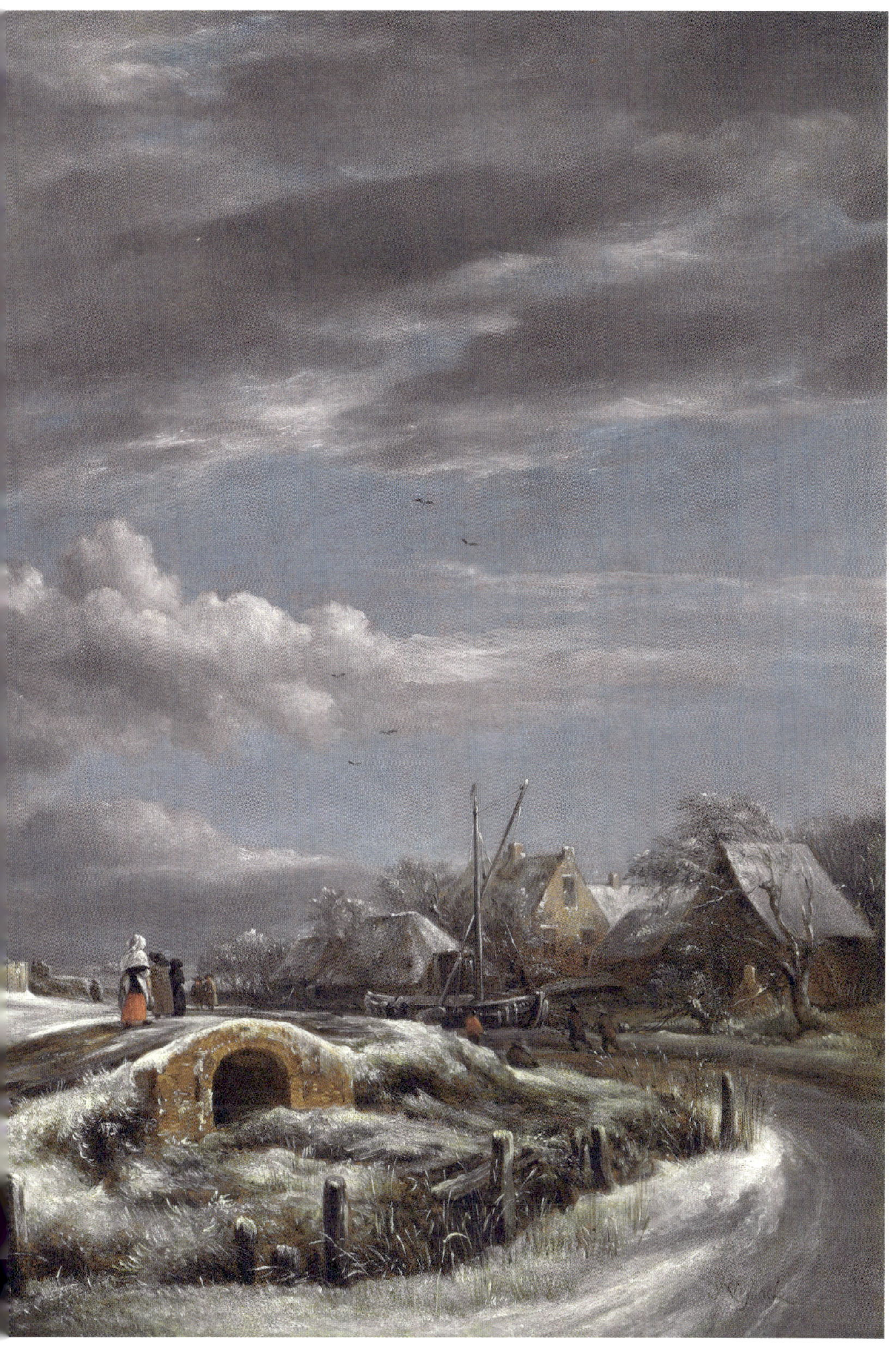

a change in the wind. The clouds are opening in that direction, which appears by the glow in the sky to be the south ... and this change will produce a thaw before the morning. The concurrence of these circumstances shows that Ruysdael *understood* what he was painting.

And so did Constable. Ruisdael's weather was not perpetual winter, just as Constable's emotions were not sealed in permafrost. Warmth would slowly return. The death of Maria had seasoned him in the process of grieving; perhaps it had taught him to look for rays of light to mitigate the darkness, for the flaring, frost-and-fire energy that, so many years later, T. S. Eliot was to call 'midwinter spring'.

Wintry landscapes appealed more to Constable as he got older. From the windows of the family home at Well Walk in Hampstead he could see for miles: 'our little drawing room commands a view unequalled in Europe,' he declared, ' – from Westminster Abbey to Gravesend.' It was an ideal weather-viewing platform, nearly as good as the heath itself. Writing to Leslie in the summer of 1833, he breaks his train of thought to exclaim *'What beautiful silvery clouds are rolling about to day!!!'* Later that year, on 7 December, he was at home when the sound of blustery wind and rain spattering against the glass caused him to look out at around three o'clock, when the light was already beginning to fade from the sky. Fetching his paper and watercolours, he rapidly sketched the weather drama that had caught his eye. As he recorded on the back of the sheet, it was a 'very stormy afternoon – & High Wind': the darkened foliage was tossing in the gusts and rain was slanting down from fast-moving clouds, making the dome of St Paul's Cathedral dissolve in a watery haze alongside the rest of London. The surface of the watercolour is marked here and there where water has blotted the pigment. Did Constable open the window to get a clearer view, inadvertently letting the rain in? If he did, the weather added its own fingerprints to his picture – just as it had, long ago, on Bowleaze Cove.

One day around this time, taking a sheet of writing paper, pen, brush and ink, he scribbled another stormy sky, with sunlight dramatically breaking through turbulent clouds. His cloud-watching must have reminded him

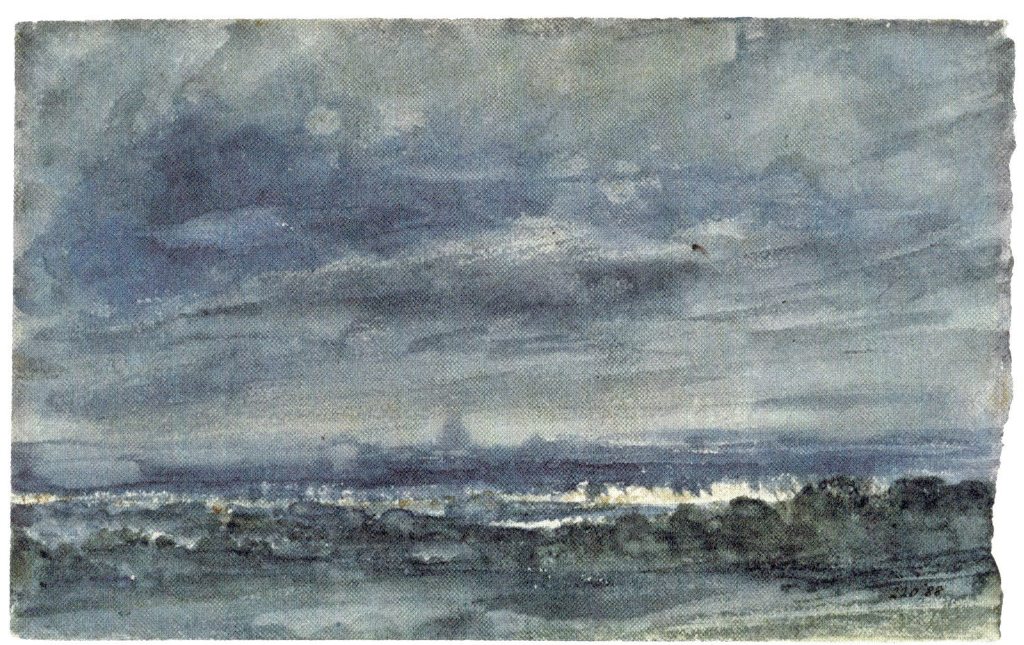

View at Hampstead, looking towards London,
7 December 1833. Watercolour on paper.

With saunt'ring step he climbs the distant stile,
Whilst all around him wears a placid smile;
There views the white-rob'd clouds in clusters driven
And all the glorious pageantry of Heaven.
Lone—on the utmost boundary of the sight,
The rising vapours catch the silver light.
Thence fancy measures—as they parting fly,
Which first will throw its shadow on the eye,
Passing the source of light; and thence away
Succeeded quick by brighter still than they.
Far yet above these wafted Clouds are seen,
(In a remoter sky still more serene)
Others, detach'd in ranges through the air,
Spotless as snow and countless as they're fair;
Scatter'd immensely wide from east to west,—
The beauteous semblance of a flock at rest.
These to the raptured mind aloud proclaim
Their mighty Shepheard's everlasting name.

Cloud study with verses from Robert Bloomfield, 1833. Pen and ink on paper.

of a section from 'Winter' in Robert Bloomfield's *The Farmer's Boy* that describes the lad climbing a stile and looking up to watch the sky, because Constable wrote out lines from the poem below the sketch:

> There views the white-rob'd clouds in clusters driven
> And all the glorious pageantry of Heaven.
> Low – on the utmost boundary of the sight,
> The rising vapours catch the silver light;
> Thence fancy measurs – as they parting fly,
> Which first will throw its shadow on the eye
> Passing the source of light; and thence away
> Succeeded quick by brighter still than they.
> Far yet above these wafted Clouds are seen
> (In a remoter sky still more serene)
> Others, detach'd in ranges through the Air,
> Spotless as snow and countless as they're fair;
> Scatter'd imensely wide from east to west, –
> The beauteous semblance of a flock at rest.
> These to the raptured mind – aloud proclaim
> Their mighty shepheard's everlasting name.

Bloomfield's close observation of cloud behaviour – not only of their shifting appearance but also their movement, their rising and ranging, which he himself could only suggest with static paint – must have delighted Constable. The Christian significance of the final lines, too: as he grew older, the spiritual temperature of his work rose. A sense of how the supernatural illuminates the natural world, of the transcendence of cloud bursts and rainbows, of the relationship of shadow to sunlight, burned ever more brightly in his paintings as the years went by.

A season of sadness

In 1829, the first year of his widowhood, Constable fell into the habit of looking back. Perhaps it was already entrenched; to create the great sequence of six-foot paintings of Suffolk he had begun ten years before, he had grown accustomed to delving as deeply into his memory as he always had into his sketchbooks, asking himself how familiar views might be changed and enriched by long reflection. Maria's death, however, pushed him into a yet more deeply retrospective mood. It was in this frame of mind, in what he described as a 'season of Sadness', that he began to publish a selection of his paintings as prints. Part of the justification for this project was the potential for financial gain that introducing his work to a wider audience might bring. But more important was the opportunity it gave him to take stock of his achievements; even to construct his autobiography in pictures.

Just as a written memoir might begin with the author's earliest years, Constable's pictorial chronicle starts with a picture of his birthplace, East Bergholt House, as the frontispiece. As he explains in the text he wrote to accompany it, the story he tells is intimately connected with the places in which his life and art were so deeply rooted.

> As this work was begun and pursued by the Author solely with
> a view to his own feelings, as well as his own notions of Art,
> he may be pardoned for introducing a spot to which he must
> naturally feel so much attached; and though to others it may
> be void of interest or any associations, to him it is fraught with
> every endearing recollection.

The prints, first published between June 1830 and July 1832 as *Various Subjects of Landscape, Characteristic of English Scenery, From Pictures Painted by John Constable, R.A.*, form a compendium of the places that had played important roles in his life: Dedham Vale, Flatford Mill, East Bergholt Common, Helmingham Park, Stoke-by-Nayland, Weymouth, Brighton, Hampstead Heath. Autobiographical, yes. But characteristic of English scenery? Not remotely. How could they be, when he had seen – and painted – so little of it? Compare a nearly contemporary work for which Turner made almost one hundred watercolours, Charles Heath's *Picturesque Views in England and Wales*, which first began to appear in 1827 (and had perhaps spurred Constable on to begin a similar project). Turner's magnificent plates range from Plymouth to Tynemouth, Caernarfon to Cambridge.

English Landscape, as Constable's work came to be known, focused on places he knew and loved; places where family and friends could be found. As Leslie observed, his subjects are nothing less than 'a history of his affections'. The project only served to underline Constable's long-entrenched habit of painting where he happened to be – a fruitful digging-down into place that makes his work resonate so powerfully today. In the London art world of the early 1830s, however, it would have been difficult to find a landscape painter less qualified to meet the expectations of a contemporary audience.

The chosen paintings were reproduced by mezzotint, a printmaking process in which a copper plate is first worked with a toothed tool that covers it with tiny indentations designed to hold ink. If, at that point, the plate were to be inked and an impression taken, it would print a uniformly rich black with a velvety bloom like the skin of a peach. The picture is created by scraping and polishing the areas that are to print grey or white, reducing or eliminating the ink-holding capacity of these parts of the copper plate. It was a strange, reverse kind of printmaking, this working from dark to light, but in skilled hands it was capable of producing images of great depth and intensity.

The skilled hands in this venture belonged to a young engraver, David Lucas. As Lucas began to prepare the plates, however, it became clear that the project was going to be far from straightforward. How could Constable not involve himself too deeply when the project was so profoundly personal? Although Lucas performed the seemingly miraculous feat of reproducing the expressive, painterly effects of Constable's brushstrokes on a copper plate, the artist was seldom satisfied. He complained; he lost his temper; he made copious notes and drew with chalk on countless proofs to show Lucas exactly where he was going wrong. One of the advantages of mezzotint was that it was possible to re-work parts of the plate: the contours of the landscape can be reshaped, for instance, or a figure be made to disappear from one spot and reappear in another. Not that such re-workings were always successful. 'I have taken much pains, with the last proof of the "Summerland",' Constable wrote to Lucas, 'but I fear I shall be obliged to reject it – it has never recovered from its first trip up, and the sky with the new ground is and ever will be as rotten as cow dung.' Throughout the letters and notes Constable sent to Lucas over the course of the project, anxiety tolls like a bell. 'My indisposition sadly worries me and makes me think (perhaps too darkly) on almost every subject', he wrote in March 1831. 'I have thought much on my book, and all my reflections on the subject go to oppress me – *its duration, its expence, its hopelessness of remuneration,* all are unfavourable.' The whole project, he lamented, had come to harass his mind 'like a disease'. 'I am now writing with the *two proofs* before me,' he told Lucas later that year, 'and I frankly tell you I could burst into tears – never was there such a *wreck.*'

Constable's outbursts of emotion were not only about specific flash points; they had a lot to do with the project as a whole. Maria's prolonged illness and premature death had ripped through the fabric of his life, leaving shreds and tatters. *English Landscape* mattered so much because it gave him the opportunity to make repairs. It was a way of retrospectively shaping his work – and his life – into a coherent story, of imposing order. It came from the same impulse that in later life led him to buy back those pictures he had sold when he got the chance, of gathering his visual story around him like a warm, protective cloak.

One might expect Constable to have used the project as a showcase for his greatest works, which tend to depict noonday scenes in high summer. But is *The Cornfield* included? No. *The Leaping Horse*? No. Where is *The Hay Wain,* that had brought him such fame in France? Also missing. One reason for his decision is that mezzotints of some of his larger paintings, necessarily scaled down, could have ended up looking like conventional reproductions, rather than the powerful works of art that Constable wanted them to be – and knew that Lucas was capable of producing. So for a significant proportion of the plates, he instead made the surprising decision to reproduce oil sketches that few but close friends would have seen. They were on a similar scale to the mezzotints, and so allowed Lucas to recreate the artist's brushwork in print, his richly velvety tones matching the expressive intensity of the original oil paint. But another reason for Constable's decision was that his oil sketches represent the landscape over a greater range of times of day and seasons of the year than his exhibited paintings. For one plate he selected the little painting based on a drawing he had made one blustery April in 1821, when East Bergholt Common was

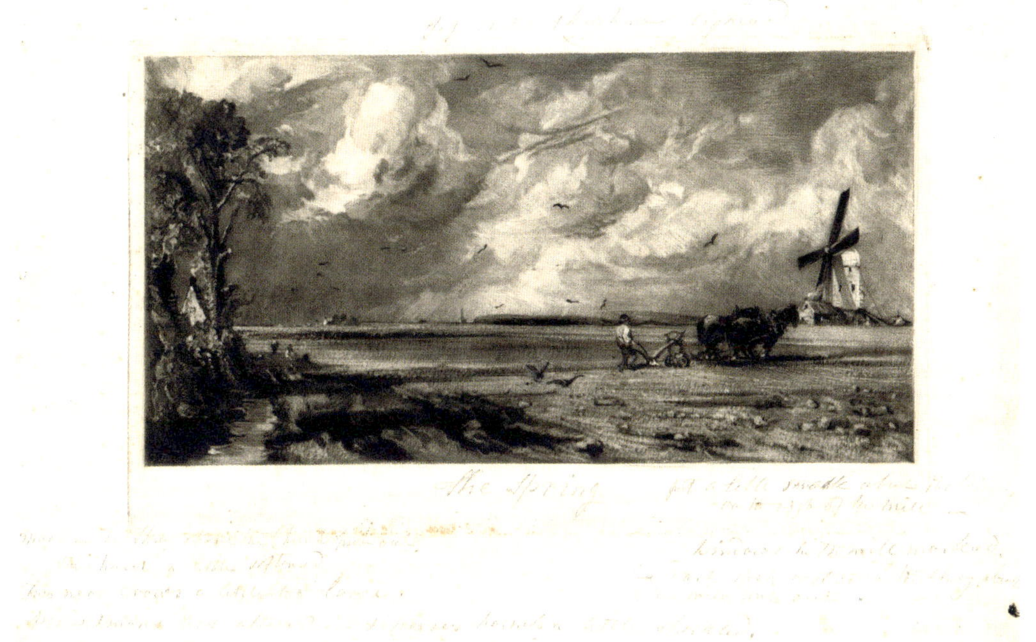

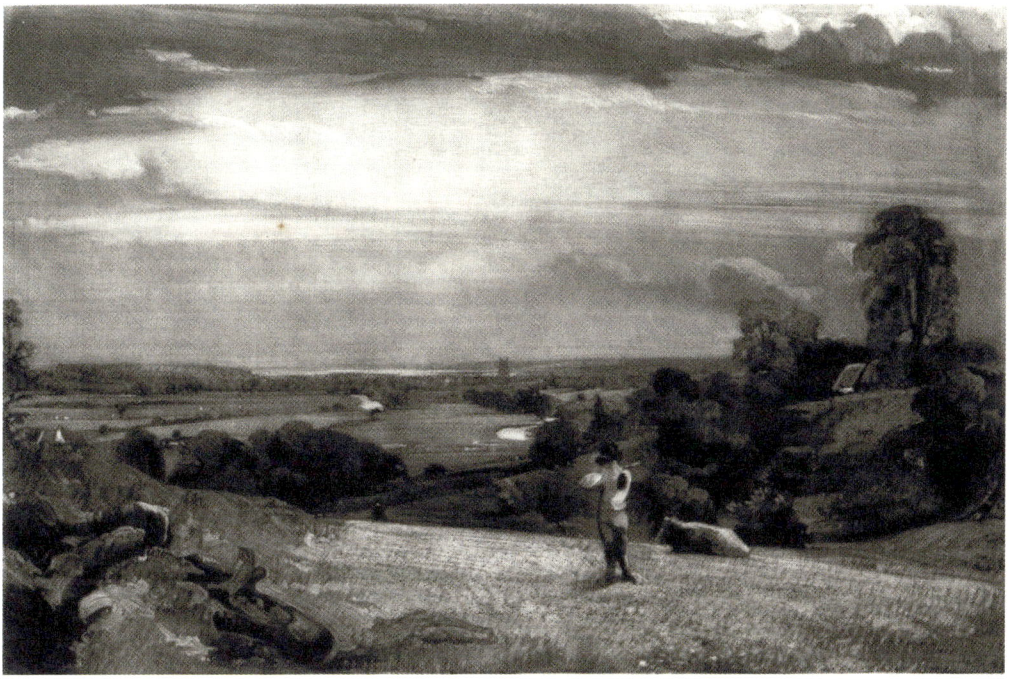

Top: David Lucas after Constable, with annotations by Constable, *Spring*, *c*. 1829. Mezzotint. The pencilled notes Constable made to David Lucas on this proof include 'Two near crows a little too large' and 'put a little smoke above the Cottages on the right of the mill'.
Above: David Lucas after Constable, *Summer Morning*, 1831. Mezzotint.

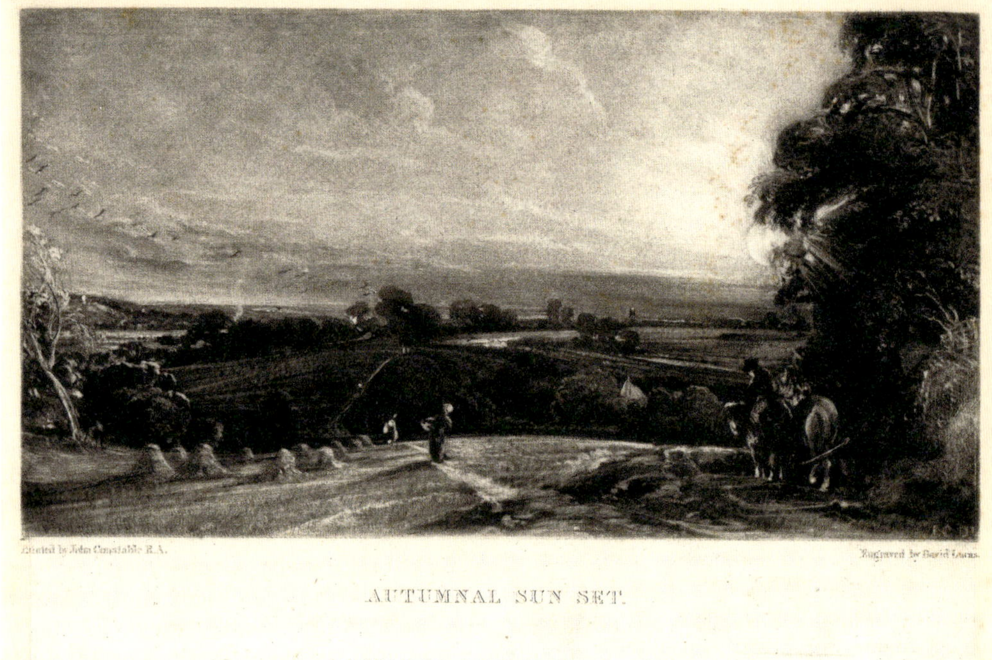

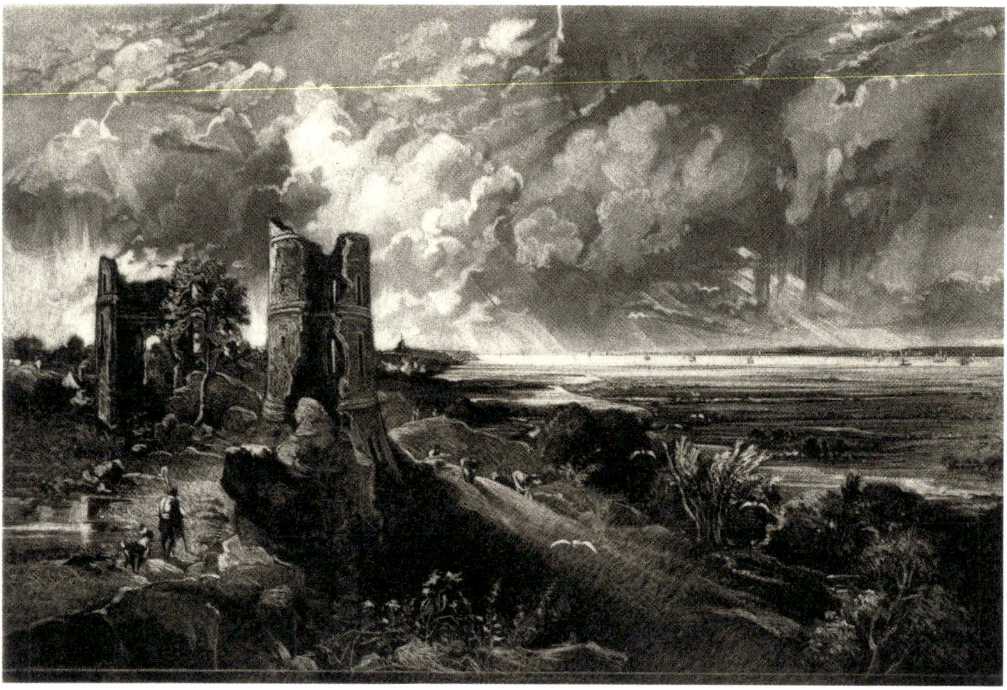

Top: David Lucas after Constable, *Autumnal
Sunset*, 1831. Mezzotint with drypoint.
Above: David Lucas after Constable, *Hadleigh
Castle near the Nore*, 1832. Mezzotint.

being ploughed, and simply called it *Spring*. He decided upon an oil sketch he had made from Langham in 1812 for a plate entitled *Summer Morning*, and a painting exhibited the same year for *Summer Evening*. He found an oil sketch of Dedham Vale that radiated golden light and called the plate *Autumnal Sunset*. The mezzotint *A Dell, Helmingham Park*, is based on one of his rare autumnal paintings; *Hadleigh Castle near the Nore* on his most wintry. The varied times of day and changing seasons described the passage of time; together, they rounded out the story of his art and his life.

Shadows

Despite the difficulties that were inevitable when a highly emotional perfectionist entrusts his work to the hands of another, Constable was fascinated by Lucas's translation of his paintings into wintry monochrome. He became preoccupied with the balance of brightness and shadow in a picture, known as 'chiaroscuro' from the Italian words for light and dark. 'It may be defined', he wrote, 'as that power which creates space; we find it everywhere and at all times in nature; opposition, union, light, shade, reflection, and refraction, all contribute to it.' These contrasts became such a pressing concern that he even updated the title of *English Landscape* when he issued a second edition in 1833: the phrase *'From Pictures Painted by John Constable, R.A.'* was substituted with *'Principally intended to mark the Phenomena of the Chiar' Oscuro of Nature'*. In his earlier years, graphite and oil had allowed him to capture the precise appearance of hedges, ploughs and the way leaves reflected sunlight; now, he had come to need a new visual language for what he found when he delved into his memory and sifted his feelings. Lucas's velvety blacks and bold chiaroscuro opened the door into exhilaratingly dramatic and emotionally charged territory.

Cloudbursts gripped his imagination. In 1830 he began *Salisbury Cathedral from the Meadows*, a painting in which thunderclouds and lightning play a leading role. 'Can it therefore be wondered at that I paint continual storms?' he asked Leslie one December day. '"Tempest o'er tempest rolled" – still the "darkness" is majestic.' Drawing imaginary landscapes was another outlet for his new obsession with chiaroscuro. A few days before Christmas in 1831, Constable was writing a letter to his sister Martha Whalley when at some point he turned the paper over. He took a brush, dipped it in the inkpot and sketched a stormy landscape, his hand moving across the sheet as swiftly as the wind to draw rain clouds above agitated ground, pushing the ink around to suggest trees silhouetted against the horizon. Over the years leading up to his death in 1837, Constable continued to make loose, tonal drawings that distilled the landscapes he kept in his mental storehouse. The ink he used – diluted to make shades of translucent mid-brown or in opaque, richly concentrated form – was the monochrome of dreams and memories. He drew a view of the Stour with the tower of Dedham church silhouetted against the sky, a vast, shadowy tree and a swoosh in the sky, either of sunrays or rain; he drew the Stour again with boats and trees, watery reflections and clouds suggested by liquid pools of ink. The fact that he did not write a date on a single one of these evocative drawings is revealing in itself. For once, it would have been meaningless. These were drawings of the Stour landscapes that had haunted him all his life, drawings of time that had passed and fallen in dense layers like autumn leaves. Of summer joys remembered in the shadows of winter. Of ghosts.

Constable's life had been beset by lateness. He had been late to enroll at the Royal Academy Schools; later still to marry; very late indeed to have been elected a Royal Academician, which only came in 1829, three months after Maria's death. (It elicited one of the saddest remarks he ever made: 'It has been delayed until I am solitary, and cannot impart it.') In the first half of the 1830s, in his late fifties – far from elderly, even by the standards of the day – he had reached the stage of life in which the death of friends and acquaintances had stopped being an occasional calamity and become a distressingly familiar occurrence. 'Thus am I almost dayly being bereft of some friend or other', he wrote unhappily to Leslie one day in 1833. And yet when death visited him in the early hours of 1 April 1837 – the cause of which was probably a heart attack – it was too early by far. As winter gave way to spring that year, he was right in the middle of things. He was busy teaching at the Royal Academy, directing the poses in the life room (he was, he grumbled to Leslie in February, 'beset with "models" in spite of this cold weather'). He had a painting on his easel of 'a beautifull subject',

A view on the Stour, *c.* 1836. Brush and ink over graphite on paper.

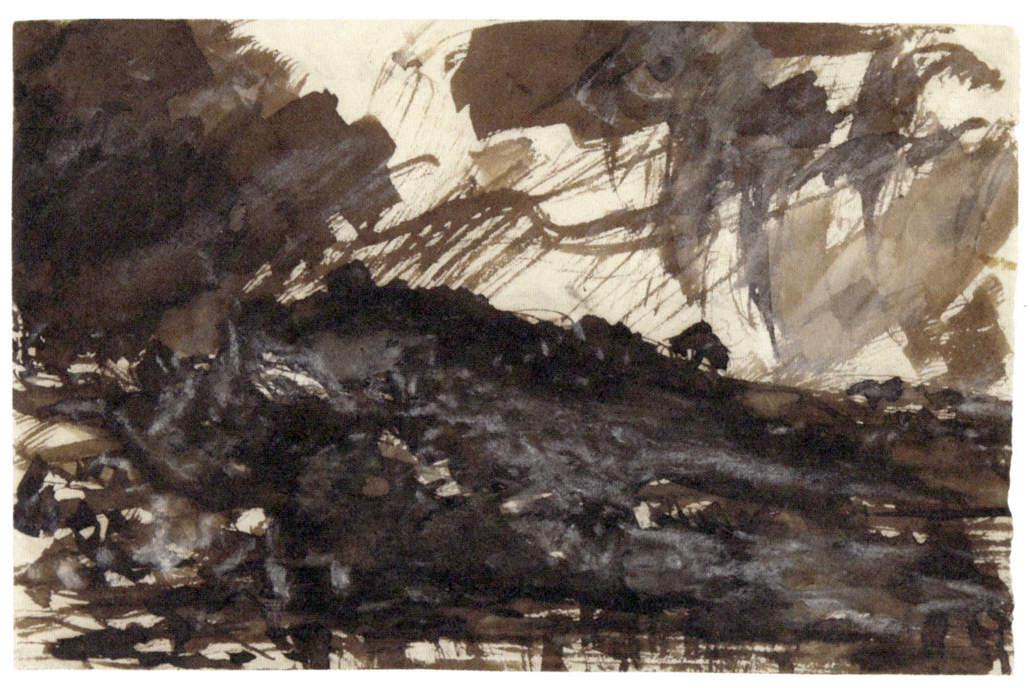

Stormy landscape, 19 December 1831. Brush and ink with white heightening on paper.

Arundel Mill and Castle, that he planned to exhibit later that year and which reminded him of Sussex, where in the summer of 1835 he had visited a close friend. He planned to marshal his observations about clouds and skies and deliver a lecture on the subject in the summer. Despite the growing roster of lost friends, he seems to have had no inkling that his own death was approaching. Leslie rushed to the house that morning as soon as he heard the news; he found Constable's pocket-watch ticking on his bedside table – he had, as usual, wound it the night before – next to a volume of the life and letters of that old favourite poet of his, Cowper.

Signs of frailty had been there to see, however. In February 1834 Constable had suffered a severe and excruciatingly painful attack of rheumatic fever from which he never fully recovered. 'I am an entire mass of helpless disease,' he wrote to his cousin, 'being unable to assist myself in even the smallest thing.' At the very end of December 1836, he wrote to Leslie thanking him for an invitation for his children to spend New Year's Day with his family. He explained how anxious he felt about making the journey to Pine Apple Place, the site of Leslie's house on the Edgware Road that overlooked open ground, although in truth it was within easy reach of Hampstead. 'This fearfull weather intimidates me,' Constable replied,

> – but it seems little likely to change. In spite however of all my
> dreads, & of all I can say about the danger of such an 'excursion
> into the country,' in this most inclement time, I can only say that
> it makes no alarm whatever in the children, & they insist on my
> coming out of my lurking hole where I had laid up for the winter.

And yet even in these last years, nature – especially of the Suffolk kind – could always lift his spirits and focus his mind on the future. 'What a fine season,' he had exclaimed joyfully to his children's tutor Charles Boner during a visit to Flatford the previous January; 'the birds are singing, the rooks busy, the meadows green, & the water & skies blue.' Even in midwinter, Constable was alive to signs of spring.

Epilogue

Constable was buried at Hampstead, in St John's churchyard on Church Row. The chest tomb that stands over the vault he shares with Maria and their eldest son glows in the spring sunshine and sparkles with frost in winter. In autumn, leaves from an oak tree fall gently onto its mossy stone.

What changes would Constable see, if he could visit his old haunts today? In Hampstead, his home on Well Walk (renumbered from 6 to 40) was up for sale in 2024 for almost £5 million. East Bergholt House, by contrast, fell into such neglect that it was demolished about three years after Constable's death, though the stable block, laundry and coach house remain. So does Old Hall, now an intentional community, and little Moss Cottage opposite, which in 1802 he rented as a painting studio – his mother called it his 'shop'. Down in Flatford, the Mill House, with its beautiful early eighteenth-century doorcase, has hardly changed. It is easy to picture Abram and Mary there, in summer with the door standing open, hearing the drone of insects from the warm surface of the millstream, or in winter, with ice frosting the water's edges. In my mind's eye I see brother Golding visiting, carrying his shotgun, a burly, outdoors figure whose movements make Mary nervous for the collection of china she has arranged on her dresser. And John, in a holiday mood, showing his two eldest the places that meant so much to him, overflowing with stories of his own childhood and staying as long as the glorious autumn weather held, only taking them back to London when the rain began to fall.

The River Stour was dangerously high when I last visited Flatford, dark and swift-flowing. It was an intensely cold day in early January and Golding Constable's dry dock was flooded. Climbing up Fen Lane and pausing to look over Dedham Vale, I saw watery fields reflecting clear skies. How often did Constable witness it like that? He described extreme weather in his letters, not his paintings; but although he did not depict these dramas – he was no Turner – they were folded into his vision. They fed his pictures, giving depth and resonance that only knowledge of the same spot over the changing seasons can bring.

But the world changed during Constable's lifespan and, 250 years after his birth, so has the weather. The effects of the industrial revolution that began near a place he once visited on a sketching tour are destabilizing the seasons themselves. A second industrial revolution, one that moves the world decisively away from its reliance on fossil fuels, is far from assured. In the anxious and unpredictable times we are living through today, the attentiveness to nature and place – the care – that shines out from Constable's brushstrokes is more necessary than ever.

Nature – whether grand or humble – mattered to Constable intensely and extravagantly. The changing seasons mattered; so did weeds, mill-ponds and the clouds in the sky. These things were more valuable to him than money; more precious, even, than his deep love for Maria – he could so easily have settled for a lucrative career and a more comfortable life for his family. As people all around the world suffer the effects of the climate crisis, Constable's stubborn refusal to compromise invites us to look at nature afresh: with his own combination of clear-eyed practicality and blazing passion.

Overleaf: A Cloud Study, Sunset, c. 1821. Oil and paper on millboard.

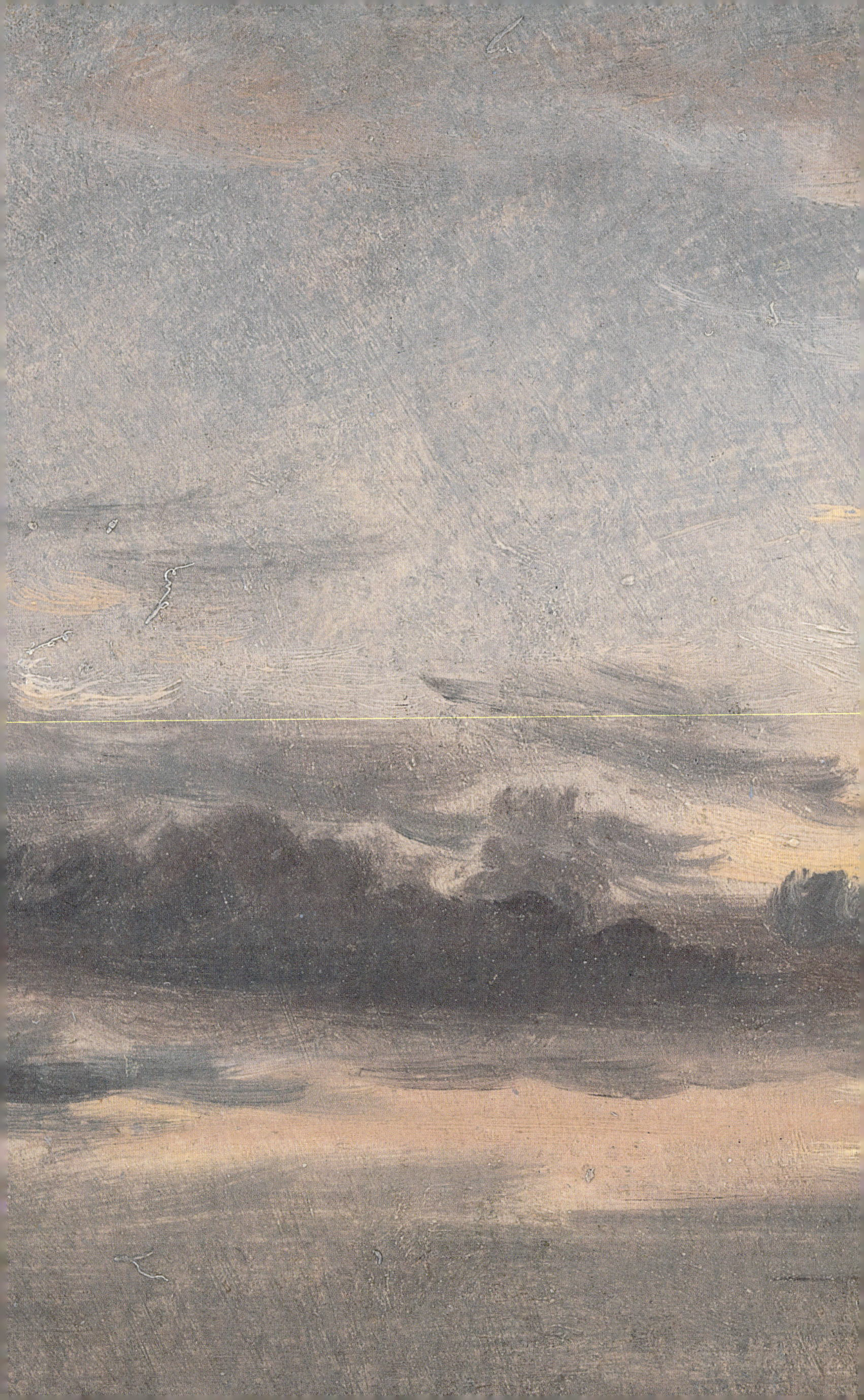

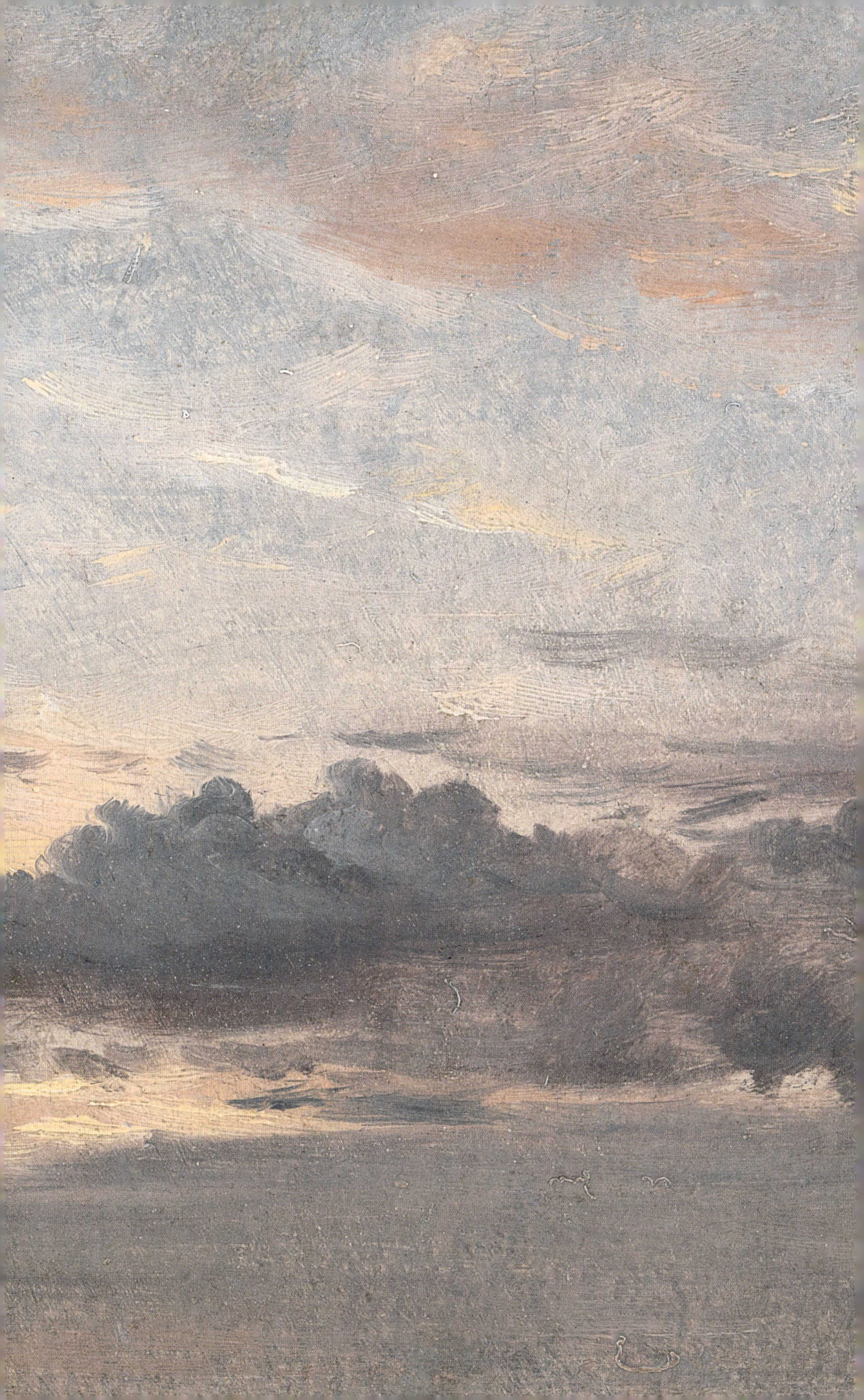

1776
John Constable, the fourth of six children, is born on 11 June at East Bergholt House to Golding Constable (1739–1816), corn merchant, mill-owner and gentleman farmer, and his wife, Ann Constable (1748–1815).

1792
At sixteen Constable leaves his grammar school in Dedham and begins training in the family business for what would ultimately be a managerial role. This involves working in his father's windmill on East Bergholt Heath, gauging meteorological conditions and familiarizing himself with the navigable River Stour, the movement of barges and the docks at Mistley, where goods are transferred from warehouses to vessels and shipped up the Thames estuary to London. Constable continues to paint and draw in his spare time, often in the company of his friend John Dunthorne, an amateur landscape painter, plumber and glazier.

1795
Ann Constable arranges for her son to be introduced to the art patron, collector and amateur artist Sir George Beaumont, then visiting his mother in Dedham. Beaumont encourages the young artist and continues to be an important mentor until his death in 1827. Constable has the opportunity of studying a greatly prized painting by Claude Lorrain, *Hagar and the Angel* (1646), in Beaumont's

collection. He described his first sight of the picture, which would exert an influence on his later work, as 'an important epoch in his life'.

1796
On a visit to stay with his uncle Thomas Allen, a brewer, at his country house in Edmonton, Constable is introduced to a group of collectors, antiquarians and connoisseurs. These include the professional artists John Cranch and J. T. Smith (known as 'Antiquity Smith' because of his predilection for antiquarian subjects). Under their guidance Constable improves his drawing skills. Cranch supplies him with a reading list on art practice.

1797
Constable experiments with etching. At Smith's request he researches Gainsborough's life and work in Ipswich. In the autumn he goes to stay with Smith in London. Although he wants to make art his profession, he informs his friend dejectedly that he must instead 'attend to my Father's business', adding: 'and now I see plainly it will be my lot to walk through life in a path contrary to that which my inclination would lead me.'

1798
Constable continues to work in his father's business and maintains contact with Smith. He makes several sketches of picturesque cottages. In the autumn he invites Smith to stay with his family

at East Bergholt, and it is his older friend's encouragement that paves the way for Golding senior's decision to allow John to study art professionally. This is the year Constable meets Dr John Fisher, who is to become an important mentor, friend and patron. Fisher is rector of Langham and canon of Windsor; he would later become Bishop of Salisbury.

1799

1799 is a decisive year in Constable's life. He is freed from the obligation to take over his father's business when his younger brother Abram, then aged sixteen, agrees to take his place, and his parents consent to him moving to London to study art. In February he presents himself, with a letter of introduction, to Joseph Farington, an influential Royal Academician who is to be an important mentor; he records many of his conversations with the young artist in his diary. On 4 March, on Farington's recommendation, Constable is admitted to the Royal Academy Schools as a Probationer and begins drawing in the Antique School. He becomes friends with fellow student R. R. Reinagle and shares lodgings with him. He returns to Suffolk in August.

1800

In June Constable receives a Royal Academy Student's ticket that permits him to draw from the living model. Having spent the first half of the year in London, in July he returns to Suffolk, where he sketches in Helmingham Park and makes a group of panoramic views of the Stour Valley as a wedding present for a friend, Lucy Hurlock. He

continues to cultivate connections with Beaumont and Farington, both of whom give him practical advice and access to Old Master paintings, prints and drawings to copy.

1801

Constable parts from Reinagle, with whom he has fallen out, and takes rooms at 50 Rathbone Place. He tells Farington that he is discouraged by some of Reinagle's remarks about his art. Between April and June he spends time with his married sister Martha Whalley and her family in the Minories, in the Aldgate area of the City of London. In late July he goes for a lengthy stay with Martha's father-in-law at his home in Fenton, Staffordshire. In August he makes a three-week tour of the Peak District, producing on average two drawings a day.

1802

Another decisive year. Constable enters a painting into the Royal Academy Summer Exhibition for the first time and it is accepted. Seeing his own landscape hanging in the context of others gives him confidence, but also makes him realize that until then he had been too reliant on the work of other artists, 'running after pictures and seeking the truth at second hand'. He decides that direct and sustained study from nature is vital for the future direction of his art. Between June and October he is in East Bergholt, where he spends an intensive period painting oil sketches outdoors. He rejects the chance of employment as a drawing master at the new Military Academy at Marlow.

1803

He exhibits four works at the Royal Academy. In April and May he makes a month-long trip down the Thames and along the Kent coast on the East Indiaman *Coutts*, which is on the first leg of her outward voyage, and produces many drawings. He then goes to East Bergholt for four months.

1804

Constable decides not to exhibit at the Royal Academy. Much of his time is taken up by painting portraits for ridiculously low prices – two guineas for a life-sized bust-length portrait and three guineas if they wanted him to include a hand (the equivalent of around £100 or £150 today).

1805

He is commissioned to produce an altarpiece for Brantham Church in Suffolk. He is in Suffolk in October and November, where he makes several watercolour views, working with a new freedom.

1806

Constable sends a large watercolour of Lord Nelson's flagship *Victory* to the Royal Academy exhibition. In August he visits cousins, the Gubbins family, at Epsom, where he makes many lively sketches of them. In September and October he spends seven weeks touring the Lake District, a trip funded by one of his uncles, David Pike Watts. He produces an average of two landscape drawings a day, most in watercolour. During his stay he meets William Wordsworth and Samuel Taylor Coleridge.

1807

He spends the year mostly in London and the near vicinity, not getting to East Bergholt until nearly Christmas. He uses drawings he had made in the Lake District as the basis for three submissions to the Royal Academy exhibition. He considers putting his name forward for an Associateship of the Royal Academy but decides against it. An introduction to the Earl of Dysart results in a commission to make copies of family portraits by John Hoppner and Thomas Lawrence. Bishop Fisher becomes chaplain to the Royal Academy.

1808

He continues to exhibit paintings based on his visit to the Lakes, and is much occupied with painting portraits. He makes many drawings at the Academy's life class at this time. In the autumn he paints naturalistic oil sketches of the Stour Valley landscape.

1809

In July he spends nearly a month in the Midlands, staying with H. G. Lewis at Malvern Hall, Warwickshire, in order to paint a portrait of Lewis's thirteen-year-old ward, Mary Freer. He tours the district and makes drawings of Warwick and Solihull. By the autumn he is back in East Bergholt, where he is reacquainted with Maria Bicknell, the twenty-one-year-old granddaughter of Dr Rhudde, the rector of East Bergholt. John and Maria fall in love. He realizes, however, that without financial security, marriage is impossible. They begin a protracted and often painful courtship.

1810

Constable renews his desire to capture the appearance of the natural landscape in outdoor oil sketches, to which he would refer in his London studio when preparing pictures for exhibition. There is a new boldness in his colours and vigour in his handling of the paint. After consulting Farington he seeks election as Associate of the Royal Academy (ARA) for the first time, but receives not a single vote. He spends around three months in Suffolk between August and November and is occupied with a commission for an altarpiece at Nayland Church. He makes a series of oil sketches and drawings in preparation for an ambitious exhibition picture for 1811, *Dedham Vale: Morning*. No painting, he later told his engraver David Lucas, had ever caused him more anxiety; 'he had even said his prayers before it'.

1811

At the Royal Academy, he exhibits *Dedham Vale: Morning*, a large landscape that he sees as a turning point in his career. In the early autumn he spends three weeks in Salisbury as the guest of the Bishop, Dr John Fisher, and his wife. There he meets Bishop Fisher's nephew, the younger John Fisher, who was to become his closest friend and confidant. On 17 December, Maria Bicknell becomes so discouraged about their prospects of being able to marry that she writes to Constable and attempts to break off their relationship; he acts decisively, jumping on the coach to Worcester to where she is staying with her aunt and successfully persuading her not to give up hope. He writes afterwards that some of the happiest hours of his life were those they spent together there – mixed with moments of 'unutterable sadness'.

1812

The year begins with Constable feeling depressed about his prospects of marrying Maria. In early January his younger sister Mary joins him in his lodgings at Charlotte Street and stays for several months to keep him company. He exhibits several works at the Royal Academy, including *Flatford Mill from the Lock* and *Summer Evening*. He then goes back to East Bergholt from mid-June and stays until early November, making numerous oil sketches. In September he is in Wivenhoe to paint a portrait of the daughter of General Slater-Rebow. His father attempts to persuade him to stay in Suffolk and to focus on portrait painting.

1813

He exhibits *Landscape: Boys Fishing* at the Royal Academy. Portrait commissions take up the early part of the year. Courtship with Maria is going badly: Maria's father disapproves of Constable writing to his daughter, and by the end of January he is no longer received at her London home, Spring Gardens. In June he goes to Suffolk where he stays until mid-November. The sketchbook he uses over those months is now in the Victoria and Albert Museum (V&A).

1814

Constable exhibits *Landscape: Ploughing Scene in Suffolk* at the Royal Academy. In February, he writes to Dunthorne asking him to send his gifted and cheerful son Johnny, then sixteen, to London to be his studio assistant, a role he performs on and off for many years. 1814 sees a change in Constable's working method. Before, he tended to work on paintings in the studio, referring to sketches made in the open air. In 1814 he begins to paint pictures outdoors, directly from nature. He goes to East Bergholt in June, and spends a fortnight with a family friend, the Rev. W. W. Driffield, at Feering and touring south-east Essex. He stays in East Bergholt until 4 November; in the V&A there is another sketchbook from these months. He confides in Maria that he feels increasing confidence in his abilities as a landscape painter. Farington tells him that people object to the apparently unfinished, sketchy quality of his pictures and recommends that he study paintings by Claude Lorrain.

1815

In 1815 he sends the maximum permitted number of exhibits – eight – to the Royal Academy exhibition, including *The Stour Valley and Dedham Village* and *Boat-Building*. The family is cast into mourning at the sudden death of Ann Constable at the end of March. Because of a clash with the dates on which works of art may be submitted to the Royal Academy to be considered for the Summer Exhibition, John does not return to East Bergholt to attend his mother's funeral. Portrait commissions keep him in London throughout June. He is able to see Maria in Putney, where her father has a house, and feels that his position is improving. In July he leaves for Suffolk and spends four months working in the fields during a period of particularly fine weather. Because of the rapid decline in his father's health, he decides to spend most of the winter in East Bergholt. Apart from visits to London in November 1815 and January 1816, he remains in Suffolk until March 1816.

1816

The Wheatfield is exhibited at the Royal Academy. His father dies on 14 May. Constable's share of the inheritance, while not large, allows him to marry Maria. He spends the earlier part of the year in Suffolk and Essex, painting and drawing from nature. 1816 is the 'year without summer', because of the eruption of Mount Tambora the previous year. In September he paints *Flatford Mill: Scene on a Navigable River*, largely out of doors. On 2 October, John Fisher marries John and Maria at St Martin-in-the-Fields, London. On their honeymoon the couple visits Bishop Fisher and his wife at Salisbury, then goes to Osmington in Dorset to stay for six weeks with the younger John Fisher and his wife Mary.

1817

Flatford Mill: Scene on a Navigable River is exhibited at the Royal Academy. In July, Constable and Maria move from his lodgings at 63 Charlotte Street, where he had lived for five years, to a house at 1 Keppel Street, Bloomsbury. From mid-July to late October the couple pay an extended visit to East Bergholt, where Constable makes detailed studies of the church, lanes and trees, as though fixing it in his memory at this pivotal point in his life. Their first child, John Charles, is born on 4 December 1817.

1818
Constable exhibits six works at Royal Academy: four oils and two drawings. He paints at least eight portraits. He fits in two brief visits to East Bergholt in July and October to make arrangements for the sale of the family home; on 28 October he makes a drawing of his parents' tomb in the churchyard at East Bergholt. In November he receives only one vote in the election for Associateship of the Royal Academy.

1819
The first few months of the year are spent working on his first 'six-footer', *The White Horse*, for exhibition at the Royal Academy. For the first time he prepares a full-scale oil sketch. The painting is purchased by Fisher for 100 guineas. In May, Constable makes a brief visit to East Bergholt before the three-day sale of the contents of East Bergholt House. The death of Dr Rhudde results in a bequest to Maria, which frees Constable from having to accept portrait commissions. On 19 July their second child, Maria Louisa (Mini or Minna), is born. In August, anxious about Maria's health, he first takes summer lodgings for his family in semi-rural Hampstead and divides his time between there and Keppel Street. Between October and November he fills a sketchbook with drawings of Hampstead, East Bergholt and Putney, now in the British Museum. On 1 November he is finally elected Associate of the Royal Academy.

1820
In February, Constable receives no votes at the election of Royal Academicians. He exhibits his second River Stour 'six-footer', *Stratford Mill*, at the Royal Academy, where it is bought by John Fisher as a gift for his solicitor. Constable takes Maria and their children to Salisbury for a long summer visit in July and August. They stay with Fisher, who in 1819 had been appointed canon residentiary of Salisbury Cathedral, a post that brought with it a spacious house in the Cathedral Close. Constable makes many drawings of the cathedral and the surrounding area, including Stonehenge and Old Sarum. After their return to London, he begins making sketches of skies and trees on Hampstead Heath. Towards the end of the year he starts work on *The Hay Wain*.

1821
In February he receives no votes at the election of Royal Academicians. His third 'six-footer', *The Hay Wain*, is exhibited at the Royal Academy. On 29 March his and Maria's third child, Charles Golding, is born. In mid-April he goes briefly to Suffolk and in June he accompanies Fisher on the latter's archidiaconal visitation of Berkshire, making drawings as they travel. On 17 June he settles with his family at 2 Lower Terrace, Hampstead. Over the summer and the autumn, he carries out an intensive campaign of what he called 'skying', observing and painting clouds, weather and light effects. In November he visits Fisher in Salisbury.

1822
In February he ties with William Daniell in the first round at the election of Royal Academicians, but loses seventeen–eleven in the second round.

He exhibits *View on the River Stour near Dedham*, his fourth six-footer, at the Royal Academy. In October Constable moves his growing family from Keppel Street to a more spacious house at 35 Charlotte Street, Fitzroy Square, the former residence of Farington, who had died the previous December. This will remain Constable's London home until his death. In the summer the family settles at 2 Lower Terrace, Hampstead, where he makes more oil studies of skies. The couple's fourth child and second daughter, Isabel, is born on 23 August.

1823

In February Constable receives three out of twenty-eight votes at the election of Royal Academicians. The house move in 1822, ill-health in the household and pressure to complete a commission from Bishop Fisher result in Constable having prepared no six-foot canvas for the Royal Academy Summer Exhibition, though he exhibits *Salisbury Cathedral from the Bishop's Grounds*, which he describes as 'the most difficult subject in landscape I ever had upon my easil'. In April he makes a brief visit to Flatford. For the summer he takes lodgings for his family at Stamford Lodge, Hampstead. In August and September he takes a three-week holiday with Fisher, during which they mainly stay at Gillingham in Dorset. In October he accepts an invitation to Coleorton Hall, the Leicestershire home of Sir George and Lady Beaumont, where he stays for six weeks.

1824

The Lock, Constable's fifth River Stour 'six-footer', is exhibited at the Royal Academy exhibition and purchased by the entrepreneur James Morrison. In May he takes lodgings for his family in Brighton, the first of several stays there; he works mostly in his London studio but travels down to be with them when he can. He begins to write hybrid diary-letters for Maria with detailed accounts of his daily life. *The Hay Wain* is exhibited at the Paris Salon and awarded a gold medal by Charles X. His reputation quickly grows in Paris, with the French art world seeing a rejection of convention and a fresh, dewy liveliness in his paintings that the English interpret as undesirable sketchiness. Constable joins his family in Brighton on 17 July and stays until mid-October, drawing and painting many Brighton scenes. The family returns to London on 2 November and by the end of the year Constable has *The Leaping Horse* in hand.

1825

Constable exhibits *The Leaping Horse*, his sixth and final River Stour six-footer, at the Royal Academy. His daughter Emily is born on 29 March; Bishop Fisher dies in May. Constable takes his family to summer accommodation at Hooks Cottage, Hampstead, but the serious illness of his eldest son John Charles causes him to transfer the family to Brighton at the end of August, where they stay until the following January. Constable remains in London and finally joins his family for Christmas, returning to London in January. His work is included in the British Institution's exhibition of modern English masters, suggesting his rising status.

1826

On New Year's Day Constable paints a view of the sea at Brighton. He receives only two votes in the second round at the election of Royal Academicians. He makes a brief visit to East Bergholt in April and exhibits *The Cornfield* at the Royal Academy exhibition. He is engaged in making replicas of *Salisbury Cathedral from the Bishop's Grounds*, *The Lock* and other, smaller pictures. In July he takes the family to Hampstead. He lets the upper half of the Charlotte Street house, keeping his studio and a few rooms for his own use, and begins to search for a permanent residence in Hampstead. His and Maria's sixth child, Alfred Abram, is born on 14 November.

1827

February sees the death of Sir George Beaumont. Constable exhibits *The Chain Pier, Brighton* at the Royal Academy. He transfers his family to 6 Well Walk in Hampstead, which was to remain Constable's home until 1834. In October he takes a holiday at Flatford with his two eldest children, John Charles and Minna; he introduces them to their aunts and uncles and makes numerous sketches on the banks of the Stour.

1828

John and Maria's seventh and last child, Lionel Bicknell, is born on 2 January. Constable is again unsuccessful in canvassing for election as a Royal Academician. He exhibits *Dedham Vale* and *Hampstead Heath* at the Royal Academy. Maria's health declines rapidly in the spring; he takes her to Brighton in May, but her condition does not improve. He takes her back home

to Hampstead at the end of July. On 23 November, she dies of tuberculosis, leaving Constable with seven children under the age of eleven. He would wear mourning for the rest of his life.

1829

On 10 February Constable is at last elected a full Royal Academician. He puts aside resentment at being overlooked for so many years and henceforth plays an active role at the Academy. As a Diploma Work, he presents *A Boat Passing a Lock*. He exhibits *Hadleigh Castle, the Mouth of the Thames – Morning after a Stormy Night* at the Summer Exhibition. He commissions the talented young engraver David Lucas to start work on a series of mezzotints reproducing both exhibited paintings and oil sketches, which he calls *Various Subjects of Landscape, Characteristic of English Scenery, From Pictures Painted by John Constable, R.A.* (usually known as *English Landscape*). Twenty-two mezzotints are published between 1830 and 1832; they are reissued in 1833 with several pages of letterpress text. In July he spends three weeks with Fisher at Salisbury, accompanied by his two eldest children; he goes back to Salisbury in November and makes several drawings and oil sketches. During this visit he decides to make a large painting of Salisbury Cathedral from the meadows.

1830

Constable takes his place on the Council of the Royal Academy, the body that took decisions on all aspects of the Academy's life from making arrangements for the annual exhibition to the amount of sherry to buy for the cellar. He exhibits *The Dell at Helmingham Park* at the annual exhibition. In July he visits Fisher briefly at Windsor. He takes his eldest son John Charles to Brighton to convalesce after an illness; it was to be his last visit there. He is at Hampstead for most of the year with his children. He spends much time and energy overseeing the *English Landscape* project, the first part of which is published in June. George IV dies in June and is succeeded by William IV.

1831

Constable serves as a Visitor in the Life Class and Painting School of the Royal Academy Schools, posing the models in imitation of works by Michelangelo and Raphael. He serves again on the selection and hanging committee for the Summer Exhibition. His own exhibit is *Salisbury Cathedral from the Meadows*. In June he takes his three daughters to stay with his married sister, Martha Whalley, now living at Dedham, and he makes another visit there in late July. On 8 September Constable attends the coronation of William IV in his capacity as a Council member of the Royal Academy. He publishes the third and fourth numbers of *English Landscape*. Towards the end of October, he becomes depressed and ill with rheumatism and other health problems.

1832

Constable exhibits *The Opening of Waterloo Bridge* at the Royal Academy exhibition, along with seven smaller exhibits. Varnishing day sees his famous stand-off with Turner, when the latter adds a dab of red paint

to his own painting, thus upstaging Constable's. In July he takes his daughter Minna to stay with her aunt Martha in Dedham. In August he visits Berkshire for four days to sketch for a painting of Englefield House. The death of his friend Fisher in late August is followed by that of Johnny Dunthorne in November, at the age of just thirty-four. He becomes friends with Charles Boner, a young man who is tutor to his children, and with George Constable of Arundel (no relation), who had written to express his admiration for *English Landscape*. Constable completes publication of this project with a fifth part, which is issued in July. In the sketchbook he uses this year he departs from his usual practice of pencil drawings and instead makes open-air studies in watercolour.

1833

Constable exhibits *Englefield House, Berkshire* at the Royal Academy, along with six other works. He begins *The Cenotaph*, a painting in honour of Sir Joshua Reynolds, from a sketch he had made at Coleorton Hall during his stay with the Beaumonts ten years before. In May he brings out a new edition of *English Landscape* with an introduction explaining his intentions. In June he gives the first of a series of lectures on the history of landscape at the Literary and Scientific Society of Hampstead. In August he takes his sons John Charles and Charley to Suffolk for a holiday and to school in Folkestone later that month.

1834

Constable exhibits the watercolour *Old Sarum* at the Royal Academy. He is seriously ill with rheumatic fever in the early part of the year and is unable to send any oils to the exhibition. In July he makes his first visit to George Constable at Arundel and is astonished at the beauty of the rugged Sussex scenery. In September he returns to Sussex at the invitation of Lord Egremont, to stay with him at Petworth House along with a houseful of other guests. Lord Egremont makes a carriage available to Constable every day so that he may see as much of the neighbourhood as possible.

1835

Constable exhibits *The Valley Farm* at the Royal Academy. He spends about a fortnight in Suffolk at the beginning of the year. In July he visits George Constable in Arundel with his eldest two children and makes numerous drawings of Arundel, Chichester and the surrounding area. He spends Christmas at Flatford. His reputation continues to grow over the channel: Thomas Uwins reported that there was 'no English painter's name known so well' in France as Constable's.

1836

He exhibits a watercolour, *Stonehenge*, and one oil, his elegiac *Cenotaph to the Memory of Sir Joshua Reynolds*, at the Royal Academy exhibition. This is the last to be held at New Somerset House; the Academy is preparing to move to the East Wing of the newly built National Gallery at Trafalgar Square. In May and June Constable delivers his lecture series on the history of landscape painting at the Royal Institution. In June he writes to Wordsworth, enclosing the gift of a copy of *English Landscape*. In December

he writes to George Constable about his intention to put his observations about clouds together as a lecture to be presented at Hampstead the following summer.

1837

In March Constable is once again Visitor at the Royal Academy Schools, teaching in the Life Class and in the Painting School. On 30 March he attends a General Assembly of the Academy in the evening; he spends the next day at his easel working on an oil painting, *Arundel Mill and Castle*. Later that evening he becomes ill. He dies, probably of a heart attack, in the early hours of 1 April, at the age of sixty. He is buried with Maria at St John-at-Hampstead. *Arundel Mill and Castle* is exhibited posthumously at the Royal Academy exhibition.

Notes

Abbreviations to Notes:
Discourses *John Constable's Discourses*, ed. R. B. Beckett (Ipswich: Suffolk Records Society, 1970)
FDC *John Constable: Further Documents and Correspondence*, ed. Leslie Parris, Conal Shields and Ian Fleming-Williams (London: Tate Gallery and Ipswich: Suffolk Records Society, 1975)
JCC *John Constable's Correspondence*, ed. R. B. Beckett, 6 vols (Ipswich: Suffolk Records Society and London: HMSO, 1962–68):
I: *The Family at East Bergholt*, 1962
II: *Early Friends and Maria Bicknell (Mrs Constable)*, 1964
III: *Correspondence with C. R. Leslie, R.A.*, 1965
IV: *Patrons, Dealers and Fellow Artists*, 1966
V: *Various Friends, with Charles Boner and the Artist's Children*, 1967
VI: *The Fishers*, 1968
Hamilton 2022 James Hamilton, *Constable: A Portrait* (London: Weidenfeld & Nicolson, 2022)
Leslie 1845 Charles Robert Leslie, *Memoirs of the Life of John Constable composed chiefly of his letters* (London: Longman, Brown, Green, and Longmans, 1845)
Reynolds 1984 Graham Reynolds, *The Later Paintings and Drawings of John Constable* (New Haven and London: Yale University Press, 1984)
Reynolds 1996 Graham Reynolds, *The Early Paintings and Drawings of John Constable* (New Haven and London: Yale University Press, 1996)
Rosenthal 1983 Michael Rosenthal, *Constable: The Painter and his Landscape* (New Haven and London: Yale University Press, 1983)
Tate 1991 Leslie Parris and Ian Fleming-Williams, *Constable*, exh. cat. (London: Tate Gallery, 1991)

Notes are listed by page number.

Introduction

7 *his umbrella*: John Constable to John Fisher, 9 May 1823; *JCC* VI, p. 116. As Beckett notes in *JCC* V, p. 69, n.4, this anecdote 'is told in many forms'.
7 *'exhilarating, fresh'*: John Constable to John Fisher, early April 1825; *JCC* VI, p. 198. The painting he describes is *The Leaping Horse*.
7 *subjects down there*: 'The Trimmers', *JCC* V, p. 69
7 *'truth at second hand'*: John Constable to John Dunthorne, 29 May 1802; *JCC* II, p. 32
8 *'I love such things'*: John Constable to John Fisher, 23 October 1821; *JCC* VI, p. 77
8 *'feeling of a country life'*: John Constable to John Fisher, 1 April 1821; *JCC* VI, p. 65
8 *annual sketching tour*: 'the birds are singing from morning till night most of all the sky larks. How delightfull is the country', John Constable to Maria Constable, 20 April 1821; *JCC* II, p. 267
8 *'works of nature'*: 'George Field', *JCC* IV, p. 172
8 *'till we truly understand it'*: John Constable, 'Lecture III: The Dutch and Flemish Schools', in *Discourses*, p. 64
10 *'home 'till night'*: John Constable to Maria Bicknell, 25 October 1814; *JCC* II, p. 134
11 *'thinks it worth picking up'*: John Constable to C. R. Leslie, 14 January 1832; *JCC* III, p. 59

SPRING

14 '*I love the exhilarating freshness of spring*':
John Constable to C. R. Leslie,
11 June 1833; *JCC* III, p. 103

16 *Thames estuary to London*: R. B. Beckett,
'Constable's Parentage', *JCC* I,
pp. 3–19 (5–6)

16 *due to epilepsy*: See Hamilton 2022, p. 17

17 *or one at a time?*: Beckett, editorial note
in *JCC* II, p. 18

17 '*through a burnt glass*': John Constable
to John Dunthorne, early Spring 1801;
JCC II, p. 26

17 '*rooted are early impressions*':
John Constable to John Dunthorne,
Spring 1800; *JCC* II, p. 24

20 '*on all the earth*': Mary Constable to
John Constable, 2 May 1825; *JCC* I,
p. 220. 'The Country does look most
beautifully', wrote Abram some years
later, 'I never remember a finer season,
do run down if you can & see it.' Abram
Constable to John Constable, 24 May
1835; *JCC* I, p. 292

20 *a farmer's eye*: the degree of Constable's
involvement in his father's business
during these years is uncertain. C. R.
Leslie states that John worked for his
father 'for about a year' (Leslie 1845,
p. 4); but he was writing many years
later, and never formally interviewed
Constable about his early life. It seems
implausible that Golding Sr would not
have taken advantage of his capable
middle son's presence at home for the
other five and a half years. For one
thing, his enterprises were complex and
demanding; for another, he had brought
up his sons to work. It is possible that
Leslie's 'year' was time Constable spent
working intensively in his father's
windmill and watermills in order to
learn the business from the ground up;
his later tasks were perhaps more ad
hoc and administrative.

21 '*life, exhilaration &c*': John Constable
to John Fisher, 26 November 1825;
JCC VI, p. 211

21 *which one it was*: *The Exhibition of the
Royal Academy, MDCCCII* (London:
Royal Academy of Arts, 1802), p. 4
<www.royalacademy.org.uk/art-
artists/exhibition-catalogue/ra-sec-
vol34-1802> [accessed 2 January 2024]

25 '*common place people*': John Constable
to John Dunthorne, 29 May 1802;
JCC II, pp. 31–32

25 *move to fashionable Bath*: John Constable
to John Thomas Smith, 18 August 1799;
JCC II, p. 16

25 '*ever seen a picture*': Leslie 1845, p. 307

26 '*dandy jetty*': John Constable to John
Fisher, postmarked 29 August 1824;
JCC VI, p. 171

26 '*Cousin Mary gave me*': Ann Constable
to John Constable, 17 January 1831;
JCC I, pp. 259; see Susan Owens, *The
Story of Drawing: An Alternative History
of Art* (New Haven and London: Yale
University Press, 2024), p. 213

27 *heard a thrush's song*: Reynolds 1996,
16.10, p. 217; Colchester Museums

27 '*gust the fields of corn*': James Thomson,
'Summer', *The Seasons* (1730), lines
1082–84

27 '*That is true fame!*': William Hazlitt, 'My
First Acquaintance with Poets', *The
Liberal*, vol. 3 (April 1823)

28 '*I drinke redde wine*': Bodleian Library
MS Digby 88; quoted in Celia and
Kenneth Sisam (eds), *The Oxford Book
of Medieval English Verse* (Oxford:
Clarendon Press, 1970), p. 485

29 '*Spring peeps forth*': Robert Bloomfield,
The Farmer's Boy (London, 1800),
'Spring', lines 57–58

30 '*on the first of May*': John Fisher to
John Constable, 3 September 1829; *JCC*
VI, p. 252

30 *excess of phlegm*: Royal College of
Psychiatrists, 'Seasonal Affective
Disorder (SAD)' <www.rcpsych.ac.uk/
mental-health/mental-illnesses-and-
mental-health-problems/seasonal-
affective-disorder-(sad)> [accessed
15 July 2024]

31 *'another race of beings'*: John Constable to Maria Bicknell, 27 February 1816; *JCC* II, p. 179

31 *'See Miltons cold Hell'*: John Fisher to John Constable, 27 April 1829; *JCC* VI, p. 245

31 *'for their inconvenience'*: John Constable to John Fisher, 4 July 1829; *JCC* VI, p. 248

32 *'nature can possibly assume'*: John Constable to John Dunthorne, 23 May 1803; *JCC* II, p. 33

32 *threat to disinherit her*: Maria Bicknell to John Constable, 13 February 1816; *JCC* II, p. 176

33 *'the Art I love'*: John Constable to John Dunthorne, 29 May 1802; *JCC* II, p. 31

33 *persuaded her to take heart*: For John and Maria's courtship, see Martin Gayford, *Constable in Love: Love, Landscape, Money and the Making of a Great Painter* (London: Penguin, 2009)

35 *'the field that grew it'*: Quoted in Richard and Samuel Redgrave, *A Century of British Painters*, ed. Ruthven Todd (London: Phaidon, 1947), p. 371

36 *'than the weather'*: Ann Constable to John Constable, 8 January 1811; *JCC* I, p. 54

36 *'"the sunshine and the shade"'*: From Constable's introduction to *English Landscape*, quoted in *Discourses*, p. 9. The words are from Byron's poem 'The Dream', stanza 6, line 19

36 *'on every thorn'*: Martha Constable to John Constable, 15 February 1831; *JCC* I, p. 260

36 *'another word for feeling'*: John Constable to John Fisher, 23 October 1821; *JCC* VI, p. 78

39 *'there, are they not?'*: Maria Bicknell to John Constable, 14 April 1812; *JCC* II, pp. 62–63

39 *as you thought*: For reassessments of the importance of Constable's Christian faith, see Timothy Wilcox, *Constable and Salisbury: the Soul of Landscape*, exh. cat. (Salisbury: Salisbury and South Wiltshire Museum, 2011), pp. 16–17;

Richard Humphreys, *John Constable: The Leaping Horse* (London: Royal Academy of Arts, 2018), pp. 36 and 53–55 and Bendor Grosvenor, *The Invention of British Art* (London: Elliott & Thompson, 2024), pp. 352–3

39 *'seems verified about me'*: John Constable to Maria Constable, 9 May 1819; *JCC* II, pp. 245–46; Beckett notes that the remark was originally made by William Wordsworth to Constable

39–40 *'tolling for the Doctor?'*: Ibid., p. 246

40 *'still more dear to me'*: John Constable to Maria Constable, 20 April 1821; *JCC* II, p. 267

40 *a panoramic view*: Reynolds 1984, 21.11 and 21.12; Hornby Library, Liverpool, B62–3 and Fitzwilliam Museum, Cambridge, 899.10

45–6 *getting it right*: On Constable's drafts for *English Landscape*, see Felicity Myrone, 'Introductions to John Constable's English Landscape', *Print Quarterly*, 24 (September 2007), pp. 273–77

46 *pace suddenly quickens*: The second extract, 'Light and shade alternate, warmth and cold, / And bright and dewy clouds, and vernal show'rs, / And all the fine variety of things', which Constable misquotes, is from Mark Akenside, *The Pleasures of the Imagination*, book I, lines 76–78; see *Eighteenth Century Poetry Archive* <www.eighteenthcenturypoetry.org/works/04279-w0010.shtml> [accessed 25 July 2024]

46 *'a pale, or lurid hue'*: *Discourses*, pp. 14–15. What Constable calls 'messenger clouds' are today called 'scud' clouds or *stratus fractus*; John E. Thornes, *John Constable's Skies: A Fusion of Art and Science* (Edgbaston: University of Birmingham Press, 1999), p. 43

47 *'the season that is past'*: *Discourses*, p. 15

SUMMER

50 *'I took several beautifull walks in search of food for my pencil this summer when I hope to do a great deal in landscape'*: John

Constable to Maria Bicknell, 4 May 1814; *JCC* II, p. 121

54 *'pursuing it uninterruptedly'*: John Constable to Maria Bicknell, 27 May 1812; *JCC* II, p. 70

54 *'subject at Flatford Mill'*: John Constable to Maria Bicknell, 10 July 1812; *JCC* II, p. 80

54 *'the voice of Nature'*: John Constable to Maria Bicknell, 22 June 1812; *JCC* II, p. 78

55 *noisy, boisterous entertainment*: Leslie 1845, p. 307

55 *'buffoonery of all sorts'*: John Constable to Maria Bicknell, 1 August 1816; *JCC* II, p. 191

55 *a pug called Yorick*: The pug tells us a lot about the Constable family's social and cultural positioning. Pugs were a fashionable breed rather than countrymen's dogs, and this particular one was named after the droll gravedigger in *Hamlet*.

55 *'plants, ferns, distances &c &c'*: John Constable to Maria Bicknell, late March 1814; *JCC* II, p. 120

60 *'a sad jealous creature?'*: Maria Bicknell to John Constable, 25 August 1813, *JCC* II, p. 111

60 *the previous year's*: John Constable to Maria Bicknell, 25 October 1812; *JCC* II, p. 89

61 *'my life were passed'*: John Constable to Maria Bicknell, 18 September 1814; *JCC* II, p. 132

61 *house in East Bergholt?*: 'For more than this week past I have been wholly engaged on a portrait of Mr. William Godfrey which was just completed in time, as he set off the next day to embark for the West Indies – I beleive they are quite pleased with it.' John Constable to Maria Bicknell, 10 July 1812; *JCC* II, p. 80

65 *'lumber'*: Golding Constable Sr to John Constable, 31 December 1811; *JCC* I, p. 74

65 *'little house at Dedham'*: John Constable to Maria Bicknell, 22 September 1812; *JCC* II, p. 86. On Constable as a portrait painter, see Martin Gayford and Anne Lyles, *Constable's Portraits: The Painter & His Circle*, exh. cat. (London: National Portrait Gallery, 2009)

65 *'during the fine weather'*: John Constable to Maria Bicknell, 6 September 1812 and *ibid.*, 28 September 1812; *JCC* II, pp. 84 and 87. The portrait, of Mary Rebow, was commissioned by her father General Rebow, who later commissioned Constable to paint his house and another small landscape in his park. John Constable to Maria Bicknell, 21 August 1816; *JCC* II, p. 196.

65 *'the best of parents'*: John Constable to Maria Bicknell, 22 July 1812; *JCC* II, p. 81

67 *'I look for fame'*: John Constable to Maria Bicknell, 28 September 1812; *JCC* II, p. 87

67 *'my pencil in my hand'*: John Constable to Maria Bicknell, 22 July 1812; *JCC* II, p. 81

67 *home of the Godfreys*: Reynolds 1996, 13.17; V&A 317-1888, p. 12

67 *'business for the Eye'*: Thomas Gainsborough to William Jackson, 1767, in John Hayes (ed.), *The Letters of Thomas Gainsborough* (New Haven and London: Yale University Press, 2001), p. 40

68 *'which is a great help'*: John Constable to John Dunthorne, 22 February 1814; *JCC* I, p. 101

68 *painting in English Landscape*: Summer ploughing was a long-established East Anglian practice, mentioned in a manorial document of the fourteenth century, *An Extent of the Manor of Horham, 1356*; George Ewart Evans, *Where Beards Wag All: The Relevance of the Rural Tradition* (London: Faber, 1970), p. 89. A contemporaneous account of the practice of summer ploughing is provided by the agriculturalist Arthur

Young: '[The farmer's] only chance is, to have abundance of patience to wait for favourable weather, and lay his account to sow very late. The motive for advising him to avoid such spring ploughings, is not derived from the practice of a few individuals, but from that of a considerable district, occupied by numerous and intelligent farmers." Arthur Young, *The Farmer's Calendar* (1808; 12th edition, London: Sir Richard Phillips and Co., 1822), p. 60. The practice continued throughout the nineteenth century. An account of summer ploughing by a farm worker, James William Seely, born at Lound, near Lowestoft, in 1894, is included by Evans in *Where Beards Wag All*, pp. 101–2.

68 *knew who owned it*: Michael Rosenthal brilliantly discusses this painting in Rosenthal 1983, pp. 70–78

68 *'cut the trees'*: John Constable to John Dunthorne, 22 February 1814; *JCC* I, p. 101

71 *'our "new neighbours"'*: John Constable to Maria Bicknell, 5 June 1814; *JCC* II, p. 125

71 *picture failed to sell*: It was purchased the following year, when it was exhibited at the British Institution.

71 *'entirely in the feilds'*: John Constable to Maria Bicknell, 18 September 1814; *JCC* II, p. 131

72 *East Bergholt House for supper*: David Lucas, manuscript annotation to C. R. Leslie's *Memoirs of the Life of John Constable* (1843), quoted in *FDC*, p. 56

72 *stumbled once or twice*: A large and detailed drawing Constable made of the garden prior to the oil paintings, perhaps in around 1814, shows dense shrubs in the space the flowerbeds later occupied; Reynolds 1996, 15.24; V&A 623-1888

72 *'pay the last rites'*: Abram Constable to John Constable, 2 April 1815; *JCC* I, pp. 122–23

72 *him to leave London*: Constable's letter to Abram has not survived, but the phrases 'critical period' and 'very urgent … business', presumably his own, were echoed by Abram in letters of 2 April and 9 April; *JCC* I, pp. 123–24

72 *3 and 4 April*: RAA/PC/1/5, p. 184. Royal Academy Council minutes, 6 January 1815. For this information I am grateful to Mark Pomeroy, Archivist of the Royal Academy.

72 *agonizingly difficult choice*: Beckett notes that Constable's absence 'may be attributed as much to an excess of sensitivity as to any preoccupation with his own affairs', and draws a comparison with his eldest son John Charles, who took after his father both physically and temperamentally, and who in 1837 'was so much overcome by the shock of his father's death that he was unable to attend the burial at Hampstead'. Editorial note to Abram's letter of 2 April 1815, *JCC* I, p. 123. It seems more likely, however, that it was attributable to the unfortunate clash of dates.

73 *'but the harvest men'*: John Constable to Maria Bicknell, 27 August 1815; *JCC* II, p. 149

73 *'almost to the grave'*: Golding Constable to John Constable, 6 May 1815; *JCC* I, p. 127

73 *ready to be harvested*: On these paintings, see Tate 1991, p. 91; and Stephen Daniels, 'Love and Death across an English Garden: Constable's Paintings of his Family's Flower and Kitchen Gardens', *Huntington Library Quarterly*, vol. 55, no. 3 (1992), pp. 433–57

80 *'continual rains'*: John Constable to Maria Bicknell, 3 November 1815; *JCC* II, p. 159

80 *'year without summer'*: See Lucy Veale and Georgina H. Endfield, 'Situating 1816, the "year without summer", in the UK', *The Geographical Journal*, 2016; <www.rgs-ibg.onlinelibrary.wiley.com/doi/10.1111/geoj.12191> [accessed 11 February 2025]

80 *'been without fires'*: Abram Constable
to John Constable, 9 July 1816; *JCC* I,
p. 137

80 *'in much need of it'*: John Constable
to Maria Bicknell, 21 August 1816;
JCC II, p. 196

83 *'much in the open air'*: Maria Bicknell
to John Constable, 5 September 1816;
JCC II, p. 200

83 *'would have done as well'*: John
Constable to Maria Bicknell, 12
September 1816; *JCC* II, p. 203

85 *'always seen each other'*: Maria Bicknell
to John Constable, 18 January 1815;
JCC II, p. 168

87 *arrive at Dedham*: Constable also began
a large painting of this scene, perhaps
over the summer of 1817, but left the
picture unfinished. See Tate 1991,
pp. 184–85

87 *'the origin of my Fame'*: Reynolds 1984,
20.43; Musée du Louvre, RF 8700.1.
I am grateful to Dr Bijan Omrani for
sharing his expertise on Neckam's
De Laudibus Divinae Sapientae (On
the Praises of Divine Wisdom) and
for finding the lines quoted in two
places in which Constable was likely
to have seen them: William Camden's
Britannia and Thomas Warton's *History
of English Poetry*.

88 *cottage beyond*: *A reaper passing a cottage
on a lane at East Bergholt*, 3 August 1817.
Reynolds 1984, 17.9; V&A 278-1888

91 *'town and country life'*: John Constable
to John Fisher, 28 November 1826;
JCC VI, p. 228

91 *'we must try the sea'*: John Constable to
John Fisher, 8 May 1824; *JCC* VI, p. 157

92 *'always varying'*: John Constable to John
Fisher, postmarked 29, presumably
August 1824; *JCC* VI, p. 171

92 *'hackneyed'*: *Ibid.*

95 *'called the country'*: Reynolds 1984, 24.17;
V&A 149-1888

95 *'taking the air'*: Reynolds 1984, 24.9;
V&A 783-1888

AUTUMN

100 *'After all this is the painter's season'*:
John Constable to Maria Constable,
25 October 1818; *JCC* II, p. 240

100 *'"in her fickle eyes"'*: John Constable
to George Constable, 12 April 1833;
JCC V, p. 11

100 *'freshness of spring'*: John Constable
to Charles Robert Leslie, 11 June 1833;
JCC III, p. 103

102 *'the painter's season'*: John Constable
to Maria Constable, 25 October
1818; *JCC* II, p. 240. In October 1815,
Constable's maternal uncle David Pike
Watts, who had funded his 1806 trip to
the Lake District, observed that 'The
Artist's View of Nature now presents the
admired October tints, which adorn the
rural Scenery; but perhaps more so at
the Lakes, than elsewhere, and chiefly at
Windermere.' David Pike Watts to John
Constable, 2 October 1815; *JCC* IV, p. 44

102 *golden foliage*: Reynolds 1984, 21.75; Yale
Center for British Art, B1981.25.126

102 *'beautifull – & lovely'*: John Constable
to John Fisher, 19 October 1823; *JCC* VI,
p. 140

102–3 *'saw in Margaret St'*: Reynolds 1996,
06.219; V&A 187-1888

103 *'knowledge of the art'*: John Fisher
to John Constable, 14 February 1821;
JCC VI, p. 61

103 *'transferred to the canvass'*: Henry
Matthews, *The Diary of an Invalid: Being
the Journal of a Tour in Pursuit of Health
in Portugal, Italy, Switzerland and France
in the Years 1817, 1818 and 1819* (2nd edn;
London: John Murray, 1820), p. 98

104 *'Ignorance appears in –'*: John Constable
to John Fisher, 1 April 1821; *JCC* VI, p. 66

104 *eye-catchingly colossal scale*: See, for
example, John Glover's brown-tinged
A Hilly Landscape in the V&A (165-1880),
almost 2 × 3 m framed, or his Claudean
Classical Landscape in Lady Margaret
Hall, University of Oxford; <artuk.org/
discover/artists/glover-john-17671849>
[accessed 20 September 2024]

105 *'the English Claude'*: John Constable to John Fisher, 30 September 1823; *JCC* VI, p. 133

105 *'a large cow-turd'*: John Constable to John Fisher, n.d. [April 1825]; *JCC* VI, p. 198

106 *down the other side*: See Ian Fleming-Williams, 'A Runover Dungle and a Possible Date for "Spring"', *Burlington Magazine*, vol. CXIV, no. 831 (June 1972), pp. 386–93

106 *mound more prominent*: Reynolds 1996, 14.34; Leeds Art Gallery, LEEAG. PA.1934.0010

109 *'almost done'*: John Constable to Maria Bicknell, 25 October 1814; *JCC* II, p. 134

109 *when he made another*: Sketchbook used July to October 1814, Reynolds 1996, 14.32, pp. 62 and 81; V&A,1259-1888

109 *'steadiness & confidence'*: John Constable to Maria Bicknell, 2 October 1814; *JCC* II, p. 133

109 *lower half of the sheet*: Reynolds 1996, 14.35 (sheet detached from sketchbook no. 14.32); V&A 437-1888

109 *'working out of doors'*: John Constable to Maria Bicknell, 25 October 1814; *JCC* II, p. 134

109–10 *'scenes of Suffolk'*: John Constable to Maria Bicknell, 12 November 1814; *JCC* II, p. 136

110 *'from my very windows'*: John Fisher to John Constable, 27 August 1816; *JCC* VI, p. 29

110 *'being lost than myself'*: John Constable to John Fisher Sr, 8 May 1824; *JCC* VI, p. 158

110–12 *tackled straight away:* For Salisbury as a subject in Constable's work, see Timothy Wilcox, *Constable and Salisbury: the Soul of Landscape*, exh. cat. (Salisbury: Salisbury and South Wiltshire Museum, 2011). Constable first visited Salisbury and drew the cathedral in 1811.

112 *Ringwood to Osmington*: Reynolds 1996, 16.44 and 16.45; V&A 268-1888

112 *Fisher preached*: Reynolds 1996, 16.49; private collection, New York

112 *'married July 2 1816'*: Reynolds 1996, 16.55 and 16.51; V&A 311-1888 (verso) and Colchester and Ipswich Museums 1940-26.7 (verso)

112 *his hosts as a gift*: Reynolds 1996, 16.80; private collection, New York

113 *in his weather journal*: Luke Howard, *The Climate of London, Deduced from Meteorological Observations, made in the Metropolis, and at Various Places Around it*, II (2nd edn; London: Harvey and Darton, J. and A. Arch, Longman, Hatchard, S. Highley [and] R. Hunter, 1833), pp. 307–13

117 *the builders' yards*: Sketchbook used in 1819, Reynolds 1984, 19.28; British Museum, 1972–6–17–15; see particularly pp. 1, 3, 6, 7, 9 and 11

118 *conduct from Hampstead*: See Reynolds 1984, 19.12 to 19.17

118 *'Gentle at S. W.'*: Reynolds 1984, 20.77; V&A 147-1888, Reynolds 1984, 20.81; private collection and Reynolds 20.82; V&A 159-1888. On Constable's sky studies, see Edward Morris (ed.), *Constable's Clouds*, exh. cat. (Liverpool and Edinburgh: Walker Art Gallery and National Gallery of Scotland, 2000); and Mark Evans, *Constable's Skies* (London: Thames & Hudson, 2018)

118 *'place of refuge'*: John Constable to John Fisher, 4 August 1821; *JCC* VI, p. 71

122 *'intimate view of nature'*: John Constable to John Fisher, 1 April 1821; *JCC* VI, p. 66

122 *'peculiar tone and beauty'*: *Discourses*, p. 15

126 *'man of clouds'*: John Constable to John Fisher, 2 November 1823; *JCC* VI, p. 142

126 *'light air from S. W.'*: Reynolds 1984, 21.45; V&A 151-1888

126 *'the night following'*: Reynolds 1984, 21.47; Royal Academy of Arts, 03/455

126 *'wind in the night'*: Reynolds 1984, 21.48; V&A 156-1888

126 *'showers had fallen'*: Reynolds 1984, 21.49; private collection

126 *'lying one on another'*: Reynolds 21.50; Yale Center for British Art, B1981.25.156 and Reynolds 21.52; Yale Center for British Art, B1981.25.147

126 *'seasons as the present'*: John Constable to John Fisher, 20 September 1821; *JCC* VI, p. 74

129 *'does not occur to us'*: John Constable to John Fisher, 23 October 1821; *JCC* VI, pp. 76–77

129 *'two evening effects'*: John Constable to John Fisher, 3 November 1821; *JCC* VI, p. 81

129 *'Hampstead Octr. 2. 1820'*: Reynolds 1984, 20.74; V&A 251-1888

130 *often as he liked*: Leslie 1845, p. 24

130 *top-lit gallery*: Hamilton 2022, p. 73

130 *'no time to lose'*: Lady Beaumont to John Constable, 10 October 1823; *FDC*, p. 146

130–31 *'will much help me'*: John Constable to John Fisher, 19 October 1823; *JCC* VI, p. 139

131 *'myself much more'*: John Constable to Maria Constable, 27 October 1823 and 18 November 1823; *JCC* II, pp. 293 and 301

131 *'streams and rocks'*: John Constable to Maria Constable, 27 October 1823; *JCC* II, p. 292

133 *take something for himself*: On Constable and copying, see Mark Evans (ed.), *John Constable: The Making of a Master*, exh. cat. (London: Victoria and Albert Museum, 2014)

133 *'Wilsons & Poussins &c.'*: John Constable to Maria Constable, 21 October 1823; *JCC* II, p. 290

133 *The Death of Procris*: Ibid., pp. 117–21. Both paintings were given by Beaumont to the National Gallery in 1826. *Landscape with the Death of Procris* (NG 55) is now considered to be a studio copy of an original painting by Claude.

133 *'a good day's work'*: John Constable to Maria Constable, 27 October 1823; *JCC* II, p. 293

134 *'confined to this house'*: John Constable to Maria Constable, 2 November 1823; *JCC* II, p. 294

134 *'done from nature'*: John Constable to Maria Constable, 9, 18 and 26 November 1823; *JCC* VI, pp. 298, 301 and 305–6

134 *'to great advantage'*: John Constable to John Fisher, 2 November 1823; *JCC* VI, pp. 142 and 144

134 *'the Claudes every night'*: John Constable to Maria Constable, 5 November 1823; *JCC* II, p. 296

134 *'that you had a wife'*: Maria Constable to John Constable, 21 November 1823, JCC II, p. 302

134 *throw it out of the window*: Maria Constable to John Constable, 21 November and 17 November 1823; *JCC* II, pp. 302 and 299

136 *'life & breezy freshness'*: John Constable to John Fisher, 2 November 1823; *JCC* VI, p. 143

138 *'see what time may do'*: Abram Constable to John Constable, 30 September 1827; *JCC* I, p. 233

138 *'"I can't think – can you?"'*: Recorded in Julian Charles Young, *A Memoir of Charles Mayne Young, Tragedian* (London and New York: Macmillan and Co., 1871), p. 134; quoted by R. B. Beckett in *JCC* V, p. 128

138 *'Suffolk very like Hampstead'*: John Constable to Maria Constable, 4 October 1827; *JCC* II, p. 440

141 *farmhouse opposite the windmill*: Reynolds 1984, 27.33; John Constable to Maria Constable, 10 October 1827, *JCC* II, p. 443; Hamilton 2022, p. 314. See also 'A Sportsman: Golding Constable shooting duck on the River Stour', Lowell Libson & Jonny Yarker Ltd British Art <libson-yarker.com/ pictures/a-sportsman-golding- constable-shooting-duck-on-the-river- stour> [accessed 7 October 2024]

141 *'weather & season is over'*: John Constable to Maria Constable, 10 October 1827; *JCC* II, p. 442

141 *'(to me & you) beautiful view'*: Abram Constable to John Constable, 30 March 1828; *JCC* I, p. 242

142 *thrashing down over the waves*: Reynolds 1984, 28.13; Yale Center for British Art, B1981.25.114

142 *Leslie's hand and wept*: Leslie 1845, p. 183

142 *'the Rectory – & its dark trees'*: John Constable to Golding Constable, 19 December 1828; *FDC*, p. 81

142 *'periods of distress'*: John Fisher to John Constable, 29 November 1828; *JCC* VI, pp. 239–40

145 *'many miles to sea'*: John Constable to Maria Constable, 3 July 1814; *JCC* II, p. 127

145 *'reflects a floating gleam'*: James Thomson, 'Summer', *The Seasons* (1730), lines 165–70

WINTER

148 *'Can it therefore be wondered at that I paint continual storms?'*: John Constable to C. R. Leslie, 15 December 1834; *JCC* III, p. 122

148 *'the scene below'*: William Cowper, *The Task* (London: Joseph Johnson, 1785), Book VI: 'The Winter Walk at Noon', stanza 2, lines 6–8

149 *'the motion of the leaves'*: 'The Trimmers', *JCC* V, p. 69

149 *'snow having fallen'*: John Constable to John Fisher, 24 May 1830; *JCC* VI, p. 258; editorial note in *JCC* III, p. 21; and Charles M. Westmacott, *A Descriptive and Critical Catalogue to the Exhibition of the Royal Academy* (London: Royal Academy of Arts, 1823), p. 13

149 *expressive handling of paint*: See Amy Concannon, 'In Focus: Salisbury Cathedral from the Meadows, exhibited 1831 by John Constable', Tate <www.tate.org.uk/research/in-focus/salisbury-cathedral-constable/the-painting> [accessed 8 January 2025]

149 *'all the frost on the trees'*: 'The Trimmers', *JCC* V, p. 69

149 *'the anatomy of trees'*: 'George Field', *JCC* IV, pp. 172–73

149 *'some picture he was about'*: 'The Trimmers', *JCC* V, p. 70

150 *'know it is severe'*: Ann Constable to John Constable, 4 January 1811; *JCC* I, pp. 52–53

150 *'the lungs and tooth ache'*: Ann Constable to John Constable, 8 January 1811; *JCC* I, p. 54

152 *'to turn a painter's mind'*: John Constable to Maria Bicknell, 23 December 1813; *JCC* II, p. 113

152 *'hardly feel the brush'*: Maria Bicknell to John Constable, 15 December 1813; *JCC* II, p. 113

152 *river towards the estuary*: Rose Staveley-Wadham, '"The Thames is Now Both a Fair and Market Too": Discovering the Frost Fair of 1814', 21 January 2019 <www.blog.britishnewspaperarchive.co.uk/2019/01/21/discovering-the-frost-fair-of-1814/> [accessed 19 October 2024]

152 *'prevent our seeing each other'*: Maria Bicknell to John Constable, 24 January 1814; *JCC* II, p. 114

152 *'equal to a winter's campaign'*: John Constable to Maria Bicknell, 12 December 1811; *JCC* II, p. 55

153 *building his reputation*: *The Diary of Joseph Farington*, ed. Kathryn Cave, vol. XVI (New Haven and London: Yale University Press, 1984), p. 5582 (21 November 1820)

153 *For fame*: This picture did make Constable famous – not in England, but in France. Having remained unsold at the Royal Academy and returned to his studio, it was bought early in 1824 by a Parisian dealer, John Arrowsmith, and later that year exhibited to great acclaim at the Paris Salon, the most influential art exhibition in Europe. As a result, Constable's painting had a profound influence on French landscape painting. See Anne Lyles (ed.), *Constable: The Great Landscapes*, exh. cat. (London: Tate Britain, 2006), p. 142, and Anne Lyles, '"Rather a more

novel look than I expected": the Making of the Hay Wain', in Christine Riding and Mary McMahon, *Discover Constable & the Hay Wain*, exh. cat. (London: National Gallery, 2024), pp. 38–51 (51)

153 *'love to any other'*: John Constable to Maria Bicknell, 5 June 1814; *JCC* II, p. 125

156 *from different angles*: The earliest known oil is Reynolds 1996, 02.13; Clark Art Institute, Williamstown, Massachusetts, USA, X12192

156 *in the depths of winter*: 'You know that I do not like to talk of what I am about in painting (I am such a conjuror)…'. John Constable to Maria Bicknell, 13 July 1815; *JCC* II, p. 146

158 *'time drew near fast'*: Abram Constable to John Constable, 25 February 1821; *JCC* I, p. 193

158 *July rather than August*: This is noted by Ian Fleming-Williams and Leslie Parris in Tate 1991, p. 163 (no. 77)

161 *'mallow, thistle, hop, &c'*: Henry Philips to John Constable, 1 March 1826; *JCC* V, p. 80

161 *'another word for feeling'*: John Constable to John Fisher, 23 October 1821; *JCC* VI, p. 78

162 *'quite at home already'*: John Constable to Maria Constable, 10, 2 and 3 September 1825; *JCC* II, pp. 390 and 381

163 *'morning could not paint'*: John Constable to Maria Constable, 11 and 12 December 1825; *JCC* II, pp. 419–21

163 *his family for Christmas*: In a letter to Fisher of 14 January 1826 (*JCC* VI, p. 212), Constable states that he had returned to London two days previously, having spent a fortnight in Brighton. It seems unlikely, however, that he joined his family after Christmas. Constable's vagueness about dates meant that he often misdated letters (see for example Beckett's editorial note in *JCC* IV, p. 360), and on this occasion he may have been writing hurriedly to Fisher without bothering to check his accuracy.

The last of his journal-letters to Maria is dated 12 December, and while a section may be missing, there is no evidence to suggest he spent Christmas with anyone but his family, as he had intended. As well as his reference on 11 December to bringing more money with him 'at Xmas', on 28 November 1825 he had written to Maria: 'Miss Arnott called to ask me, with her mother's compliments, to dine there on Christmas Day. I told her I had a wife, and must needs go and see her'; *JCC* II, p. 415

166 *always felt at the shore*: John Constable to Maria Bicknell, 3 July 1814; *JCC* II, p. 127

166 *'life & worldly prospects'*: John Constable to C. R. Leslie, 4 September 1832; *JCC* III, p. 79. Confirmation that cholera was the cause of Fisher's death came some months later; see John Constable to Dominic Colnaghi, 23 March 1833; *JCC* IV, p. 162

167 *'seems in a fit state'*: John Constable to C. R. Leslie, 4 September 1832; *JCC* III, p. 80

167 *'always to be with me'*: John Constable to John Fisher, 17 November 1824; *JCC* VI, p. 181. See Hamilton 2022, p. 252

167–70 *'what he was painting'*: John Constable, 'Lecture III: The Dutch and Flemish Schools', in *Discourses*, p. 64

170 *'midwinter spring'*: T. S. Eliot, *Little Gidding* (London: Faber & Faber, 1942), line 1

170 *'Westminster Abbey to Gravesend'*: John Constable to John Fisher, 26 August 1827; *JCC* VI, p. 231

170 *'rolling about to day!!!'*: John Constable to C. R. Leslie, 16 August 1833; *JCC* III, p. 105

173 *'shepheard's everlasting name'*: 'Cloud Study with Verses from Bloomfield', Tate <www.tate.org.uk/art/artworks/constable-cloud-study-with-verses-from-bloomfield-t01940> [accessed 21 November 2024]

174 *enriched by long reflection*: On Constable's late work, see Anne

Lyles, *Late Constable*, exh. cat. (London: Royal Academy of Arts, 2021) and Alexandra Harris, 'John Constable's Last Decade', *RA Magazine*, 26 October 2021 <royalacademy.org.uk/article/john-constable-exhibition-ra-magazine> [accessed 10 January 2025]

174 *'season of Sadness'*: John Constable to William Wordsworth, 15 June 1836; Mark L. Reed, 'Constable, Wordsworth, and Beaumont: A New Constable Letter in Evidence', *The Art Bulletin*, vol. 64, no. 3 (September 1982), pp. 481–83 (481)

174 *'every endearing recollection'*: *Discourses*, p. 12

174 *Weymouth, Brighton, Hampstead Heath*: On the *English Landscape* project, see Andrew Wilton, *Constable's 'English Landscape Scenery'* (London: British Museum Publications, 1979); Tate 1991, pp. 319–57; Stephen Calloway, 'Canon: the "Chiar' Oscuro of Nature"', in Mark Evans (ed.), *John Constable: The Making of a Master*, exh. cat. (London: Victoria and Albert Museum, 2014), pp. 183–207; and Felicity Myrone, 'No Mercenary Views: Constable's English Landscape', in *Tate Papers* (vol. 33), 2020 <www.tate.org.uk/research/tate-papers/33/no-mercenary-views-constable-english-landscape> [accessed 2 January 2025]

175 *'a history of his affections'*: Leslie 1845, pp. 316–17

175 *reappear in another*: This technical peculiarity is the principle behind M. R. James's ghost story 'The Mezzotint', first published in *Ghost Stories of an Antiquary* (London: Edward Arnold, 1904)

175–6 *'as rotten as cow dung'*: John Constable to David Lucas, 26 February 1830; *JCC* IV, p. 325

176 *'like a disease'*: John Constable to David Lucas, 12 March 1831; *JCC* IV, p. 344

176 *'never was there such a wreck'*: John Constable to David Lucas, 4 December 1831; *JCC* IV, p. 360

176 *the original oil paint*: I am grateful to Stephen Calloway for this plausible suggestion.

176 *than his exhibited paintings*: James Hamilton makes a similar point in Hamilton 2022, p. 334

179 *'all contribute to it'*: *Discourses*, p. 62

179 *'the "darkness" is majestic'*: John Constable to C. R. Leslie, 15 December 1834; *JCC* III, p. 122

180 *'cannot impart it'*: Leslie 1845, p. 186

180 *'some friend or other'*: John Constable to C. R. Leslie, 16 August 1833; *JCC* III, p. 105

180 *'this cold weather'*: John Constable to C. R. Leslie, 25 February 1837; *JCC* III, p. 147

180–83 *visited a close friend*: John Constable to George Constable, 17 February 1837; *JCC* V, p. 37

183 *subject in the summer*: John Constable to George Constable, 12 December 1836; *JCC* V, p. 36

183 *favourite poet of his, Cowper*: Charles Robert Leslie, *Autobiographical Recollections*, I, ed. Tom Taylor (London, 1860), p. 158

183 *'even the smallest thing'*: John Constable to Mary Allen, 20 February 1834; *JCC* V, p. 172; and see editorial note from Beckett, *ibid.*

183 *'laid up for the winter'*: John Constable to C. R. Leslie, 30 December 1836; *JCC* III, p. 145

183 *'water & skies blue'*: John Constable to Charles Boner, letter postmarked 16 January 1835; *JCC* V, p. 178

Epilogue

240 *folded into his vision*: For example, 'There is sad ravage made with the trees, owing to the wind and the weight of snow hanging on the foliage – one would think there had been a battle of Waterloo in Mr. Godfrey's park, and the roads are impassible for the broken boughs & fallen trees,' John Constable to Maria Constable, 24 October 1819; JCC II, p. 186

Year by Year

188 *'epoch in his life'*: Leslie 1845, p. 6

188 *'inclination would lead me'*: John
Constable to J. T. Smith, 2 March 1797;
quoted in Leslie 1845, p. 8

189 *'truth at second hand'*: John Constable
to John Dunthorne, 29 May 1802;
JCC II, p. 32

190 *£100 or £150 today*: *The Diary of Joseph
Farington*, ed. Kenneth Garlick and
Angus Macintyre, vol. VI (New Haven
and London: Yale University Press,
1979), p. 2340 (1 June 1804); see also
<www.nationalarchives.gov.uk/
currency-converter> [accessed
2 January 2025]

191 *'said his prayers before it'*: Note
made by David Lucas in the
margin of Leslie's *Memoirs*;
FDC 1975, p. 55

191 *'unutterable sadness'*: John Constable
to Maria Bicknell, 24 December 1811;
JCC II, p. 57

193 *clouds, weather and light effects*:
John Constable to John Fisher,
23 October 1821; JCC VI, p. 76

194 *'I ever had upon my easil'*:
John Constable to John Fisher,
9 May 1823; JCC VI, p. 115

195 *Constable's home until 1834*:
see Hamilton 2022, p. 349

197 *'name known so well'*: Charles Boner
to John Constable, 19 January 1835; JCC
V, p. 179

Works of Art

213 *lack of success*: Ian Fleming-Williams
and Leslie Parris, *The Discovery of
Constable* (London, 1984), p. 5

214 *'admired at Paris'*: John Fisher
to John Constable, 10 May 1824;
JCC VI, p. 158

A Constable Bookcase

The literature on Constable is like a large wood: at the centre stand some magnificent venerable trees surrounded by many well-established specimens, and it expands every year as vigorous saplings spring up. A conventional bibliography was likely to wander too far under the canopy and end up enumerating more than would be useful to most readers as new avenues opened up and invited exploration. In the context of this book, I felt that suggestions for 'follow up' reading on particular subjects would be easier to find in endnotes, so that is where I have put them. What follows here is less a formal bibliography than a description of the sections of my bookshelves devoted to the books that were most useful to me when writing this one. Although it is highly selective, I hope it will serve as a useful guide to the Constable wood and individual specimens to be found there.

On the most accessible shelf of my Constable bookcase – rarely off the table, in fact – is the two-part catalogue raisonné by Graham Reynolds, *The Early Painting and Drawings of John Constable*, 2 vols (New Haven and London, 1996) and *The Later Paintings and Drawings of John Constable*, 2 vols (New Haven and London, 1984), with additions in the more recent of the two. Any student of Constable owes a gigantic debt of gratitude to Reynolds, who joined the staff of the Victoria and Albert Museum in 1937, became Keeper of Paintings from 1959 to 1974 and Keeper of the Department of Prints and Drawings from 1961 to 1974. His catalogue raisonné, which discusses Constable's paintings and drawings in the context of the artist's life and his other work, is one of the two great cornerstones of Constable scholarship.

Keeping company with the four Reynolds volumes is the other cornerstone: six volumes of *John Constable's Correspondence*, edited by R. B. Beckett and published by the Suffolk Records Society and HMSO between 1962 and 1968. These comprise letters to the artist's family (vol. I); to early friends and his fiancée then wife Maria Bicknell (vol. II); to his friend and future biographer C. R. Leslie (vol. III); to patrons, dealers and fellow artists (vol. IV); to various friends with Charles Boner and the artist's children (vol. V); and to his great friends the Fishers (vol. VI). Together they give insights into the artist's character and daily life that can hardly be had into any other artist. Beckett's extensive annotations are exemplary: both judicious and entertaining. Alongside two further volumes – *John Constable's Discourses* (Ipswich, 1970), also edited by Beckett, and *John Constable: Further Documents and Correspondence*, ed. by Leslie Parris, Conal Shields and Ian Fleming-Williams (London and Ipswich, 1975) – they provide a highly detailed portrait of the man. The experience of reading Constable's letters alongside Reynolds's catalogue is of getting to know the mind and heart of a man who lived two hundred years ago to an almost uncanny degree.

On the next shelf are biographical studies. The first was written by a fellow artist who became a close friend of Constable's in around 1819, Charles Robert Leslie. As his title suggests, Leslie based *Memoirs of the Life of John Constable composed chiefly of his letters* (London, 1843; 2nd, fuller edition, 1845) heavily on the artist's surviving correspondence as well as his personal recollections. An edition edited by Jonathan Mayne, former Assistant Keeper of Paintings at the V&A, was published by Phaidon in 1951 and is available today as a modern reprint. *The Diary of Joseph Farington, 1793–1821*, ed. by Kenneth Garlick, Angus Macintyre, Katherine Cave and Evelyn Newby (New Haven and London, 1978–98) contains numerous first-hand accounts of conversations between Constable and one of his early mentors. More recent biographies include Anthony Bailey's *John Constable: A Kingdom of his Own* (London, 2006) and Martin Gayford's *Constable in Love: Love, Landscape, Money and the Making of a Great Painter* (London, 2009), the latter an absorbing study of a crucial period of the artist's life, both in terms of his life and his work. A recent addition to the bookcase is an elegantly written and highly readable biography by James Hamilton, *John Constable: A Portrait* (London, 2022).

Next come art historical studies. Books that address Constable's whole career include Graham Reynolds's *Constable: The Natural Painter* (London, 1965); Michael Rosenthal's thought-provoking *Constable: The Painter and his Landscape* (New Haven and London, 1983) and his later *Constable* (London, 1987), written for Thames & Hudson's World of Art series; Malcolm Cormack's *Constable* (Oxford, 1986); *Constable*, an exceptionally informative and judicious catalogue of an exhibition held in 1991 at the Tate Gallery, edited by Ian Fleming-Williams and Leslie Parris; William Vaughan's *Constable* (London, 2002); Jonathan Clarkson's *Constable* (New York and London, 2010); Gillian Forrester's *John Constable* (London, 2024); and Nicola Moorby's *Turner & Constable: Art, Life, Landscape* (London, 2025). The fascinating story of Constable's posthumous rise to fame is told by Ian Fleming-Williams and Leslie Parris in *The Discovery of Constable* (London, 1984).

Occupying another shelf are books concerned with specific themes or periods within Constable's work. These include the series of 'six-footer' landscapes that established his career, explored in depth in *Constable: The Great Landscapes*, the catalogue of an exhibition held at Tate Britain in 2006, curated by Anne Lyles. Lyles also curated an exhibition at the Royal Academy in 2021, 'Late Constable', accompanied by a catalogue that contains a notable essay on the late drawings by Matthew Hargraves. Drawings themselves are the subject of the exhibition catalogue *Constable: A Master Draughtsman* (Dulwich Picture Gallery, 2004), edited by Ian Fleming-Williams, which includes an excellent essay by Anne Lyles, 'The Landscape Drawings of Constable's Contemporaries: British Draughtsmanship *c*. 1790–1850'. In 2011 Mark Evans, a successor to Graham Reynolds as Head of Paintings at the V&A, wrote *John Constable: Oil Sketches from the Victoria and Albert Museum*. He followed that in 2014 with *John Constable: The Making of a Master*, with contributions by Stephen Calloway and myself, an exhibition catalogue exploring the artist's working methods and his close relationship with the work of Old Masters such as Claude Lorrain, Ruisdael and Cuyp. *Constable's Portraits: The Painter & His Circle* by Martin Gayford and Anne Lyles is the catalogue of an exhibition held at the National Portrait Gallery in London in 2009.

The subject of the sky in Constable's work has been a source of such fascination that it fills a section of its own. It is investigated by Kurt Badt in *John Constable's Clouds* (London, 1950); by Louis Hawes in 'Constable's Sky Sketches', *Journal of the Warburg and Courtauld Institutes*, vol 32 (1969), pp. 344–65; by John E. Thornes in *John Constable's Skies* (Birmingham, 1999); by Edward Morris in *Constable's Clouds*, the catalogue to an exhibition held in 2000 at the Walker Art Gallery in Liverpool and the National Gallery of Scotland in Edinburgh; and by Mark Evans in *Constable's Skies* (London, 2018).

A final shelf contains books on individual works and particular places. *The Leaping Horse* by Richard Humphreys is a focused monograph published by the Royal Academy of Arts in 2018, while *Discover Constable & The Hay Wain* by Christine Riding and Mary McMahon was published by the National Gallery, London, in 2024 to accompany an exhibition of the same name. Constable's relationship with place is explored in Alastair Smart and Attfield Brooks's *Constable and his Country* (London, 1976); in Timothy Wilcox's exhibition catalogue *Constable and Salisbury: the Soul of Landscape* (Salisbury and South Wiltshire Museum, 2011); in Andrew Loukes's *Constable at Petworth* (London, 2014); and in Shân Lancaster's *Constable and Brighton: Something out of Nothing* (London, 2017).

Works of Art and Picture Credits

No illustration or digital image, no matter how high the resolution, can replace the experience of being in the presence of a work of art. It is the difference between seeing a view through a window and going out for a walk. It is fortunate, then, that a great many works of art by Constable are in public collections. Ironically, it was Constable's lack of success during his lifetime (it has been estimated that he sold, exchanged or gave away around one hundred pictures, a small proportion of his total output) that directly resulted in many more being placed in museums and public galleries than would otherwise have been the case. The towering reputation he holds today is a posthumous phenomenon, one that has been driven by this visibility.

The Victoria and Albert Museum holds the most comprehensive collection of works by Constable in existence. The person largely responsible for this is the artist's daughter, Miss Isabel Constable, who in 1888 made a gift to the museum of what remained of the contents of her father's studio – ninety-five oil paintings and sketches, two hundred and ninety-seven drawings and watercolours and three sketchbooks – and at her death that same year bequeathed a separate group of oil paintings and watercolours. At a stroke, the V&A became the principal study centre for Constable. Collectors, too, made gifts that range from major exhibition paintings to the full-scale oil sketches for *The Hay Wain* and *The Leaping Horse*. A selection of paintings and oil sketches is always on display in the Paintings Galleries, and works on paper may be seen in the Prints and Drawings Study Room.

At the time of her gift to the V&A, Miss Constable also presented many drawings to the British Museum and gave or bequeathed eleven paintings and sketches to the National Gallery. Following the creation of a separate National Gallery of British Art (later known as the Tate Gallery), some of these were transferred to Tate Britain. Because pictures by artists born earlier than 1790 were permitted to remain at Trafalgar Square, a group of Constable's major paintings, including *The Hay Wain* and *The Cornfield*, can still be seen in the National Gallery. The Royal Academy has Constable's Diploma Work, *A Boat Passing a Lock* (1826), the picture presented by the artist on finally being elected a Royal Academician in 1829; it also holds a fine group of oil sketches, also presented by Miss Constable. The Courtauld Gallery's collection contains numerous drawings and sketches by Constable.

Outside London, the Fitzwilliam Museum in Cambridge, the Ashmolean Museum in Oxford, Christchurch Mansion in Ipswich and Anglesey Abbey (National Trust) near Cambridge all have significant collections of Constable's works. At Gainsborough's House in Sudbury is a permanent display of items on long-term loan from the Constable family collection, including works of art by Constable himself and by his children, and memorabilia such as his paintbox, studio props and his pocket watch.

Constable is exceptionally well represented in North American collections, in particular the Yale Center for British Art in New Haven, Connecticut, and the Huntington Art Museum, San Marino, California. Other notable collections include the Museum of Fine Arts in Boston; Harvard Art Museums; the Frick Collection, New York; the Philadelphia Museum of Art; the John G. Johnson Collection, Philadelphia; the National Gallery of Art, Washington D.C.; The Phillips Collection, Washington D.C.; and the Clark Art Institute, Williamstown, Massachusetts. In Australia, a fine group of pictures can be seen at the National Gallery of Victoria in Melbourne.

Constable's work received widespread recognition and acclaim in France long before it did in England, beginning in 1824, when *The Hay Wain* was exhibited at the Paris Salon and awarded a gold medal by the King of France. As Fisher remarked at the time, it was 'surely a stride up three or four steps of the ladder of popularity. English boobies, who dare not trust their own eyes, will discover your merits when they find you admired at Paris.' Outside a small circle of friends and admirers, Constable's merits took longer to be appreciated in England than Fisher predicted, while in France his work exerted an influence on artists from Eugène Delacroix to Claude Monet. So it is fitting that an extensive collection of his paintings, watercolours, drawings and sketchbooks should be found in the Musée du Louvre in Paris.

33 × 50.8 cm (13 × 20 in.). Ipswich Borough Council Museums and Galleries, Suffolk (R.1955-96.2). Photo Colchester & Ipswich Museums Service/Bridgeman Images **76-77** Oil on canvas, 33 × 50.8 cm (13 × 20 in.). Ipswich Borough Council Museums and Galleries, Suffolk (R.1955-96.1). Photo Colchester & Ipswich Museums Service/Bridgeman Images **79** Graphite, 9.3 × 15 cm (3¾ × 6 in.). The Morgan Library & Museum, New York. Gift of Richard S. Davis (1960.13) **81, 82 (detail)** Oil on canvas, 101.7 × 127 cm (40⅛ × 50 in.). Tate (N01273). Photo IanDagnall Computing/Alamy Stock Photo **84** Oil on canvas, 30.5 × 25.1 cm (12⅛ × 10 in.). Tate (N02655). Photo classicpaintings/Alamy Stock Photo **86** Graphite, 11.5 × 18.6 cm (4⅝ × 7⅜ in.). Victoria & Albert Museum, London (298-1888). Photo Bonhams, London/Bridgeman Images **89** Graphite. 59.1 × 49.5 cm (23⅜ × 19½ in.). Victoria & Albert Museum, London (320-1891). Bridgeman Images **93** Oil on paper, 14.6 × 24.8 cm (5¾ × 9⅞ in.). Victoria & Albert Museum, London (591-1888). Bridgeman Images **94** Oil on paper, 16.2 × 30.8 cm (6½ × 12¼ in.). Victoria & Albert Museum, London (149-1888) **96-97** Oil on paper, 23.5 × 32.6 cm (9⅜ × 12⅞ in.). Royal Academy, London (03/1390) **98-99 (detail)** Oil on paper, 24.1 × 29.2 cm (9½ × 11½ in.). Private collection **101** Oil on paper, 17.1 × 33.6 cm (6¾ × 13¼ in.). Victoria & Albert Museum, London (127-1888). Bridgeman Images **107, 108 (detail)** Oil on canvas, 55.6 × 77.8 cm (22 × 30¾ in.). Photo Museum of Fine Arts, Boston/Warren Collection. William Wilkins Warren Fund (48.266)/Bridgeman Images **111** Graphite, 8.7 × 11.3 cm (3½ × 4½ in.). Private collection **114-115** Oil on millboard, 45.2 × 24.7 cm (17⅞ × 9¾ in.). Victoria & Albert Museum, London (330-1888).

Photo Smith Archive/Alamy Stock Photo **116** Oil on canvas, 25.4 × 30 cm (10 × 11⅞ in.). Victoria & Albert Museum, London (122-1888). Photo The Stapleton Collection/Bridgeman Images **119** Oil on paper, 24.1 × 29.8 cm (9½ × 11¾ in.). Victoria & Albert Museum, London (151-1888) **120-121** Oil on paper, 24.1 × 29.2 cm (9½ × 11½ in.). Private collection **123** Oil on paper, 24.8 × 30.3 cm (9⅞ × 12 in.). Yale Center for British Art, Paul Mellon Collection, New Haven, CT (B1981.25.156) **124-125** Oil on paper, 21.2 × 29 cm (8⅜ × 11½ in.). Yale Center for British Art, Paul Mellon Collection, New Haven, CT (B1981.25.147) **127** Graphite, 23.3 × 16 cm (9¼ × 6⅜ in.). Victoria & Albert Museum, London (251-1888) **128** Oil on panel, 16.6 × 22.1 cm (6⅝ × 8¾ in.). Tate (T03903) **132** Graphite, 18.1 × 26.2 cm (7¼ × 10⅜ in.). Victoria & Albert Museum, London (356-1888) **135** Oil on canvas, 132 × 108.5 cm (52 × 42¾ in.). National Gallery, London. Bequeathed by Miss Isabel Constable as the gift of Maria Louisa, Isabel, and Lionel Bicknell Constable, 1888 (NG1272) **137** Graphite, 17.9 × 14.6 cm (7⅛ × 5¾ in.). The Trustees of the British Museum (1896,0821.15) **139** Pen and wash, 32.5 × 22.5 cm (12⅞ × 8⅞ in.). Private collection. Courtesy Christie's **140** Graphite, 22.5 × 33.2 cm (8⅞ × 13⅛ in.). Lowell Libson & Jonny Yarker, Ltd **143, 144 (detail)** Oil on canvas, 122 × 164.5 cm (48⅛ × 64⅞ in.). Yale Center for British Art, Paul Mellon Collection, New Haven, CT (B1977.14.42) **146-147 (detail)** Oil on canvas, 58.1 × 70.8 cm (22⅞ × 27⅞ in.). Private collection. Photo Christie's Images/Bridgeman Images **151** Woodcut. Yale Center for British Art, Paul Mellon Collection, New Haven, CT (B1977.14.17924) **154-155** Oil on canvas, 131.5 × 187.8 cm (51⅞ × 74 in.). The Frick Collection, New York (1943.1.147)

157 Oil on paper, 24.1 × 18.1 cm (9½ × 7¼ in.). Victoria & Albert Museum, London (166-1888r). Photo Luisa Ricciarini/ Bridgeman Images **159, 160 (detail)** Oil on canvas, 130.2 × 185.4 cm (51⅜ × 73 in.). National Gallery, London. Presented by Henry Vaughan, 1886 (NG1207). Photo The National Gallery, London/Scala, Florence **164-165** Oil on paper, 17.3 × 23.9 cm (6⅞ × 9½ in.). Tate (N02656) **168-169** Oil on canvas, 58.1 × 70.8 cm (22⅞ × 27⅞ in.). Private collection. Photo Christie's Images/ Bridgeman Images **171** Watercolour, 11.5 × 19 cm (4⅝ × 7½ in.). Victoria & Albert Museum, London (220-1888) **172** Pen and ink, 33.5 × 21.1 cm (13¼ × 8⅜ in.). Tate (T01940) **177 above** Mezzotint, 15.5 × 25.6 cm (6⅛ × 10⅛ in.). The Trustees of the British Museum (1842,1210.84) **177 below** Mezzotint, 17.6 × 25.3 cm

(7 × 10 in.). The Trustees of the British Museum (1842,1210.118) **178 above** Mezzotint with drypoint, 17.6 × 25.4 cm (7 × 10 in.). The Trustees of the British Museum (1842,1210.94) **178 below** Mezzotint, 18.3 × 25.5 cm (7¼ × 10⅛ in.). The Trustees of the British Museum (1842,1210.47) **181** Brush and ink over graphite, 20.3 × 16.9 cm (8 × 6¾ in.). Victoria & Albert Museum, London (249-1888) **182** Brush and ink with white heightening, 11.7 × 18.5 cm (4⅝ × 7⅜ in.). Princeton University Art Museum. The John B. Elliott, Class of 1951, Collection (1998-869) **186-187** Oil on paper on millboard, 15.2 × 24.1 cm (6 × 9½ in.). Yale Center for British Art, Paul Mellon Collection, New Haven, CT (B1981.25.128)

Acknowledgments

My introduction to John Constable came in 1995, when I found myself working
for several months at the Great House in Burford, West Oxfordshire, helping to
catalogue the extraordinary print collection assembled by the late Christopher
Lennox-Boyd. Christopher owned a group of mezzotints from Constable's *English
Landscape* project, including rare proof impressions taken from copper plates
before completion so that the artist could check the image as it came into being.
Constable himself had drawn on some of these to show the printmaker changes
he wanted to have made. It was electrifying to hold these working proofs in my
hands: it felt as though I had been granted a glimpse over this perfectionist's
shoulder as he marked corrections with decisive dashes of the chalk, the final
outcome still hanging in the balance. My task was to attempt to arrange these
prints in chronological order, navigating by changes: the disappearance and
reappearance elsewhere of a figure, for example, or a sudden flight of birds in
a previously blank sky. I subsequently catalogued another group in the Department
of Western Art at the Ashmolean Museum in Oxford, and I was hooked.

In 2007, when I became Curator of Paintings at the Victoria and Albert
Museum, I found myself working with the National Collection of works by
Constable, which forms part of one of the most extensive collections of landscape
art in the UK. My understanding of Constable was shaped by having curatorial
responsibility for his drawings, watercolours, oil sketches and exhibition paintings
– discussing them with colleagues and researchers, writing about them and
preparing them for display or loan. I should like to offer warm thanks to Mark
Evans, former Head of Paintings at the V&A, eminent Constable expert and good
friend, with whom I have been talking about the artist on and off for the best part
of twenty years. He has kindly supported the present book from the outset.

I should also like to thank the distinguished Constable scholar Anne Lyles for
her encouraging words on the initial proposal for this book and for subsequently
sharing her knowledge with me. The authors of two recent biographical works
on Constable, Martin Gayford and James Hamilton, have also been generous with
their expertise and insights. This book has benefitted greatly from conversations
with George Carter, Daniel & Clara, Bendor Grosvenor, Fred Ingrams and Thomas
Marks; and from the expertise of the following within museums, collections and
other institutions: Ruth Hibbard and Katharine Martin at the V&A; Annabel Kishor
at Christie's; Nicola Moorby at Tate Britain; Annette Wickham and Mark Pomeroy
at the Royal Academy of Arts; Elenor Ling at the Fitzwilliam Museum; Fatema
Ahmed and Sophie Barling at Apollo Magazine; Joachim Homann at Harvard
Art Museums; Lucinda Lax and Edward Town at the Yale Center for British Art
in Newhaven; and Katie Hanson of the Museum of Fine Arts in Boston. Closer
to home, Penny Deben and Richard Wilson, respectively President and Chairman
of the Friends of Ipswich Museum, have been a valued support. I should also like
to offer warm thanks to Donato Esposito and James Cahill, Trustees of the Cosman
Keller Art & Music Trust, for inviting me to give the 2025 Milein Cosman Slade
Lecture which gave me the opportunity to debate some of the ideas in this book.

Heartfelt thanks are due to my friend Bronwen Burgess, who was there at Burford at the very beginning. She brought her precise writer's eye to the manuscript and made a wealth of insightful comments and suggestions (any errors are, of course, my own). For encouragement and friendship, I should also like to thank: Peter Davidson, Jane Greenwood, Mark and Rosie Haworth-Booth, Alan Hollinghurst, Lucy Holmes, Kirstin Kennedy, Samantha Knights, Bijan Omrani, Peter Sheppard, Tessa Solomon, Jane Stevenson, Veronica Watts, Reinhild Weiss and Xanthe Wilde.

At Thames & Hudson it has been a pleasure to work once more with Ben Hayes, Commissioning Editor, and Kate Edwards, Senior Editor. My thanks also go to Associate Editor, India Jackson; to Maria Ranauro for her picture research; to Anna Perotti for her elegant design; and to Celia Falconer for expertly steering the book through the production process. I gratefully acknowledge the support of my agent, Andrew Gordon, and the friendly efficiency of his assistants David Evans and Emmanuel Omodeinde.

By good fortune, the date this book was commissioned meant that each chapter could be written in the appropriate season. I began writing 'Spring' in a mild, blustery March and completed 'Winter' just as February brought the first few brighter days to what had been a particularly cold, damp season. In the course of that year, I revisited the places Constable knew intimately and – in most cases – loved: East Bergholt and Flatford, Brighton, Salisbury and Hampstead. My husband Stephen Calloway was by my side through it all and has been a constant sounding board and inspiration. As ever, my special thanks and love go to him.

Index

Page references in *italics*
indicate illustrations

A
Aikin, John 28
Allen, Thomas 188
Arundel, Sussex 197

B
Balloon 88
Bannister, Jack 21
Beaumont, George, 7th
    Baronet 25, 130–1, 133,
    134, 136, 188, 189, 194, 195
Beaumont, Margaret
    (née Willes) 130, 131
Bicknell, Maria *see*
    Constable, Maria
    (née Bicknell)
Blake, William *127*
Bloomfield, Robert 29, *172,*
    173
Boner, Charles 183, 196
Bowleaze Cove 113,
    114–5, 170
Brantham Church, Suffolk
    190
Brighton 26, 91–2, *93, 94,*
    95, 141–2, 162–3, *164–5,*
    166, 174, 194–5, 196
British Institution, London
    27, 65, 85, 195
British Museum, London
    193
Bruegel, Pieter the Elder 148
Byron, George Gordon,
    Lord 36, 80

C
Camden, William 87
Charles X 163, 194
Charlotte Street, London
    33, 141, 191, 192, 194, 195
Chelmsford, Essex 55
chiaroscuro 179–80

Chichester, Sussex 197
Colchester, Essex 55, *59*
Coleorton Hall,
    Leicestershire 131, 133–4,
    136, 194
Coleridge, Samuel Taylor
    27, 28, 190
Collins, William 105
Constable, Abram (brother)
    16, 27, 72–3, 80, 136, 138,
    141, 153, 158, 184, 189
Constable, Alfred Abram
    (son) 136, *137,* 195
Constable, Ann (mother) 33,
    39, 72–3, 149–50, 188, 192
Constable, Ann (sister) 26
Constable, Charles Golding
    (son) 134, *137,* 138, 193, 197
Constable, Emily
    (daughter) *137,* 138, 194
Constable, George (of
    Arundel) 100, 196, 197
Constable, Golding
    (brother) 16, *140,* 141,
    142, 184
Constable, Golding (father)
    16, 32, 39, 45, 61, 65, 67, 71,
    73, 78, 149, 188, 189, 192
Constable, Isabel (daughter)
    136, *137,* 138, 194
Constable, John
    appearance 17
    birth 188
    burial place 184, 197
    death 180, 183, 197
    education and training:
        artistic 14, 16, 188, 189;
        management of family
        business 10–1, 16, 20,
        45, 188
    exhibitions: British
        Institution 27, 85, 195;
        Paris Salon 163, 194;
        Royal Academy *see*
        Royal Academy of Arts

    homes: Charlotte Street
        33, 141, 194, 195; East
        Bergholt House *18–9,*
        39, 72, 73, 109, 156, 174,
        184, 188, 193; Hampstead
        91, 118, 129, 138, 142, 170,
        184, 193, 194, 195; Keppel
        Street 85, 90, 118, 141,
        153, 192, 193, 194
    influences: Gainsborough
        25; Lorrain 102–3, 188
    journal-letters to Maria
        162–3, 194
    landscape painting: and
        artistic conventions
        7–8, 22, 25–6, 47, 102–5;
        capturing motion in
        35–6, 50, 54, 68, 149; and
        chiaroscuro 179–80;
        copies 133–4, 136, 167;
        emotional resonance of
        36, 60–1, *62,* 65, 67, 78,
        87–8, 112, 129, 145, 156,
        161, 167; from memory
        156, 161–2, 174, 180; in
        open air 71–2, 109, 192;
        poems quoted in 27,
        29, 36, 45, 87, *172,* 173;
        skying 122, 129, 193;
        studies of light and sky
        46, 117–8, 122, 126, 129;
        unfinished look of 31, 35,
        192; vividness of 7, 21,
        95, *96–7;* wildness of 113
    lectures 8, 167, 170, 183, 197
    mentors: Beaumont 25,
        130–1, 133, 134, 136, 188,
        189, 194, 195; Bishop
        Fisher 103, 110, 189, 190,
        191, 192, 194; Farington
        153, 189, 191, 192, 194;
        Smith 188–9
    portraits of *15,* 17
    relationships: children
        134, 136, 138, 141, 195;

Dunthorne, John 60, 158, 188; Dunthorne, Johnny 158, 167; father 16, 61, 65, 67, 73, 78; Fishers *see* Fisher, John (Archdeacon of Berkshire); Fisher, John (Bishop of Salisbury); Maria *see* Constable, Maria; mother 33, 72–3, 149–50; Reinagle 189; siblings 17, 20, 27, 33, 72–3, 136, 138, 141
and Royal Academy: as student 189; associate member 32, 103–4, 180, 193; Council member 196; exhibitions *see* Royal Academy of Arts; Royal Academician, votes and election 103–4, 180, 193, 194, 195; teaching 183, 196, 197
and seasons: knowledge of changes in 20, 27, 46, 161; reactions to 14, 31–2, 40, 45–6, 54, 80, 100, 102, 109, 134, 163, 170, 183; weather diary 8, 10, 36, 122
sketchbooks 55, 85, 109, 138, 141, 191, 192: emotional resonance of 87–8, 90, 112; 'little scraps' 55, *58, 59,* 60–1, *64,* 67–8; skying 122, 126, 193
subjects: agricultural labour 9, 27, *58, 59, 66,* 67–8, 71, 156, 158, 161–2; beaches 92, *93,* 113, *114–5;* boats and boat building 69, 70, 71–2, 92; churches 54, 55, *59,* 60, 88, 110, *111,* 112, 149, 179, 192, 194, 195, 196; clouds and sky 46, 95, 118, 122, *123, 124–5,* 126, 129, *172,* 173; dunghill 106, *107, 108;* familiar places 85–

90 *see also* East Bergholt, Dedham, Stour, Flatford, Hampstead; riverine landscape 80, *81, 82,* 83, 153, 180, *181, 182;* ruins *143, 144,* 145; sea *164–5,* 166; snow 149; trees 88, *89,* 90, *127, 132;* urban scenes 153; windmills 16, *43, 44, 45, 94, 95*
travels: Berkshire 193; Brighton 91–2, 95, 141, 163, 166, 194–5, 196; Coleorton Hall 131, 133–4, 136; Dorset 112, 192; Kent 190; Lake District 50, 190; Salisbury 110, 192, 195–6; Sussex 197; Warwickshire 190
views on: Brighton 91–2; feeling *versus* conventions in landscape painting 103–5; spiritual dimension of nature 39, 173
Constable, John (works by)
Arundel Mill and Castle 183, 197
Autumnal sunset 100, *101,* 102, *178,* 179
A barge on the Stour at Flatford Lock 51
Boat-Building near Flatford Mill 69, 70, 71–2, 105, 156, 161, 192
A Boat Passing a Lock 195
Bowleaze Cove, Weymouth Bay 113, *114–5*
Branch Hill Pond, Hampstead 116, 117
Brighton beach with colliers 92, *93*
A cart on a lane at Flatford 35–6, 37, 38
Cenotaph to the Memory of Sir Joshua Reynolds 135, 136, 196, 197
The Chain Pier, Brighton 195
Cloud study 124–5

Cloud study with verses from Bloomfield 172
commissioned paintings 61, 65, 83, 105, *107, 108,* 190, 191, 194
The Cornfield 21, 27, 195
A Cottage in a Cornfield 158, 161
Dedham Vale 195
Dedham Vale, a lane and farm workers 58
Dedham Vale, evening 23, 24, 25–6, 141
Dedham Vale, morning 191
The Dell at Helmingham Park 196
East Bergholt fair 55, 56–7
Elm trees in Old Hall Park, East Bergholt 88, *89,* 90
Englefield House, Berkshire 196
English Landscape (prints collection) 40, 45–7, 68, 87, 174–6, *177–8, 179,* 195, 196, 197
The entrance to the lane from East Bergholt to Fen Bridge 86, 87–8
Fir trees at Hampstead 127, 129
Flatford Mill from the Lock 191
Flatford Mill: Scene on a Navigable River 80, *81, 82,* 83, 156, 161, 192
Golding Constable's Flower Garden 73, 76–7, 78
Golding Constable's Kitchen Garden 73, 74–5, 78
Hadleigh Castle, the Mouth of the Thames – Morning after a Stormy Night 143, 144, 145, *178, 179,* 195
Hampstead Heath 195
Hampstead Heath, looking towards Harrow, at sunset 120–1, 126
The Hay Wain 7, 118, *154,* 156, 158, *159, 160,* 161–2, 163, 193, 194

John Charles and Maria Louisa Constable fishing from a barge at Flatford *139*, 141
A Landscape 21
Landscape: Boys Fishing 191
Landscape: Noon see *The Hay Wain*
Landscape: Ploughing Scene in Suffolk (A Summerland) 29, 66, 67–8, 71, 105, 175, 191
Landscape with a double rainbow 6
Landscape with a fallen tree 78, 79
The Leaping Horse 194
The Lock 194, 195
Maria Constable with two of her children 128
Mary Constable reading 33, *34*
The nursery *137*
Old Sarum 196
The Opening of Waterloo Bridge 118, 153, 163, 196
Portrait of Maria Bicknell *84*
A rainstorm over the sea 96–7
The rectory from East Bergholt House 62–3
Salisbury Cathedral from the Bishop's Grounds 149, 194, 195
Salisbury Cathedral from the Meadows 179, 196
The sea at Brighton 163, *164–5*, 166
A sportsman shooting duck on the River Stour *140*, 141
Spring: East Bergholt Common 40, *42–3*, 45, 47, 176, *177*
Stonehenge 197
Stormy landscape 180, *182*
The Stour Valley and Dedham Village 105–6, *107*, *108*, 192
Stratford Mill 153, 193

Study of altocumulus clouds *123*, 126
Study of sky and trees 119
Study of tree trunks 41
Summer Evening 191
Summer morning, Dedham from Langham 52–3, 54–5, *177*, 179
A threshing yard and a house by a church in Colchester 59, 60
Trees in a lane at Staunton Harold, Leicestershire 131, *132*, 133
The Valley Farm 197
View at Hampstead, looking towards London 170, *171*
View on the River Stour near Dedham 194
A view on the Stour 180, *181*
The Wheatfield 192
The White Horse 153, *154–5*, 193
Willy Lott's house 156, *157*
A windmill near Brighton 94, 95
Winter (after Jacob van Ruisdael) 166, 167, *168–9*, 170
Constable, John Charles (son) 90, *137*, 138, *139*, 141, 193, 194, 195, 196, 197
Constable, Lionel Bicknell (son) 141, 195
Constable, Maria (née Bicknell) burial place 184 children 20, 85, 90, *128*, 136, *137*, 138 and Constable: artistic tributes by *93*, 129; courtship 32–3, 73, 83, 85, 113, 150, 152, 190, 191; journal-letters 162–3, 194; letters between 30–1, 39–40, *41*, 54, 55, 60–1, 65, 67, 71, 73, 80, 83, 109–10, 131, 133–4, 145, 150, 152; marriage 78, 110, 192

death 142, 166, 170, 174, 195
family homes 61, *62*, 73, 150
ill health 9, 90–1, 141–2, 166, 193, 195
inheritance 32, 193
portraits of *84*, *128*, *137*
Constable, Maria Louisa 'Minna' (daughter) 90, *137*, 138, *139*, 141, 193, 195, 196
Constable, Martha (sister) *see* Whalley, Martha
Constable, Mary (sister) 20, 33, *34*, 136, 184, 191
Constable, Nancy (sister) 141
Cousins, Samuel 134
Cowper, William 9, 148, 183
Cranch, John 188

D
Daniell, William 193
Dedham *52–3*, 54, 87, 105, *107*, *108*, 180
Dedham Vale *23*, *24*, 25, 55, *58*, 60, 65, 67, 130, 141, 174, 185
Diary of an Invalid, The (Matthews) 103–4
Driffield, W. W. 192
Dughet, Gaspard (Gaspar Poussin) 102, 103, 104, 133
Dunthorne, John 17, 20, 22, 31, 33, 60, 68, 131, 158, 188, 192
Dunthorne, Johnny 158, 167, 192, 196
Dysart, Wilbraham Tollemache, 6th Earl of 190

E
East Bergholt 9, 16, 17, 20, 22, 25, 39, 50, 54–5, 60, 61, *64*, 68, 71, 85, 87, 100, *101*, 102, 138
fair 55, *56–7*
Old Hall 61, 88, *89*, 90, 105
rectory 61, *62–3*, 73, 142

St Mary's church *18,*
54, 60, 88, 110
West Lodge 25
East Bergholt Common 40,
42–3, 45, 47, 174, 179
East Bergholt House *18–9,*
39, 72, 73, 109, 156, 174,
184, 188, 193
East Bergholt Mill *44*
Egremont, Lord 197
Eliot, T. S. 170
Englefield House, Berkshire
196

F
Farington, Joseph 153,
189, 191, 192, 194
Farmer's Boy, The
(Bloomfield) 29, *172,* 173
Field, George 149
Fisher, John (Archdeacon
of Berkshire)
death 166–7, 196
letters from Constable 8,
36, 91–2, 102, 103–4, 122,
126, 129, 130–1, 134, 161,
167
letters to Constable
29–31, 103, 110, 142
paintings bought 153, 193
visits from Constable 9,
83, 87, 102, 112–3, 118, 153,
192, 193, 194, 195, 196
Fisher, John (Bishop of
Salisbury) 103, 110, 189,
190, 191, 192, 194
Fisher, Mary 112, 113
Fitzhugh, Thomas 105
Flatford 16, 25, *37, 139,* 156
see also Lott, Willy, house of
Flatford Lock *51,* 153, *154*
Flatford Mill 54, *69, 70,* 71,
80, *81, 82,* 83, 136, 138, 174,
184
Fleet River 90
Francia, François Louis
Thomas 21
Freer, Mary 190
Frost Fair on the Thames,
London *151,* 152

G
Gainsborough, Thomas
25, 67, 188
Galen 30
George IV 91, 196
Gilpin, Sawrey 21
Glover, John 103, 104–5
Godfrey, Peter 90, 105
Godfrey, Philadelphia
105, 106
Godfrey, William 61, 65
Gubbins family 190

H
Hadleigh Castle *143, 144,* 145
Hampstead 50, 90–1, 126,
138, 142, 170, 184, 193, 194,
195
Hampstead Heath 8, 26,
116, 117–8, *120–1,* 122, 126,
127, 129, 174, 193
Helmingham Park 174
Hippocrates 30
Hoppner, John 190
Howard, Luke 113
Hurlock, Lucy 189

I
industrial revolution 9, 26

K
Keppel Street, London
85, 90, 118, 141, 153, 192,
193, 194

L
Labours of the Months
(medieval verses) 28, 148
Lake District 50, 190
landscape painting,
conventions and
traditions in 7–8, 22, 25,
47, 102–5, 148
Langham 39, *52–3,* 54,
100, 179
Lawrence, Thomas 190
Leslie, C. R. 45, 100, *127,*
142, 166, 167, 170, 175, 180,
183
Lewis, H. G. 190

Literary and Scientific
Society of Hampstead 197
Lorrain, Claude 25, 26,
102–3, 104, 130, 131, 133,
134, 136, 188, 192
Lott, Willy, house of 50, *154,*
156, *157,* 158, 162
Lucas, David 175–6, *177–8,*
179, 191, 195

M
Matthews, Henry 103–4
mezzotint 175–6 *see English
Landscape*
Michelangelo 136, 196
Military Academy, Marlow
33, 189
Mistley, Essex 16, 17, *55,*
71, 88, 150, 188
Morrison, James 194

N
National Gallery, London
133, 136, 197
Nayland Church 191
Neckam, Alexander 87
Netley Abbey 112

O
Old Hall, East Bergholt 61,
67, 88, *89,* 90, 105
Osmington, Dorset 83, 110,
112, 192

P
painter's season 47, 100, 102
Paris Salon 163, 194
Peel, Robert 166–7
Philips, Henry 161
Pitt's Mill 45
Poussin, Gaspar *see* Dughet,
Gaspard

R
Raphael 136, 196
Rebow, (Francis Slater)
General 83, 191
Reinagle, Ramsay Richard
15, 17, 189
Rembrandt 129, 130

Reynolds, Joshua, cenotaph to the memory of *135*, 136, 196
Rhudde, Dr 32, 39–40, 73, 78, 190, 191, 193
Roberts, Mrs 25
Romanticism 28
Royal Academy of Arts (RA), London
Summer Exhibition (overview) 14
RA exhibitions with Constable's works: *Cenotaph to the Memory of Sir Joshua Reynolds* 136, 197; Constable's first 21, 189; *The Cornfield / The Chain Pier, Brighton / Dedham Vale / Hampstead Heath / A Boat Passing a Lock / Hadleigh Castle, the Mouth of the Thames* 195; *Dedham Vale* 141; *Dedham Vale: Morning / Flatford Mill from the Lock / Summer Evening / Landscape: Boys Fishing* 191; *The Dell at Helmingham Park / Salisbury Cathedral from the Meadows / The Opening of Waterloo Bridge / Englefield House, Berkshire / Old Sarum* 196; *Hadleigh Castle, the Mouth of the Thames* 145; *Landscape: Ploughing Scene in Suffolk* 29, 191; *The Valley Farm / Arundel Mill and Castle* 197; *Salisbury Cathedral from the Bishop's Grounds* 149, 194; 'six-footer' paintings (*The White Horse / Stratford Mill / The Hay Wain / View on the River Stour near Dedham / The Lock / The Leaping Horse*) 153, 193, 194; *The Stour Valley and Dedham Village / Boat-Building / The Wheatfield / Flatford Mill: Scene on a Navigable River* 72, 192; *Victory* 190
membership 32–3, 103–4
Royal Academy Schools, London 14, 16, 180, 189, 196, 197
Royal Institution, London 197
Rubens 130
Ruisdael, Jacob van 166, 167, *168–9*, 170

S
Salisbury 83, 102, 110, *111*, 112, 118, 192, 193, 195–6
seasons
and Constable: knowledge of changes in 20, 27, 46, 161; reactions to 14, 31–2, 40, 45–6, 54, 80, 100, 102, 109, 134, 163, 170, 183; weather diary 8, 10, 36, 122, 126, 129
effects on health and mood 29–32
unseasonal weather 80, 113, 152
Seasons, The (Thomson) 27–9, 45, 145
Smith, George 102
Smith, J. T. 'Antiquity Smith' 188–9
Southampton 112
St John-at-Hampstead 184, 197
St Mary's church, East Bergholt *18*, 54, 60, 88, 110
Staunton Harold, Leicestershire 131, *132*
Stoke-by-Nayland, Suffolk 25, 100, 174
Stour 8, 16, 20, 50, *51*, 54–5, 71, 110, *140*, 141, 153, *154–5*, 158, 180, *181*, *182*, 184–5, 188, 193, 194
Stour Valley 25, 105, 106, *107*, *108*, 189, 190
Summer Exhibition *see* Royal Academy of Arts
Swanevelt, Herman van 134

T
Tambora eruption 78, 80, 192
Telegraph 88, 92, 150
Thames 16, 90, 145, *151*, 152
Thomson, James 9, 27–9, 45, 145
Trimmer, Henry 149
Turner, J. M. W. 50, 54, 174–5, 185, 196

U
Uwins, Thomas 197

V
Victoria and Albert Museum, London 55, 191, 192
Victoria, Queen 26

W
Warton, Thomas 87–8
Waterloo Bridge 118, 153, 163, 196
Watts, David Pike 190
weather *see* seasons
West Lodge, East Bergholt 25
Weymouth, Dorset 112, *114–5*, 174
Whalley, Martha (née Constable) 36, 180, 189, 196
White, Gilbert 122
William IV 196
Wilson, Richard 102, 103, 130, 133, 136
windmills 16, *42–3*, *44*, 45, 46, 47, *94*, 95
Wordsworth, William 28, 136, 190, 197

Y
year without summer 80, 192

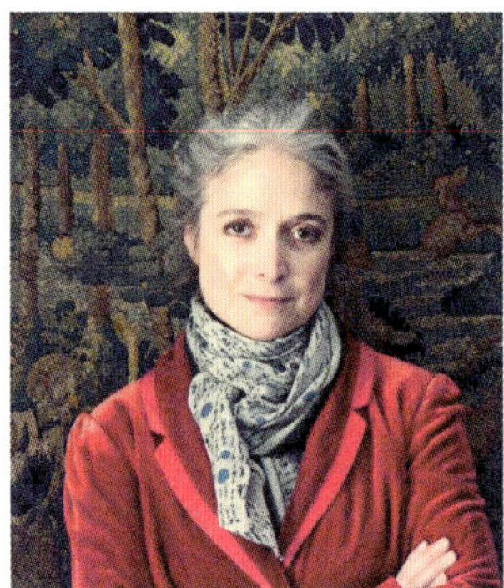

Dr Susan Owens is an art historian, award-winning writer and former curator at the Victoria and Albert Museum. Her previous books include *The Story of Drawing* (2024), *Imagining England's Past* (2023) and *Spirit of Place* (2020).

Photograph by Stephen Calloway

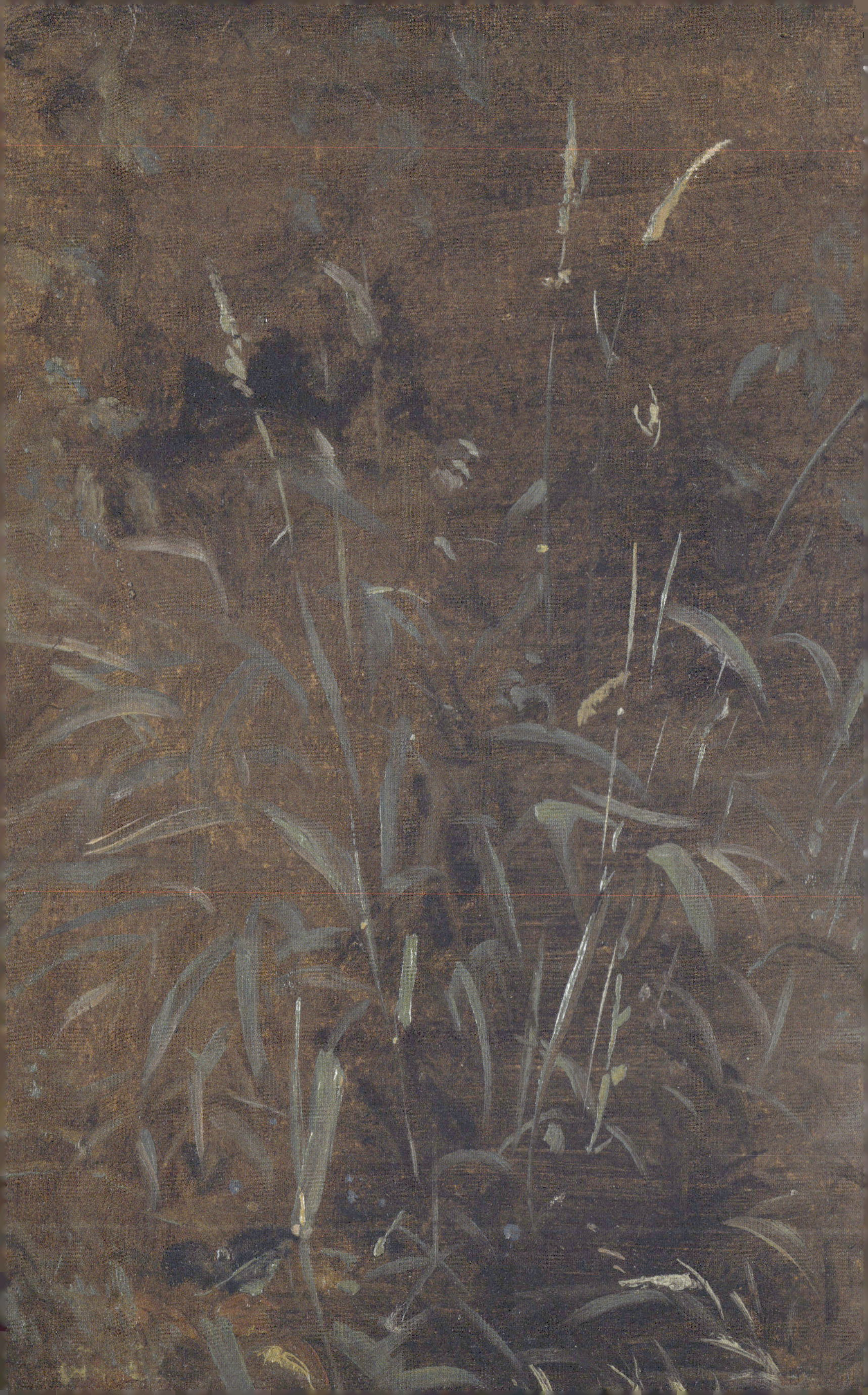